GEORGE

Also by Sean Smith

GEORGE

SEAN SMITH

HarperCollins*Publishers*

HarperCollins*Publishers*
1 London Bridge Street
London SE1 9GF

www.harpercollins.co.uk

First published by HarperCollins*Publishers* 2017
This edition published 2018

1 3 5 7 9 10 8 6 4 2

A catalogue record of this book is
available from the British Library

ISBN 978-0-00-815564-3

Printed and bound in Great Britain by
CPI Group (UK) Ltd, Croydon

For David and Marian

CONTENTS

PART ONE

GEORGIOS KYRIACOS PANAYIOTOU

1

YOGI

―――――――

The boy who would grow up to become George Michael had
an unruly shock of black curly hair, a sensitive nature and the
weight of parental hopes on his shoulders. He was much loved
and indulged, in keeping with his status as the only male child
in a Greek-Cypriot household, but was aware of his responsi-
bilities from a young age. He needed to make something of
his life.

His mother and father toiled long hours to give their
family the best possible life. He witnessed his beloved mum
endlessly scrubbing her hands to rid them of the smell from
the local fish and chip shop where she worked extra hours
to help provide for her son and his two elder sisters. Their
labours eventually paid off and by the time George was
a teenager, they lived in an affluent neighbourhood and
he could treat his girlfriend to a drive in his dad's swanky
Rolls-Royce. That luxury had been a million miles away
when he was born Georgios Panayiotou in a modest house
in Church Lane, an unprepossessing street in East Finchley,
North London.

His beginnings were only relatively humble, however, especially when compared to his father's start in life as one of seven children sharing a house in the rural Cypriot village of Patriki on the north-eastern Karpas Peninsula of the island, about twenty miles from the fishing port of Famagusta. In 2004, George released a song called 'Round Here', a nostalgic contemplation of his origins. It began with the memorable line: 'My daddy got here on the gravy train', which suggested his father had an easy time of it, making lots of money for very little effort. Perhaps he was having a gentle joke at his father's expense, because that certainly wasn't the case.

Patriki was not a place for an ambitious young man like Kyriacos Panayiotou to make his fortune. There was no easy money to be had in Cyprus where, traditionally, the men rolled up their sleeves and worked as farm labourers and fishermen while the women stayed home and raised often very large families. In this conventional community, the father of the house was very much the boss.

Nowadays, Cyprus is a wonderful destination for tourists, thrilled to sample its rich history and legends, its fabulous Mediterranean cuisine, to gaze at calm seas, olive and lemon groves and bask in the countless hours of warm sunshine. This, as the tourist guides will tell you, is Aphrodite's island, where in Greek mythology the goddess of love was born in the sea foam and drifted to the eastern shore in a seashell. One of the most famous paintings of all, Botticelli's *The Birth of Venus*, depicts her arrival.

Cyprus, historically, had always been vulnerable to military aggression. It was a gateway to both East and West and therefore of great strategic value. The island was still part of the

British Empire when Kyriacos was growing up. In the early 1950s, when he left school and started trying to find work, tensions were tightening between the majority Greek population and the Turkish communities.

When he was eighteen, Kyriacos took the bold step of seeking to establish a new life overseas. He chose to try his luck in Britain. In the post-war years, the United Kingdom was suffering from a chronic labour shortage and sought to recruit workers from Commonwealth countries by encouraging immigration with promises of a better life.

He found an ally in his cousin, Dimitrios Georgiou, known to his friends as Jimmy, who was an apprentice tailor and looking to build a career abroad. Kyriacos had little training to fall back on – just the work he had been able to pick up as a waiter back home. Jimmy's son, Andros Georgiou, explained, 'Our fathers came off the banana boat together. Though they didn't admit it, part of the reason they came was to flee National Service. They arrived in London with less than a pound in their pockets.'

Although the comment is slightly tongue-in-cheek, it's true that the young men avoided being called up for two years in the military, which was the law at that time. Leaving such a tight community was a wrench for both of them, and they would always try to send a few pounds back to their families from the little they earned in London. They arrived in Britain in 1953 at a time of some optimism that a new age was beginning, best epitomised by the Coronation in June of the new Queen, Elizabeth II. At Epsom, Gordon Richards finally won the Derby and in August the Ashes were regained. And rationing was coming to an end at last.

The cousins headed for the burgeoning Greek-Cypriot community in North London where they could find cheap lodgings. Jimmy found work as a tailor's assistant in South London while Kyriacos made do with menial jobs in shops and restaurants. They both enjoyed the freedom of their new adventure. Aware that his name was a mouthful for prospective employers, neighbours and, most importantly girlfriends, Kyriacos Panayiotou decided to call himself Jack Panos. He worked hard and played hard, having no shortage of female admirers around the coffee shops and dancehalls of North London.

The age of rock and roll was just beginning, when the sound of Bill Haley & His Comets and later Elvis Presley made going out so much more fun than it used to be. Jack revelled in his new freedom, far away from the disapproval of his father. He also looked the part with a fifties-style quiff and chiselled movie-star looks. 'When he was very young, my dad was very handsome,' recalled the adult George in his autobiography, published when he was still in his twenties.

At one dance, Jack met a radiantly pretty local girl called Lesley Harrison, who lived at home with her family in one of a labyrinth of then depressing and poor streets between Archway and Highgate. Lulot Street was a typical example, consisting of a line of Victorian terraced houses with outside toilets that George later described as 'very working class'. His grandfather, George Harrison, had worked for the Post Office as a telephone mechanic. The street itself was demolished in the 1970s to make way for modern flats. In 'Round Here', George was perhaps more accurate in his description of his mother, saying she had a 'real bad start to the game'.

Lesley was always well spoken with a soft and easy manner – she never sounded as if she should be behind the bar of the Queen Vic. According to George, it was only when her own mother – George's grandmother, Daisy – died that she discovered she was half Jewish. Apparently, she had been disowned by her wealthy Jewish family for marrying a gentile.

The families who lived in her neighbourhood of North London were back then very old-fashioned in their views regarding immigrants. Greeks were placed firmly in the unwelcome category. George would later hear stories of those days from his parents: 'There were places that would say, "No blacks, no Irish, no Greeks, no dogs" kind of thing.' That attitude failed to deter Lesley, who fell in love with her dancing partner. 'My parents were rock and roll dancers,' George explained. 'They met at a dance and my father used to throw my mother all over the show.'

They were good enough to enter competitions, and one teenage girlfriend of George remembers him showing her an old black-and-white photograph of his parents dancing. She recalls, 'They looked amazing, with glamorous hairstyles and clothes like something out of the movie *Hairspray*. I remember wishing that we learned how to dance like that, proper couples dancing, not just disco.'

Lesley was clearly very proud of her darkly handsome boyfriend. She even entered his picture in a competition run by the now defunct *Reveille* magazine called 'Search for a TV Star'. He reached the final and his photograph was published with the memorable caption: 'Jack Panos is chased down the street by girls wherever he goes'. That may have been a slight exaggeration, but his son would be very impressed by his dad's achievements, which were kept hidden when he was growing up.

Jack and Lesley were married in 1958. Her father didn't attend for the simple reason, according to George, that the groom was Greek: 'In those times, he saw that as absolutely the same as marrying someone of a completely different colour.' One unavoidable fact was that Lesley from Lulot Street was now Lesley Panayiotou. It was a bold and strong-minded thing to do at the time, following your heart and hoping for a better life.

Jack was twenty-three and his new wife twenty-one. Their prospects didn't look good as they settled down to married life. The young couple's carefree dancing days ended to a certain extent when they faced up to the responsibility of raising their first child, a girl they named Panayiota but who everyone called Yioda. Their first daughter was born that October in the maternity annexe of the Royal Free Hospital in the Liverpool Road. At the time, Jack was working on the counter in a grocer's and they were living in Kentish Town, one of a number of homes around North London in which they had rooms before they managed to buy their own house.

Almost exactly two years later, in October 1960, Lesley gave birth to a second daughter, Melanie, which is a name that sounds very English but is derived from 'Melania', the Greek for 'dark'. Jack was now a waiter and they had moved a few neighbourhoods away to Muswell Hill.

The couple longed for a male child and their wish was eventually granted on 25 June 1963. They named him Georgios Kyriacos. The Greek pronunciation of Georgios is 'Yorios', which was a bit difficult for his elder sisters, so they called their brother Yogi, a pet name that stuck with him during his early years.

By the time of his son's birth, Jack had worked his way up to be an assistant manager in a local restaurant. It would be many years before Georgios fully appreciated his father's work ethic and commitment to improving the status of his family. 'The honest truth is that the average Greek-Cypriot is a lot more hard-working than the average English man,' he observed somewhat controversially. He described his father as the 'absolute archetypal 1950s immigrant from Cyprus – very determined and every single member of his family made something of themselves. They were typical immigrants that worked their arses off and reaped the rewards.'

On his mum's side, Georgios never knew his Uncle Colin, her elder brother. He died, aged thirty-eight, in January 1964 from an overdose of barbiturates at the house in Lulot Street when his nephew was six months old. His death certificate grimly contained the words 'schizophrenia' and 'did kill himself'. The tragedy was hidden from Georgios growing up, but much later, as George Michael, he wrote a very personal song, 'My Mother Had a Brother', in which he revealed that his uncle was a gay man who had been unable to declare his sexuality because of the times in which he was born. He also said Colin killed himself on the day he was born, but this was dramatic licence.

The family moved yet again, to a small flat above a launderette in Holmstall Parade in Edgware, which was a small group of shops on the main A5 road with a bingo hall on the corner. The flat had a view of a dusty and shabby backyard on one side and the busy road on the other. It was hardly a step up from the familiar streets of North London that Lesley had been loathe to leave, but it better suited Jack's ambitions.

While still very much London, Edgware had a more suburban feel to it than the old haunts of Archway and Kentish Town. The media liked to talk of 'Swinging London' and the 'Swinging Sixties' in terms of young Britain finding a new and exciting culture, finally free from the shackles of the Second World War. Jack and Lesley, however, were faced with a much more uninspiring life, trying to save enough to drag themselves out of their working-class monotony while keeping three young children clothed and fed.

At least now they were in the catchment area of a good school. Roe Green Infant and Junior Schools were in Princes Avenue, Kingsbury, less than a mile away from the flat. The junior school boasted the motto 'Be The Best You Can Be', a sentiment that resonated in the Panayiotou household and one that, professionally, George Michael was destined to follow.

In the summer of 1968, just before Yogi was due to start school, Jack took his family to Cyprus for the first time. He had not been back there for fifteen years and much had changed. The country had achieved independence in 1960 and joined the Commonwealth a year later. But it was not a stable time and the year of his son's birth had seen the beginning of violence between Greek and Turkish Cypriots. Greece wanted to absorb Cyprus back into the motherland – a policy known as Enosis – which inevitably led to bloodshed and the destruction of property on both sides. The adult George Michael would remember standing in front of the gates that led to the Turkish sector in Famagusta and being warned by his dad not to go in there because he might legally be shot by the armed patrols.

Jack's cousin Jimmy and his young family went along on the holiday as well. The two men would still try to see each other in London at weekends despite their work commitments and Georgios became particularly close to Jimmy's son, Andros, a friendship that would continue into adulthood.

During his time away, Jack's father had died. The adult George would later comment that he was in little doubt that the grandfather he never knew was extremely strict with his children. He had a very old-fashioned Greek attitude that almost certainly included a degree of physical punishment: 'I never met my grandfather because he died before my parents met, but everything I have heard points to the fact that he was loved and respected but feared.' Jack, too, expected his children to be well behaved and respectful of elders, but he didn't rule by fear. 'He's in no way a violent man – he's a very gentle man,' said George. Young Georgios received a clip from his father on just two occasions growing up. On the first, he was whining to his tired and overworked dad about a torch he wanted. He was, he admitted, like a dog with a bone and wouldn't stop going on about it. The second would be a few years later while on another family holiday to Cyprus.

On his return from his first Cyprus trip, Georgios, aged five years and three months, faced his first day of school. To a small boy, Roe Green seemed enormous and forbidding. By a stroke of luck, he walked through the gates at the same time as another Greek–Cypriot boy, Michael Salousti. They were both terrified, leaving their mums watching anxiously as their teacher gathered together her small charges to take them into class. The two boys quickly hooked up with a couple of other Greek-Cypriot children, including George Georgiades, whose parents were also in the catering trade and knew Jack: by coincidence, the two best friends Georgios had at primary school were called George and Michael.

They asked him if his mother was Cypriot as well and he was quick to correct them: 'No, she's not. My dad is only.' He also told them he was 'special' when they asked him about the flaky eczema on his legs. His mum had thoughtfully told him to say that so he wouldn't worry about the condition, which he endured as a youngster.

His new friends called him Yogi and, though he was shy at first, Georgios soon settled into a happy daily routine. Often, if his mother was working in the fish and chip shop, he would go round to the Georgiades' house after school for his tea and a play before Lesley came to pick him up. The boys would enjoy fish fingers or beans on toast and then sit round and sing along to an LP of *The Sound of Music*, which they loved. The soundtrack to the popular Julie Andrews film was the second-biggest-selling album of the decade and every home seemed to have a copy. The Georgiades household was no exception, and Yogi would happily join his pal at the coffee table in the lounge to sing 'Do-Re-Mi', their favourite tune, which so memorably began with 'Doe a deer, a female deer'.

The year after Georgios began at Roe Green proved to be a turning point in the fortunes of his family. His father went into partnership with two others in his first restaurant, called Angus Pride, in Station Road, a busy and cosmopolitan street the other side of the Edgware Road. He also had his eye on buying a house in one of the tidy streets that ran between the school and the flat where they were living at the time. He found a three-bedroom, semi-detached house in Redhill Drive, Burnt Oak, which he secured with a mortgage of £4,000. Nowadays it would cost more than half a million.

Redhill Drive is a wide and quiet residential street and a good location to bring up a young family. While the brown, slightly drab-looking house was quite modest at the time, it represented a huge step up the social ladder for his family, in effect from working class to lower middle class. The improvement in status didn't mean they had an easier life. Lesley was permanently exhausted as she juggled looking after three children with various jobs that included shifts at the restaurant. Jack was mostly absent because of the long hours he spent at work turning the business into a success. He may not have been at home as much as his young son would have liked. He may not have been there to take Georgios to the park as often as the other dads. But he set an example that would prove invaluable. He gave his son the gift of determination.

2

DAYDREAMER

Georgios was thrilled to have his own room at last at the back of the house, overlooking the garden and, beyond, an old overgrown tennis court that everyone called 'the field'. The patch of green would prove a happy hunting ground for a young boy interested in nature or just wanting to while away some time picking blackberries or kicking a ball around with friends.

While Georgios did not particularly like his next-door neighbour on one side, a woman he regarded as a 'real old cow', he got on famously with the O'Reillys. They were a large Irish Catholic family who lived on the other side. He would often play in the field with their son Kevin and was happy to be watched by Mrs Maureen O'Reilly if his mum was busy. He called her 'Auntie'. In the Greek-Cypriot community, boys would refer to other mums that way as a mark of respect and regard. Georgios would always do that. Maureen thought Yogi was a lovely little boy with his black curly hair and little glasses. She still recalls him knocking on the front door one day. He had a big grey cat in his arms.

'Auntie, my cat is dead,' he told her mournfully, gazing sadly at the motionless creature. 'Oh, Yogi,' said Mrs O'Reilly, 'I am so sorry. Is your mother in? Why don't you go and tell her?'

In the 2005 documentary *A Different Story*, George remembered living in the house. He would lie in bed each morning waiting for the sun to come out so that he could go and explore. One summer day, he rose early, crept out of the house and was nowhere to be seen when his mother called him down to breakfast. A frantic search followed until he was spotted in his pyjamas in the field, collecting all manner of bugs that Lesley might not have welcomed into the house. In some ways, Yogi was much more like a young Gerald Durrell than a budding Elton John.

Redhill Drive was one of those streets where everyone knew each other. Yogi made friends with another little boy called David Mortimer, who lived a few doors away. Their mothers had started chatting in the street one day when they were walking with their sons. It turned out that David was also at Roe Green but was a year older, so they saw little of each other at school but in the evenings would play together; it was the start of a lifelong friendship.

As he grew up, leaving the infants' and moving on to the junior school, Yogi grew in confidence. Michael Salousti recalls, 'He looked quite eccentric with his curly hair and glasses. He had quite a funny sort of fuzzy hair but, always, a really nice happy smile. He was sensitive though and was very conscientious about teasing other children.' Yogi was always quite stocky and big for his age, so, while he would never get into scraps at school, he was perfectly happy to stand up to bullies if they were picking on another boy. Michael adds, 'We were both bigger kids and would stop kids being bullied. We weren't heavy-handed about it. It was more a case of trying to explain to another boy, "Why would you want to bully that youngster?"' It would be stretching the point to suggest that Georgios had a social conscience at such a young age, but he did show kindness, particularly to one boy who was smaller and always the target for the class tormentors.

He thrived at junior school under the watchful eye of his form teacher, Mrs Anne Ash. These were the days when pupils had to show their teachers the utmost respect. In return, Mrs Ash treated the boys and girls with consideration: 'She was a lovely teacher,' recalls Michael. 'Things may have changed now but there was no rudeness back then. There was no talking while she was talking.' Georgios was a very polite boy. Every morning he would greet his teacher, 'Good morning, Mrs Ash', and she would respond courteously, 'Good morning, Georgios.'

He joined the school choir and sang in the Harvest Festival and Christmas concerts in front of proud parents, including Jack and Lesley, who would crowd into the school hall. This was not, however, the start of a golden school singing career for Georgios. The teacher in charge of the choir would not stand for any indiscipline and she was very tough on any talking. On one occasion, Georgios forgot the golden rule and was whispering away to Michael at the back of the class when the teacher pointed them out and dismissed them from the choir there and then. He was not particularly upset: growing up, Georgios had shown very little interest in music. He didn't care for the Greek folk music his father would insist on playing around the house. Indeed, Jack's only artistic talent seemed to be an ability to balance a plate or a drink on his head while dancing.

Georgios wasn't the least bit sporty, although he could run fast as a boy. He was more of a geek, read a lot for his age, was articulate, and useful at arithmetic and algebra. He was always a bit lazy academically, bright enough to do the minimum and still pass all his exams. He was never much of a team player, didn't follow a football team and didn't join in the games of rounders or French cricket at break times or in the park after school. His principal interest was still nature until an event occurred, one he later described as 'very strange': he fell down the staircase at school when he was running for lunch. It was his Damascus moment.

He told Greek television, 'I had a very bad fall, cracked my head and, in the year consequent to the accident, not only my interests but my abilities seemed to change. Before the accident, I was very interested in nature and biology. I was a fairly good mathematician and obsessively read books all the time. But after the accident, literally within two weeks, I brought home a violin – unfortunately a violin – and within months was obsessed with music. I had lost the ability to do any maths and lost my interest in nature and bugs, insects and stuff. So, my interests changed dramatically after that event. Not my personality though. But I have to believe that I wouldn't have been a musician. It is possible that a flight of stairs contributed to musical history.'

Interestingly, in that particular interview George Michael was asked the questions in Greek but responded in English. As a boy he joined his sisters for Greek lessons at weekends but didn't enjoy them, mainly because they were held on a

Saturday when he had far better things to do aged seven or eight than to learn a very difficult foreign language. Every weekend a 'crappy little van' would collect them and other local children and drive a few miles to Willesden, where they would sit in a classroom for private lessons. Georgios gave the impression of making progress, but in reality after two years he could speak only a few words, although he did understand more than he let on. He was at a disadvantage compared to his friends at school who had two Greek-speaking parents. Lesley never bothered much with the language and she always spoke English to her children. It might have been different if Jack had been able to spend more time at home with them when they were growing up.

Jack's determination to provide a better life for his family was beginning to pay off in terms of the presents he could buy his children and the holidays they could now afford more easily. Georgios loved the bicycle he was given on his seventh birthday. It was purple and blue and his most prized possession. He could now cycle up the road to see his pal David, who had actually moved to another house further up the same street, to the 'posh end' as George would later laughingly describe it.

You can often tell how well a family is doing by the things they chuck away. One afternoon after school Georgios was messing about in the garage when he came across an old wind-up gramophone that his mother had thrown out. It was the sort of retro piece of equipment that would be highly desirable now, but then it was just a dusty old antique. The record player became his principal preoccupation, especially when his mum gave him three old 45s to play – two tracks from The Supremes, the premier sixties girl band, and one from the leading British vocalist of the age, Tom Jones.

He would come home from Roe Green and, instead of dashing out to the field, he would hide away in his bedroom with his music: 'I was totally obsessed with the *idea* of the records. I loved them as things and just being able to listen to music was incredible.' George Michael would never have much in common with Tom Jones, the epitome of Welsh masculinity, but some of the later dance tracks of Wham! would have an affinity with the easy soulfulness of Motown. Lesley would have loved to dance to them if she hadn't been so busy in the chip shop. At least Tom and Diana Ross were much cooler early influences than the Julie Andrews songbook.

For his next birthday, his parents bought him a cassette player with a microphone and he was able to tape the latest hits from the radio. He loved recording things; he and David became 'The Music Makers of the World', the name they gave themselves, and prepared to take pop by storm from the comfort of their homes in Redhill Drive. They also started to make their own tapes, of funny moments and little sketches that would have them howling with shared laughter. It was a pastime that Georgios continued to enjoy through much of his life.

Georgios had never bought a record. That was to change on the annual trip to Cyprus when he was ten and splashed out on 'The Right Thing to Do' by Carly Simon, which was a minor hit in the UK in 1973 when it was the follow-up to her best-known track, 'You're So Vain'. Carly Simon was one of the hugely popular group of female singer-songwriters of the early seventies that included Joni Mitchell and Carole King. They combined catchy melodies with heartfelt, introspective lyrics that often told a story of damaged love. She was the perfect choice for a sensitive boy like Georgios Panayiotou who, regardless of any future image, was always in touch with his feelings. 'The Right Thing to Do' was a song about Carly's relationship with her then husband, James Taylor, another acclaimed musician of that age. The sentiment is a romantic one – 'Loving you's the right thing to do' – but there's a tinge of realism, of fading attraction and the need for reassurance … 'Hold me in your hands like a bunch of flowers'.

This particular trip to Cyprus also marked the second time Georgios received a scolding from his father. He was with his cousin Andros when they developed a taste for nicking things from a local shop. They began by stealing sweets, some they ate while others they hoarded. Eventually their thieving got out of hand when they made off with a carton of Dinky toy cars. The shopkeeper realised it was them, found their stash and told their parents. Jack without further ado smacked his son around the legs, which effectively prevented Georgios from becoming Cyprus's most wanted.

At least Georgios paid for 'The Right Thing to Do'. Carly Simon had a touch more credibility than his other favourite record of that year: 'Daydreamer' by teenage heart-throb David Cassidy, who made a successful transition from television actor to pop star. David first found fame as Keith in the popular early seventies sitcom *The Partridge Family*. He sang lead vocals on a number of hits as part of the TV cast, including the number one 'I Think I Love You', before breaking through as a solo artist with hit singles 'How Can I Be Sure' and 'Could It Be Forever'.

For a while, when 'Daydreamer' was at the top of the charts, Cassidy's face stared down from the walls of a million adoring young teenage girls. He was blue-eyed, with immaculate teeth and hair, and, most of all, he was non-threatening; he was clean-cut and safe. Georgios liked both the song and the image of Cassidy. He never forgot the first time he saw the American star on television, heading a football on the roof of the LWT building on the South Bank. The camera panned to the ground below and there were thousands of girls screaming at him. He saw the adulation that Cassidy's fame brought him and, although he was only ten, realised he wanted that for himself. Georgios longed to be put on a pedestal and adored from afar – famous but untouchable.

For a while Cassidy seemed to be on *Top of the Pops* every week. The long-running programme was essential viewing on Thursday evenings, and the following day it would be a major topic of conversation in the playground. He would join his friends to sing along to most of the chart hits, as did boys and girls all over the country.

On one rainy autumnal day the weather was too dismal to go outside, so everyone had to stay in the classroom for break. At that age, the boys tended to stick together at one end of the room and the girls would be grouped at the other. Georgios and Michael Salousti sat underneath a table and proceeded to give a rousing rendition of 'Daydreamer'. 'We were just singing away, minding our own business,' Michael recalls. 'You can imagine the scene – a bunch of kids making a lot of noise. We thought we couldn't be heard amongst all the chatter. We didn't notice, however, when it all went very quiet. Mrs Ash had walked in and there we were still singing, "I'm just a Daydreamer, I'm walking in the rain …"

'Suddenly, all we could hear were the other children laughing away. And there was Mrs Ash looking down at us, trying her best not to chuckle away as well. You could tell she was desperate to burst into laughter. So we had to creep out from under the table completely red-faced and embarrassed.'

Georgios didn't regard this as his first public singing performance, preferring to remember the less awkward gang shows that he took part in as a member of the local scout troupe. They used to meet in a hall near the school and he would wander down every week with Kevin O'Reilly from next door.

Mostly, his musical tastes were very much middle-of-the-road and focused on the charts and what was playing on Radio 1. This was an age of flamboyance and the rather feminine world of glam rock, where pop stars seemed most worried about blow-drying their hair and pouting for the camera – and that was just the men. Image ruled as acts such as The Sweet, Mud and Gary Glitter hogged the charts. There was little room for autobiographical contemplation in the lyrics of hits like 'Tiger Feet' and 'Blockbuster'.

The ten-year-old Georgios Panayiotou was impressed, but the three acts that had most impact on him then were Queen, Roxy Music and Elton John. They had much more credibility among music critics. Queen first appeared on *Top of the Pops* in March 1974, performing their debut hit 'Seven Seas of Rhye'. Georgios became an instant fan, much to the amusement of his friend Michael, who would tease him about it: 'I used to laugh at it. I would say, "Queen are rubbish, Georgios. Who likes Queen? Nobody likes Queen."' Surprisingly perhaps, he did not choose a Queen track when he appeared on *Desert Island Discs* in 2007, although he didn't forget all his childhood favourites. He picked 'Do the Strand', released by Roxy Music when he was ten.

None of his friends were particular fans of Elton John. He was never an artist that inspired great devotion, but over the years he was a huge influence on the music of George Michael. The melodies of the suburban superstar from Pinner were a pleasure best enjoyed in quieter moments. He liked the catchy hit 'Crocodile Rock' and could often be heard singing, 'I remember when rock was young, me and Suzie had so much fun' in the garden. He much preferred it to the more aggressive 'Saturday Night's Alright for Fighting' that often ended Elton's shows.

The man born Reg Dwight had become one of the biggest superstars in the world despite a less-than-promising appearance. He was chubby, short-sighted, with an ongoing fixation with his hair, or lack of it, but was an aspirational figure for an impressionable ten-year-old boy from the suburbs – who was chubby, short-sighted and struggling with his hair.

At that age, Georgios pretty much liked everything in the charts, and that even included The Wombles; they featured in a school project he devised. 'He could be very inspirational about certain things,' observes Michael. 'In our last year at junior school, we were put into groups and had to come up with a social project. So Georgios had the idea that we should all be Wombles. They were really popular at the time, clearing rubbish and keeping Britain tidy. The idea was to make things from the rubbish you collected. Georgios was very much the lead and took it upon himself to do the whole thing. He decided he wanted to be Orinoco, who was basically the most popular character. I had to make do with Uncle Bulgaria.

'The best part was devising banners and posters with Mrs Ash that explained why you should keep the school tidy. We put them up around the school. It was such a success that we got commended by the headmaster in assembly.'

Once Georgios felt comfortable, he had the confidence and ability to take control and make something a success. It was one of the traits he inherited from his father.

Before he left Roe Green, further evidence of the precocious artistic nature of Georgios Panayiotou came to light. He contributed two poems to the junior school's 1974 yearbook. They demonstrate a highly developed and mature sense of rhythm and imagination in someone so young. Neither is particularly cheery. The first, 'The Story of a Horse', is signed by Georgios Panayiotou, 4S. It began:

> Once there was a lonely horse,
> weeping on a stack of hay
> The gun was ready, the bullet was hot,
> the horse had broken a
> leg that day

The second, entitled 'Sounds in the Night', was a freestyle verse signed Professor WhatsIsname (Alias G. Panayiotou 4S):

> … Now what have I forgotten to tell you,
> I'm sure something slipped my
> Tongue. Ah! Now I remember, you'll guess what I have
> To say to you … I am BLIND!!!

Georgios didn't have far to go when he started senior school at Kingsbury High: it's next door to Roe Green. He would not be settling in for the long haul, however. Jack had plans to take his family up to the next stage of middle-class Englishness: he wanted them to move to the countryside.

In January 1975, Jack bought a house on Oakridge Avenue, Radlett, that would be the family home for Georgios throughout his teenage years. The detached four-bedroom white house was simply stunning, although it required a great deal of initial building work to convert it into the spacious, stylish, open-plan Mediterranean-style mansion that Jack had set his heart on. It was at the end of the road; just green fields lay beyond, with trails that were a dog walker's paradise. The back route into the centre of the pretty Hertfordshire town and its railway station was a brisk ten-minute walk.

They couldn't move in immediately, so had to live in the flat above the restaurant in Station Road for a few months. Being able to eat in the Angus Pride all the time wasn't ideal for his waistline and Georgios, who was prone to gaining a few extra pounds, was on the chubby side when they finally moved.

The restaurant was proving to be a great success. Some people found Jack Panos a little brash and extrovert, but his son was very gracious about what he called his dad's 'heroic effort'. Inevitably, Georgios was the product of both his father and his very English mother. Jack was an astute businessman; material wealth mattered to him. Lesley was a kind and generous soul who cared little for money. Georgios, too, was never motivated by money – much easier not to be when you have some – but he had his father's strong will to succeed. He was, however, raised in very much a female household, spending most of his time with his mum and two sisters. The two girls also had a profound and underestimated influence on him: Yioda was thoughtful, serious and contained. Melanie was much more flamboyant and extrovert; she was also something of a mother hen where her kid brother was concerned. Georgios would prove to be a mix of both personalities.

The sisters had it much tougher than the son of the house, although he was indulged rather than spoiled. The girls were not even allowed to have boyfriends. And if they went out together, perhaps to the ice rink, then their younger brother would have to go along, too. A close friend observed that the sisters did have some difficult times dealing with their tough, patriarchal dad, particularly during their teenage years. As a boy, Georgios felt guilty that he always seemed to get his way whereas his two 'wonderful' sisters never did. He recalled, 'I was always the one who was going to get the easy ride.'

Georgios would have to change schools when they eventually moved. As part of Jack's master plan of social improvement for his family, he was keen to send his son to private school, but this was not greeted with any enthusiasm. In an early indication of his stubbornness and resolution, Georgios refused, feeling he would be more comfortable in a state school. He would soon be an adolescent teenager with the usual anxieties of that age; it would be hard enough in any new school but particularly one where he was concerned he would feel out of place: 'My friends would have called me a sissy. Plus I would have been intimidated by it and I really didn't want to be with those kinds of people.'

Faced with his son's immovable 'force field', Jack relented and let Georgios have his way. Instead, he was enrolled in Bushey Meads School in Coldharbour Lane, Bushey, five miles away from his new home. There, he would soon meet someone who was to change his life.

3

BLACK MAGIC

———

Georgios was clearly a bit lost. He was carrying his violin case in his left hand and peering through thick-lensed glasses at his unfamiliar surroundings, trying to ignore the playground sniggers that inevitably follow when a new boy faces his first day at a strange school. The golden rule is not to stand out, but with his wild hair he was fighting a losing battle on that score from day one.

Then came the embarrassment of being introduced to his new classmates by a teacher struggling to get her tongue around the name Georgios Panayiotou. He fully expected there to be no takers when the teacher asked for a volunteer to show him around and make sure he knew where to go and what to do. To his surprise, a hand shot up from the back of the class. 'I'll do it, Miss. Give him to me.' It was a tanned, very good-looking boy called Andrew Ridgeley, who chose that day to do something to alter their destinies.

At first, there was no indication that the two would hit it off, until break time, that is, when the lads were playing a juvenile playground game called 'King of the Wall'. Andrew was the reigning king and goaded the seemingly shy and brooding Georgios to have a go at dislodging him. He got his comeuppance when the stocky new boy pulled him off, clambered over him and established himself as the reigning monarch. It was a simple thing but earned him the glimmer of respect needed to establish a proper friendship. They simply clicked and were a stronger unit together than they were individually.

Jack and Lesley didn't care for their son's new pal when he brought him home. They thought him too cocky and sure of himself for someone so young. Jack commented, 'He was extremely confident.' Andrew noticed their initial frostiness: 'His parents didn't like me for quite a while. There was always a bit of tense air when I went round there.'

Lesley, in particular, was worried he might be a bad influence on her Yogi. Andrew failed to call her 'Auntie Lesley', a mark of respect that would have got him on her right side immediately. While he seemed very relaxed, in reality he was very impressed with how much money his new friend's family had. The house in Oakridge Avenue was undeniably a beautiful home. He also noticed that Georgios seemed very unaffected by his affluent surroundings and certainly didn't bring any kind of superior attitude to school.

Andrew didn't appreciate at first that the Panayiotous had dragged themselves up from a humble start to this more opulent lifestyle. Although his parents had had more educational opportunities, they too had worked hard and faced many battles to improve their family's position. Now they were a well-established and distinctly middle-class family living in Bushey.

Andrew and Georgios were second-generation immigrants and there are some striking similarities in their heritage. Both their fathers came on a 'banana boat' to the UK and arrived in the 1950s with nothing, although Albert Mario Ridgeley had received a privileged education at the English school in the ancient Egyptian port of Alexandria, where he was born. His mother was Italian and his father an Egyptian Jew, and from an early age he had to deal with a lot of racially based prejudice.

Andrew has always been appreciative of his father: 'He is a very liberal man and I grew up under the impression that everyone was equal because I was never taught anything different.' For his part, Albert considered his family to be the main motivation of his life. He explained, 'People should realise the family is the basis of all human society and should play an important part in day-to-day lives.' It's a view that would always resonate with the Panayiotous.

Albert had a spell in the RAF, studied Russian and German at St Andrews University and married a teacher called Jenny. He was working for a Surrey camera company when their two sons were born: first, Andrew in January 1963 and then Paul a year later. The elder Ridgeley boy was almost six months older than Georgios. The Ridgeleys moved from Windlesham to Bushey when Andrew was five, and became pillars of the local community. Jenny went back to work and became a teacher at the Bushey Heath Primary School, where she also served as a governor.

Albert was a tireless volunteer for good causes. He was at one time treasurer of Bushey Old People's Welfare Committee and a part-time voluntary ambulance driver as well as working tirelessly on behalf of the local Rotary club. One of Andrew's school friends and neighbours remarked, 'Everyone loved Andrew's dad. He was a really lovely man, a real gentleman. He was one of those people about whom my parents would have said, "He is a nice man, that Mr Ridgeley."'

Bushey was very much a small world. Andrew Ridgeley grew up in a very solid and respectable family unit, and the subsequent public image he cultivated, as a pleasure-seeking playboy of pop, didn't reflect his upbringing.

Georgios was always welcome in the Ridgeley household in Bushey and hit it off with younger brother Paul, not least because he too had a drum kit in his bedroom. Georgios had been given drums for Christmas in 1975, a present that Lesley came to regret as she listened daily to the incessant beat of her son playing along to the hits on Radio 1.

To a certain extent, Lesley was correct in worrying that the confident Andrew would exert an influence on her son, although how bad that was is open to doubt. He was a leader. He probably brought out Georgios' lazy side because he too cared little for school and neither boy would think twice about skipping a day here and there. Even though his mum was a teacher, Andrew was looking forward to leaving school at the earliest opportunity. While Georgios was no school lover either, he didn't want to upset his parents and resolved to stay and pass his exams, just in case he needed qualifications.

The two boys would just sit around and chat about how they were going to be famous. Their musical taste was very similar and they discovered that they both owned a copy of *Goodbye Yellow Brick Road*, arguably Elton John's most celebrated work. It was a double album, so that was practically a whole afternoon taken care of, whichever house they were in.

Andrew didn't much mind how he made it and would have been perfectly pleased to achieve his ambition through being a footballer. He already looked like a young pop star though, even in his green blazer. Today, he would probably be the youngest competitor on *Britain's Got Talent* or *The X Factor*, charming everyone with his youthful charisma and being told by Simon Cowell that he has a great future.

Georgios wasn't there yet. He was a work in progress, although, encouraged by Andrew, he did begin to take more care of his appearance. His sister Melanie, who wanted to be a stylist, cut his hair into something more manageable and then he persuaded his parents that he wasn't too young for contact lenses. They agreed, provided he didn't wear them all the time.

He now had a nickname. On his first visit to Oakridge Avenue, Andrew heard his sisters refer to their brother as 'Yorg'. Mischievously, he took the name back to school and told classmates that, at home, Georgios was known as 'Yoghurt'. It was a bit of schoolboy fun but the name stuck. He was now called Yoghurt, or 'Yog' for short, which, unsurprisingly, he preferred. From the start, he called his friend 'Andy'.

Yog went to his first live gig in May 1976 when he joined his mother and sisters to see Elton John at Earls Court. He thought it was 'fantastic'. He couldn't get over the size of the show: 'He was spot on, brilliant, especially considering how big Earls Court is.' Elton didn't perform 'Crocodile Rock' on the *Louder than Concorde (But Not Quite as Pretty)* tour but he did sing a ballad that would have a much greater impact on the career of George Michael. 'Don't Let the Sun Go Down on Me' was an instant classic and its sad sentiment of rejection perfectly fitted the themes of George's own more introspective songs. Time and time again in the future George Michael would infuse his slower songs with the melancholy of loss.

Two other more obscure Elton compositions from 1976 would also feature in the future repertoire of George Michael. Again, both 'Idol' and the exquisite, elegiac 'Tonight' are ballads. It seemed Elton's songs were particularly suited to George's pure vocals and sensitive interpretation.

Gradually, Yog was coming out of his shell. It wasn't easy, joining a school a year after his contemporaries. Cliques had already been formed and if it hadn't been for Andrew he might have remained an outsider. He was still in his friend's shadow, however, when the following year they both went to the Watford Empire one Saturday afternoon to see a new film that was receiving plenty of publicity. It was *Saturday Night Fever* and Yog was transfixed. He was determined to be John Travolta or, more precisely, his character in the film, Tony Manero, who had a dead-end job in a hardware store by day and then was transformed into the strutting, white-suited king of the dance floor at night.

The soundtrack, stacked full of disco classics, became the soundtrack to life in Oakridge Avenue, with George either belting out the beat to 'Stayin' Alive' on his drums or trying to copy some of Travolta's steps. As 'Yog Manero' he felt confident enough to start going to school discos with Andrew, who was in his element.

'He really was a great dancer,' observed Andrew. 'It was then he began to express his physicality and his sexuality.' In effect, Georgios Panayiotou was able to perform and stand out in the crowd by acting a role. In this case, he was a flamboyant disco champion. They went out and bought trendy clothes, including dungarees, a must-have for any disco dancer. Yog had to earn money for such luxuries by taking on babysitting or doing jobs around the house and garden.

Andrew decided it was time Yoghurt had a girlfriend. He was coming up to fifteen and getting more kisses from his mum and sisters than from any of the teenage girls around school. In class, Georgios had caught the eye of a very pretty girl with a fashionable frizzy perm called Lesley Bywaters, who clearly enjoyed his company. But he was doing nothing to take it any further than the occasional coy glance and tentative smile. It was time his more dynamic buddy took charge.

Andrew got together with Lesley's friends to engineer a meeting between the two teenagers by the ice cream van in the playground at break time. Andrew was very firm with Yog, saying that this would be the opportunity to make his move and ask Lesley out on a date. He had done his homework and knew that Lesley liked Georgios. She recalls, 'He just really had the best personality. You wouldn't have found a wittier, funnier guy. When we were in a group in class, he was always amusing. He was very intelligent and would make us all cry laughing. Yog was hilarious.'

Despite his tentative makeover, at this time in his life the teenage Georgios was not blessed with the natural good looks and charm of Andrew Ridgeley. 'He was certainly a bit chubby,' observes Lesley. 'He didn't like that and could get very upset about it. He was never huge but he was uncomfortable about being a little bit portly.'

That didn't bother her as she nervously made her way towards their assignation. It was not a dazzling conversation in the manner of a Hollywood rom-com: 'We kind of muttered and mumbled. He sort of said let's go out on a date and that was it and we kind of shuffled off. Obviously he liked me and I liked him.'

On the evening of their first date, Georgios arrived at the door with a box of Black Magic chocolates. They weren't for Lesley, however; they were for her mother, Joyce: 'He gave them to my mum and she was so delighted. He was a real gentleman. And I remember her saying to me later, "Oh, what a lovely boy!" It was very grown up. His mum had so obviously said that he had to make a good impression and should take the mother a box of something.'

For their first date, Yog took her for dinner to the Angus Pride, where she was introduced to his mother and father: 'We walked in and they were both there. His mum was so lovely to me. She was really friendly and smiley and so excited that her son had brought a girl. She was chuffed because her name was Lesley and, of course, that was my name as well: the two Lesleys. I remember warming to her more than his dad, who seemed terribly scary. He wasn't really, but I was fifteen and he seemed old.'

The family restaurant may have been a surprising and mature choice for a first date, but at least the food was far better than burger and chips in a fast-food chain. This was a proper date. They both had steak, which was delicious, but Lesley was ill at ease throughout the meal: 'I felt very self-conscious,' she recalls.

The evening went well enough though for them to start dating properly – although, more often than not, Andrew would tag along as well. Lesley didn't mind this, not seeing three as being a crowd. She was one of the Bushey Meads group who had grown up together and she had known Andrew since primary-school days. She didn't find him cocky or brash: 'He was just a nice lad – always a good laugh.'

Both boys looked older than they were and had little trouble getting into discos. Teenage girls like Lesley would be let in as a matter of course. So the three musketeers were happy to jump onto the number 142 bus and head down the Edgware Road and into town for a night of dancing at Cherry's nightclub.

Lesley, who had no idea that her slightly overweight boyfriend could shake some moves, was astonished: 'He was a very good dancer and I was very surprised. Him and Andrew went mad and I was just hanging back, thinking, "Blimey!"'

Yog had moved on from 'Stayin' Alive' and his favourite dancing track now was the timeless classic 'You Make Me Feel (Mighty Real)' by Sylvester. 'He loved that,' recalls Lesley. 'He was absolutely mad on that.' The song, which featured Sylvester's distinctive light falsetto gospel voice, became one of the great anthems of disco when it was released in 1978, reaching the top ten in the UK in October. Every club played it at least once a night.

Sylvester James Jr, known affectionately as the Queen of Disco, was at the forefront of many cataclysmic events that hit society in the twentieth century – racial discrimination, gay rights and a truly sad demise from AIDS (acquired immune deficiency syndrome). He was from a comfortably-off, middle-class black family in Los Angeles and, from a young age, was open about his sexuality, celebrating his feminine androgynous side in the Castro area of San Francisco, where he settled. The author Vince Aletti memorably described him as 'gay in a fuck you way'. Sylvester became friends with Harvey Milk, the 'Mayor of Castro', who was the first openly gay man to be elected to public office and was portrayed so memorably by Sean Penn in the film *Milk*.

Sylvester's life and career had some interesting similarities to the one that George Michael would later lead. He sued his record company, he was arrested by police and his partner, an architect, contracted the HIV virus and died from complications associated with AIDS in 1987.

A year later, Sylvester too succumbed to the condition at the age of forty-one. The freedom and joie de vivre of the seventies in the gay community had given way to fear and sadness as so many friends and family were buried, and society and in particular the media sought to come to terms with what was happening. Sylvester left his estate to be split between two charities, the AIDS Emergency Fund and Project Open Hand, which was founded in the mid-eighties to serve nutritious meals with love and a smile to those living with the condition.

Such matters were far removed from the suburban world of Georgios Panayiotou and his friends at Bushey Meads. George Michael would later say that he had his first homosexual stirrings when he was fourteen, but he told no one and was happy to be dating Lesley. He would invite her back to the house in Oakridge Avenue; on the first occasion it was much to the surprise of his elder sisters. 'I remember the first time, walking casually past his sisters and Yog saying to them, "Oh, this is Lesley". I think they were quite interested that he had actually managed to hook a girlfriend. I was so worried that I would run into his parents, because you are at that age. So we shuffled off to his bedroom, which sounds really suspect but it wasn't at all. We listened to music and there was a bit of kissing but that was it.'

He took her to see the another disco classic of 1978, *Thank God It's Friday*, at the Odeon, Edgware Road, which featured the incomparable Donna Summer singing the Oscar-winning 'Last Dance' and the Commodores performing 'Too Hot Ta Trot'. Whenever the film was showing, cinemas around the country would turn into disco halls for the night. Lesley observes, 'Literally, everyone was dancing in the aisles – including us.'

Yog loved all the cheesiest tunes of the time. He liked the hits of ELO and would sing along to 'Evil Woman' and 'Mr Blue Sky'. One of his party pieces in the common room at school was singing 'When You're in Love with a Beautiful Woman', a UK number one for Dr. Hook. There was nothing cool about his tastes and he was not going to surprise everyone by putting Lou Reed or Iggy Pop on the turntable.

Classmates got used to seeing Yog and Lesley together. 'We were quite excited about it. I think people thought it was rather sweet because he hadn't dated anyone before and I hadn't dated anyone in school,' she remembers. They would walk down to the baker's at the end of the road during lunch periods or share tuck-shop duties. They were happy times for Lesley because her boyfriend was always entertaining, quite often unintentionally: 'We were singing along in the tuck room and Yog was giving it the full treatment when a big box of Crunchie bars fell on his head and knocked him to the floor.'

He liked nothing better than playing along to his favourite tracks on the drum kit in his bedroom at Oakridge Avenue.

Lesley recalls, 'He was very into the drums. We did a summer concert at school – something they did every year – and Yog did a drum solo. To be honest, it was very boring.'

He was listed in the programme for the concert in the school's main hall in July 1978 under his name, Georgios Panayiotou. He was performing his 'own composition'. Afterwards he inscribed Lesley's programme in his distinctive left-handed scrawl: 'nominated for an Oscar for his marvellous contribution to the Bushey Meads Musical Appreciation Society for the old, blind and deaf all over the world'. He signed it with the Greek version of his name, spelt out in capitals.

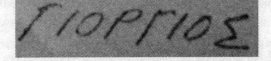

Lesley was thrilled and went off on her summer holidays happy to be his girlfriend. That is, until she met Mark from Chipping Sodbury: 'I was on my summer holiday with my parents and my cousin and I met this bloke. I really had a bit of a crush on him. It was never going anywhere. We didn't have any mobiles or computers or anything. There was no way we would be in contact again. But I came back to Bushey and my heart was full of Mark.'

Poor Yog had no idea he was about to be thrown over until he received a phone call from Joyce Bywaters. Lesley recalls, 'It's very funny, looking back. I got my mum to phone him and dump him. Isn't that awful! It was a nightmare really because I didn't know what to do. I don't think there was any particular bad feeling because I still saw him on occasion after that and we got on all right. I don't think he was heartbroken.'

Lesley was the first girlfriend of Georgios Panayiotou. They were young teenagers and sex was not on the agenda. Bizarrely, he later said that he had lost his virginity before he even had a girlfriend. He claimed he was just twelve when an older girl jumped on him. 'She was a right old dog,' he said, ungallantly. He hated the whole thing and told no one, not even to win bragging rights over classmates at school. A subsequent girlfriend observed that she could well believe that he had experienced something he found traumatic. He certainly didn't want to try sex again for a very long time.

Georgios was prone to sudden bursts of moodiness. In an interview with Chris Evans in 1996, George Michael said he had been at a party with Lesley and was sitting between her legs when she leaned forward, took off his thick glasses and told him, 'Haven't you got beautiful eyes.' He thought she was taking the 'piss out of me' and, so he said, he got up, left the party immediately and went straight home. The incident was an early indication of just how quickly Georgios Panayiotou could switch moods, a characteristic he took with him when he became George Michael superstar. His future manager, Simon Napier-Bell, described it memorably: 'He could shoot mistrust from his eyes like fire from a flamethrower.'

For her part, Lesley can remember the party but hasn't a clue what he was talking about. Sometimes it happens like that, especially as teenagers. Georgios, egged on by Andrew, had his revenge of sorts at Lesley's sixteenth birthday party at her house the following April. The drink was flowing and everyone was having a great time. Lesley glanced out the window and there in the garden were the two future stars of Wham! They were peeing into the fishpond.

4

EXECUTIVE DECISIONS

Yog was surprisingly coy about his musical talents. He was dismissive about his abilities, perhaps as a result of being teased. He always seemed concerned that the instrument was uncool in some way, even though he was comfortably the best violinist in Bushey Meads and played lead violin throughout his school career. He impressed the new music teacher, Joy Mendelsohn, when he was a fourteen-year-old O-level student: 'He was very good, although it wasn't his favourite instrument. He probably wanted to give it up but I wouldn't let him.' The young musicians weren't playing Beethoven or Bruch; Joy would arrange popular tunes like 'Trains and Boats and Planes' and 'King of the Road' as well as many old Beatles hits to suit their capabilities. They would perform at end-of-term and Christmas concerts in the big school hall. 'Now, I wish he'd done the arrangements,' laughs Joy. She was, nevertheless, pleased with her interpretation one year of Slade's perennial favourite, 'Merry Christmas Everybody'.

Yog would lead about six first violins and six second violins, depending on who was available. He made an impression on

Joy because he could play so many instruments and was a quick learner:'He had a natural talent. The others would have to work at it. He could be quite self-deprecating, though.'

He much preferred the drums to the violin and had proper percussion lessons at school that led to that enthusiastic drum solo at one of the concerts. He also played some guitar, another ability he also kept hidden. Joy's job was to try and get Yog to overcome a natural shyness: 'He would never show off his talent,' she recalls simply.

Not many students took music seriously at Bushey Meads; Andrew, for instance, was never interested. Yog was one of just four pupils in Joy's first O-level class, which, in the 1970s, consisted of exclusively classical set works. He would spend a lot of time in the new music block taking advantage of the individual practice rooms. He had a superb ear for music:'He excelled at anything to do with listening to music and he was able to write out rhythms,' Joy remembers. 'If I played him something, he could sing it back to me or write it down and notate. He was lazy about his homework, but then he was a boy.'

Yog was one of only two students who went on to study music theory at A-level. Unfortunately that small number meant that the school could not justify Joy continuing to teach them, so he would join Ruth Woodhead, who played the flute, for lessons twice a week at the Watford School of Music in Nascot Wood Road. Ruth was another student who had grown up in Bushey and knew everyone from primary-school days. In fact, Andrew Ridgeley proposed to her at Ashfield Junior School when she was eight. She turned him down, considering him to be a particularly naughty boy:

'I always remember him being at the back of the class and being called to sit at the front and behave himself.'

For their trips to Watford, Yog's mum Lesley would pick them both up from school and drive them the four miles to their lessons. Ruth was as shy as Yog in company and was quite in awe of his smartly dressed mother with the nice hair. Neither of the two teenagers enjoyed their music theory, which was very heavy going, and conducted by an elderly, old-fashioned teacher. There was the occasional laugh: Yog, in particular, had a fit of the giggles when they were discussing the pheasant-plucking song in class.

After struggling through it for a year, Yog gave up music theory. He realised it had no place in his future plans. But, like many other things in his life, he kept his accomplishments and intellect hidden. That did not mean he did not have confidence in his abilities. He knew he was good and was certain that he could have a career in music. 'It was always just music,' observed his father, Jack.

He did have one last hurrah for Joy, when he starred in the Christmas pantomime – her version of *Aladdin* containing lots of in-jokes about teachers and students. It was all good fun and instantly forgettable, except that it gave everyone at school the first opportunity to hear Yog sing, although the songs would never feature in the George Michael back catalogue.

He played a character called Wazir. 'He really came into his own,' says Joy, fondly. 'I wrote him awful songs to sing. It was all very corny. "Wazir was here" – and all that sort of thing. But I think everyone thought he was good, both as an actor and a singer.'

Bushey Meads may have been slow to realise he could sing, but commuters outside Green Park Tube station in Central London already knew. From the age of fifteen, Yog would bunk off school, usually on a Friday, to meet up with his childhood pal David Mortimer to try their luck in the bustling world of busking.

Even though Andrew was now his best buddy, he still saw David regularly and they would rendezvous at his house in Burnt Oak before heading off into the West End with a microphone and David's twelve-string guitar. While Andrew dabbled a little with guitar, David took his music seriously and was a more than useful musician.

Yog and David were not the most successful busking duo; it wasn't as simple as merely choosing a spot and getting on with it. No sooner had they found a promising place than the police would appear out of nowhere and move them on, so it was very difficult to make any money. Green Park was their favourite station because they might manage twenty minutes before uniform showed up. 'We were actually very good,' maintained Yog. 'We just got crap money because to make money you had to get these pitches where the police would leave you alone. But to have those you had to arrive at 5.30 in the morning, which was beyond the call of duty for me, even at fifteen. Sometimes the little money we made would be nicked.'

It was good practice to sing in public. They would perform a selection of very middle-of-the-road standards by The Beatles, Elton John and Queen and try and sneak in a few bits and pieces they had tentatively written together, although that would generally mean people turning round, wondering what on earth they were listening to.

Busking was an adventure and far better than school. On one occasion, however, they were alarmed to see a large skinhead wearing a bright red Fred Perry jumper careering down the escalator. He was obviously fleeing the long arm of the law. Yog recalled how funny it was: 'There was no one else about and there's me and Dave singing "Hey Jude" and he comes charging over and says to me, "Give us your fucking jumper." And I'm like, "This is my favourite jumper actually." "Give us your fucking jumper!" So I am standing there, taking off my best jumper and thinking, "This is so humiliating." I am thinking, "Dave, hit him with your guitar." But eventually I have to swap it.' Poor Yog then had the humiliating ride on the Tube home wearing a red jumper three sizes too big for him; he had to wear it because it was a freezing cold day. David, naturally, was laughing his head off at his friend's embarrassment even though Yog muttered unconvincingly, 'I quite like it, actually.'

At least they usually made enough for a night out. It became their Friday routine: Yog would keep his fashionable clothes at David's house and change into what he assumed was the latest trendy outfit before heading out clubbing. As usual, he never had trouble getting into places because he looked older than he was.

Georgios Panayiotou was a different person away from Bushey Meads. From an early age he could keep different aspects of his life entirely separate; he could compartmentalise. His friends outside school had no idea that he was enthusiastically embracing pantomimes, reading books and playing the violin. While, for their part, his classmates little realised that he was at last making a start on the music career he wanted for himself.

Andrew had been pushing for them to start a band from almost the first day they met. 'Let's get a band together' would be his daily refrain. Yog kept putting him off and being sensible about it, telling him he wasn't going to do anything about it until after O-levels, all of which he passed comfortably. After that, he delayed even more by saying he wanted to take his A-levels first.

A further obstacle was that Andrew was hardly ever around after he left Bushey Meads. He enrolled at Cassio College in Langley Road, Watford, met a new circle of friends and revelled in the environment of a sixth-form college where he was treated as an adult. Yog was unimpressed: 'Suddenly, he was a serious fashion victim. He was wearing really outrageous clothes that looked absolutely terrible and taking drugs and stuff.' George Michael later confided that he was put off trying LSD after learning that Andrew had a very bad experience after trying the hallucinogenic drug for the first time. Andrew subsequently avoided a drug-influenced lifestyle, much preferring alcohol as the stimulant of choice.

Although it was still great to dance to, the allure of disco was fading for the two suburban soul boys. They had never embraced punk in any shape or form so they were looking for a new direction to spark their interest. They found it in a relatively short-lived revival of ska music, a variation of reggae that originated in Jamaica in the late fifties and early sixties. It was pioneered by the legendary Prince Buster, a former boxer and gang leader who made the new sound popular throughout the world and had a breakthrough hit in 1967 in the UK with his song 'Al Capone'.

The new take on ska became known as 2 Tone, an edgier sound masterminded by Jerry Dammers, the songwriter and keyboard player with The Specials, a collective from Coventry. He wanted to create something that could represent harmony at a time when racial conflict and the exploits of National Front extremists were gathering far too many headlines. He started his own label, 2 Tone Records, which featured a logo that defined the style and fashion of the movement: a figure sporting a black suit with a white shirt, black tie, white socks, black loafers and sunglasses, all topped off with a porkpie hat. This uniform would be the basis for much of what George Michael wore throughout his professional career. The enterprising Dammers signed many of the bands that became synonymous with 2 Tone, including The Selecter, Bad Manners, The Beat and, most famously, Madness with the 'nutty sound' of Camden Town.

For Andrew and Yog, 2 Tone was a winning combination of music and fashion. It also seemed to be a gateway to instant success for this raft of previously unheard-of groups. In 1979, The Specials reached the top ten with 'Gangsters', a reworking of 'Al Capone', and 'A Message to You, Rudy'. Madness changed their name from Morris and the Minors to Madness in honour of Prince Buster's song 'Madness is Gladness'. Their first hit was called 'Prince' and their second a reworking of his song 'One Step Beyond'.

Andrew and Yog were fans of both bands, but they needed to jump on the bandwagon or miss out altogether. Eventually Andrew had had enough of his friend's hesitation and insisted they have a rehearsal the following night. Yog finally relented, but only if David Mortimer came up from Edgware. Fortunately, he could make it, and their first tentative steps towards stardom were made in the living room in Oakridge Avenue.

They made quite a noise; luckily, Jack was working in the restaurant that Saturday night. Yog's mother Lesley tactfully suggested that perhaps in future, if they were going to continue, they might alternate rehearsals between Radlett and Andrew's home in Bushey.

They came up with their signature tune at the very first rehearsal. 'Rude Boy' was their idea of a 2 Tone anthem. Yog scrawled the lyrics on a scrap of paper. Basically, it consisted of Andrew and Yog chanting the title and it was very catchy.

> Rude boy rude boy rude boy rude boy
> Rude boy rude boy rude boy rude boy
> Rude boy rude boy rude boy rude boy
> This ain't your party
> No one invited you …

The boys started rehearsing more seriously in preparation for their first live gig. They recruited Andrew's younger brother Paul on drums and classmate Andy Leaver on guitar. Their first choice as bassist dropped out, but the Ridgeleys used to live across the road from another Bushey Meads old boy, Jamie Gould, who was a few years older, owned a Rickenbacker bass and was already playing in a band. He enjoyed reggae, so was happy to join them. They were now six in number, which may have seemed an extravagance, but Madness too were a sextet.

Andrew and Yog had equal standing as leaders of the group. They were both singers and the intention was for them to share the vocals. Jamie gives a surprising verdict on their capabilities: 'I would have said that Andrew was actually the better singer at the time. It was obvious that Yog was quite focused on everything. He worked at it. He had an exceptional voice but Andrew was the one whose voice rang out over the top of everything. He had a more powerful voice.'

The two singers would bicker constantly like an old married couple in a television sitcom. The rest of the boys would let them get on with it. Andy Leaver was very popular: 'He was really bubbly and happy. Just a lovely chap,' recalls Jamie, who used to spend most of rehearsals jamming with Paul. The younger Ridgeley had developed into an excellent drummer, modelling his technique on Stewart Copeland, the virtuoso drummer with The Police. He had provided the distinctive beat on their many hits that included two number ones in 1979: 'Message in a Bottle' and 'Walking on the Moon'.

Sometimes Yog would sit down and play the drums, always good for getting rid of some frustrations. Rehearsals were a bit of a trial for everyone. Jamie observes, 'It often got to the point where you thought it was pointless. You would come in and rehearse for two hours and had played just two three-minute songs!'

By November 1979, despite the constant arguments, they were ready for their first gig. They played a very short set after the fireworks on Bonfire Night at the St Andrew's Methodist Church Hall in Bushey Heath, known to all locally as the Scout Hut. The hall, which was about ten years old, was a typical village space in that it played host to all sorts of activities, including a youth club, Sunday school and a bridge club; the boys wondered what the mysteriously named 'Wives Club' might be. The dark wooden floor was laid out as a badminton court with a stage at one end where the band set up.

An exuberant and noisy rendition of 'Rude Boy' was the highlight of the night. They did well enough to be asked back. The band were also given permission to practise from time to time at the hall, which gave their parents a rest. Prospects looked even brighter when a young A&R man called Michael Burdett came to watch them rehearse. Michael had been taken on as a talent scout by Sparta Florida Music Group, a small music publishing company based in Knightsbridge. His job was to find the next big thing, although that was proving quite difficult. His bosses had already passed on one unsigned band he was keen on: they were from Dublin and called U2.

The history of pop music is, of course, littered with missed opportunities, so Michael continued to see new bands practically every night. His girlfriend's younger sister knew Paul Ridgeley, so he agreed to drift over to the Scout Hut one evening, have a listen and maybe offer some advice. He was happy to do that even though he was only nineteen and still a novice himself.

Michael immediately liked the band who, as yet, didn't have a name: 'The two singers immediately impressed me. There was something about their commitment to performance that I'd only seen before in well-known, more successful bands. Andrew was warm, intelligent, good-looking and great company. He already looked like a terrific performer and had a good voice. The other singer, who seemed slightly more serious but just as committed, was introduced to me as Yoghurt. Together they had real chemistry. They weren't the finished product by any means, but I couldn't get "Rude Boy" out of my head.'

Michael thought the band had real potential, but he also enjoyed spending time with them. Andy Leaver had a knack of keeping spirits up with what Michael describes as his 'comedic, self-deprecating manner'. Yog was the most serious: 'He seemed to prefer one-to-one conversations to being in a large group. In those one-to-one chats, he was just delightful and had a certain empathetic quality to him.'

Michael started going to more rehearsals, usually at Radlett or at Andrew's parents' new house in Bushey, and recorded them: 'I wanted to listen back so I could hear where they were going wrong, or more importantly, where they were going right.' He played these very early recordings to his bosses at Sparta Florida, but they passed on the band. He had been hoping they would provide a little seed money so that the band could make a proper demo, but they could not be persuaded.

Plan B was for everyone to share the expense of recording time at a real studio. They each put in £12 to pay for it, and soon after New Year 1980 Michael found a sixteen-track facility in the picturesque village of Wheathampstead, just north of St Albans. He was able to book the time at the Profile Recording Studios under the band's chosen name. They had written a song called 'The Executive' and decided to call themselves that. Michael wasn't so sure: 'I wasn't a fan of the name and expressed disappointment. I can see that Andrew was probably already imagining them in bowler hats, looking quite dapper and, of course, that might have worked.'

Yog's very first day in a recording studio began in an exciting fashion. The boys had piled into a van driven by saxophonist Noel Castelle, another local musician, who had agreed to play sax at the session. The van skidded across the road and narrowly missed traffic before swerving back amid much shouting and honking of horns. It could have been a disaster. Everyone arrived for the big day thoroughly shaken.

Fortunately, things improved after that near disaster. Michael brought a friend, Simon Hanhart, along to help with engineering and song structures. He was a trainee engineer at the Marquee Studios behind Wardour Street. He would subsequently become one of the most respected producers in the business, working with David Bowie, Marillion and the London Symphony Orchestra, as well as producing the acclaimed BBC charity record 'Perfect Day', which featured an all-star cast, including Elton John, U2 and the song's composer, Lou Reed.

Here he was helping his mate on a chilly morning in the middle of the Hertfordshire countryside. They decided to record two songs. 'Rude Boy' was the first. Andrew and Yog set about laying down their harmonies like seasoned professionals. 'They weren't fazed at all,' recalls Michael. At the end, everyone gathered behind the microphone and made party sounds, shouting and whooping and clinking bottles.

Unusually, the second track was an instrumental version of Beethoven's 'Für Elise', featuring David on lead guitar and Yog and Andrew vocally improvising and chanting on the off-beat, which was the style with ska music at the time. On the day, the version ends memorably with David making a small mistake and exclaiming, 'Oh, shit!'

Michael observes, 'It was a good fun day and none of them seemed overwhelmed. I remember Yog in particular asking questions about recording techniques. The only downside of the experience was the facilities at the studio. The reverb would only work on one side of the stereo, so they were never fully mixed.'

Simon and Michael were not unhappy, however, because the two tracks clearly showed The Executive's potential. Afterwards, everyone adjourned to The Cherry Tree pub in Wheathampstead to unwind and discuss the day. All agreed it was a good experience. Now all they had to do was persuade a record company to sign them.

5

CALL ME GEORGE

Jack Panos never tired of telling his son that he couldn't sing. His opinion did nothing to shake Yog's resolve. Now that he'd enjoyed his first taste of real recording, he was more eager than ever to make it work and still keen to win his sceptical father's approval.

One chilly day after school, he enthusiastically played the demo to his father: 'Rude Boy' blared out from the sound system of Jack's new Rolls-Royce. The atmosphere inside the car was no warmer. Hearing his son incessantly chanting 'Rude Boy' didn't change Jack's view that his son was being naive and wasting precious time with his musical obsession. Yet again, he was making his well-worn point that this was not a career option.

For Yog, who invariably treated his father with great respect despite being a teenager, this seemed like the final straw, especially when Jack casually observed, 'All seventeen-year-olds want to be pop stars.' He exploded: 'No, Dad! All twelve-year-olds want to be pop stars.'

Michael Burdett was much more confident than Jack Panos that Andrew and Yog would succeed. Over the next month or two he booked meetings with A&R managers at leading record companies in London, including WEA, Virgin, EMI, Chrysalis and Island. They all passed, but he kept trying.

An optimistic Yog, meanwhile, went back to school after the winter break to continue his A-levels. One of the rites of passage for English students in the UK is a coach trip to Stratford-upon-Avon, and the sixth form of Bushey Meads was no exception. In February 1980, Yog dutifully joined the other A-level pupils to see Ronald Eyre's production of *Othello*. The anguished Moor of Venice was played by Donald Sinden, who managed successfully to bridge the gap between critical acclaim and being a much-loved comedy and television figure.

Yog did not care much for Shakespeare. He found the Bard a bore and Sinden's perfectly enunciated performance did not change his mind. The trip wasn't a complete waste of time, however, because his eye was caught by an older girl from school, who was brunette, slim and statuesque. Her name was Helen Tye and, in Yog's opinion, she should definitely have been a model. He was delighted, therefore, to discover on his return to school that she would be in his painting class even though she was in the upper sixth.

At first, Yog was taking three subjects at A-level: English, Art and Music Theory, and it was widely assumed that he would go on to university. His parents were keen for him to be the first in the family to make that academic leap forward. He clearly had the intellect, although it never figured in his future plans at all.

He enjoyed the art lessons, particularly because Helen was at the easel next to him. She was struck by his precise eye for detail when painting a landscape, although it was obvious he wasn't really interested in art as a career subject. His conversation was full of music and his excitement at the prospect of a record deal for The Executive. She observes, 'He was absolutely clear the whole time I knew him that he was going to have a career in music.'

Helen liked him right from the start. He was not some sort of classroom Adonis but someone who was fun to talk to and much more interesting than the other boys: 'You could have a lively discussion with him about a lot of different subjects. When you are that age, most boys seemed to be either boring or weird.' For his part, Yog too liked their conversations. 'He was an intelligent person and I think he enjoyed being around somebody who had thoughts and opinions,' she adds.

They both had a social conscience and strong views about fairness and equality. As teenagers, they liked to complain about the views of their parents and would have voted Labour if they had been old enough. Helen explains, 'We were both at a state school at a time when the prevailing culture was in favour of higher taxation in order to pay for housing and education. The National Health Service, for example, was taken totally for granted. Student loans would have been something a bit American and unthinkable. I think we relished being a bit provocative against our parents. We were spoilt brats, really, because we both came from middle-class, pretty well-to-do families.'

Helen also felt empathy with Yoghurt – the name the majority at school still called him – because they were both partial outsiders. She explains, 'My mother is Swedish so I have never really felt a hundred per cent English. It's a ridiculous generalisation but I didn't feel most of the English people I met were very interesting. At the time Bushey was very white and very suburban. There was no diversity at all really, so even somebody who was Greek was exotic. He spoke with this very North London accent which is a bit different somehow to the Bushey accent. And he was just like an ordinary bloke – except that he wasn't ordinary at all.'

Yog hadn't dated anyone since Lesley Bywaters, and that was more than a year before, so it was time to try again. He correctly foresaw that a date with Helen would do wonders for his credibility as a budding pop star and that they would look good together.

'Do you like dancing?' he asked her casually, paintbrush in hand. 'Yeah, of course,' she answered. He told her that there was a disco close to his dad's restaurant and wondered if she might like to go with him. She did. 'Call me George,' he said.

He had decided that he would start calling himself George Panos, which he thought sounded a lot better than Georgios Panayiotou. He couldn't opt for Yoghurt or Yog as that made him sound like the bassist in a heavy-metal band.

Helen and the new 'George' started dating. George's dancing was getting better all the time and while The Executive were a 2 Tone band, he still liked nothing better than showing off his latest moves to 'Boogie Wonderland' by Earth, Wind & Fire or 'Contact', a big disco hit for Edwin Starr that had the cheesy chorus hook, 'Eye to eye, contact'. George proved very adept at the hand movements and the stare.

An evening out would always finish with dinner at the Angus Pride. He told Helen she could order what she liked, although he himself was going through a very picky stage with his eating: 'He always ordered the same thing. It was like a deep-fried, very thin fillet of pork. He didn't like green vegetables. So he would have that and then he would have taramasalata with pitta bread. It wasn't a very healthy diet! I would try different things because the food was excellent there.'

Jack would come out into the restaurant at some point and walk about the tables, saying hello to people and having a friendly word, eventually making his way over to his son and his new girlfriend. 'He was always very pleasant to me,' remembers Helen, who was a crucial two years older than his first girlfriend when she met George's father and less in awe. 'He was somewhat preoccupied, in the same way that my mother would be. Business owners are always busy and preoccupied and not really "people" people in the same way.'

Jack did cause great excitement in her street on the occasion he drove George round to give them both a lift to the restaurant. He was behind the wheel of his silvery blue Rolls-Royce with its personalised KP number plate, proof indeed that he had become a successful man. The net-curtain-twitchers had a field day. Helen had never been in a Rolls before and felt very grand as they made their way serenely to Edgware.

Most of the time George's mother Lesley would ferry them about in her less-impressive brown Triumph Herald. Helen got on famously with his mum and enjoyed the times she spent in the kitchen of their Radlett home, chatting away to Lesley and the two sisters, Yioda and Melanie.

Lesley no longer took George to school every day. He was happy to catch the bus. But he was still her boy and she would do anything for him. 'She was an angel and was devoted to him,' observes Helen, who thought his mother was wonderful from the first time George invited her over to the house.

'They had a big open kitchen with a large table in it and she would always say, "Have a cup of tea and are you hungry?" And George would answer, "Yes, can you fry me an egg?" She was just super-nice. She was genuinely interested in having a conversation with George and with me. She treated us like adults and she wanted to know what we thought about things. I think that was a real eye-opener for me. She was very empathetic and just treated us as people she would enjoy having dinner with.'

Helen's observations about Lesley Panayiotou reveal why her son regarded his mother – and not Andrew, David or Andros – as his best friend: 'She treated her son with respect. She spoke to him as if he had interesting things to say … and so he did.'

Helen also got on well with his sisters: 'They were very different. Melanie was more glamorous. She had beautiful long black hair and was very into makeup and hair. Yioda was very sort of natural and didn't care what she looked like. She was more of a tomboy. Melanie was fun-loving and fashion-conscious whereas Yioda was more thoughtful and intellectual. I really liked both of them and we would have long conversations.'

It was fortunate for George that Melanie was so keen on hair styling, because she was continually asked to practise on her brother. If there was one aspect of his looks that he felt insecure about, it was his hair. Helen observes, 'His hair was a big saga. He just didn't like it. He didn't like the way it was naturally. Melanie was forever styling and changing his hair.'

His unruly mop became more of an issue when for the first time he had to face up to having his picture taken for publicity purposes. To everyone's excitement, Arista had shown interest in the demo tape and had asked the obvious question: 'What do The Executive look like?'

Michael Burdett came round to the house in Radlett and took a number of pictures of the six band members inside and out in the garden. He placed them on the stairs in a direct imitation of the well-known Madness picture that had publicised 'One Step Beyond'. Yog's hair was moderately wild but he had shaved off the teenage beard he was growing; The Executive was beginning to look like a proper band.

Arista approved of the pictures and still seemed interested. Meanwhile, Michael's publishing company Sparta Florida wanted to secure publishing rights for the song 'Rude Boy' and offered a contract to Andrew and Yog that even Michael, their own employee, thought was embarrassing – especially as they weren't actually offering a financial advance. Fortunately, Jack, despite his cynicism, knew a record producer who ate in his restaurant and was able to get some proper advice for the boys. They turned it down.

Jack was also there when Michael organised an evening when the band's parents could be told how things were progressing and what a life in the spotlight might mean. It was a little presumptuous but these were young men swept along by the excitement of it all. Jack was as downbeat as ever about the prospects, although he did promise a celebratory dinner at his restaurant if a deal was ever signed.

Just when a breakthrough seemed within touching distance, Arista cooled – so much so that they stopped taking Michael Burdett's calls. It was disappointing.

At least George's relationship with Helen was progressing nicely. He was a romantic boyfriend who enjoyed kissing and holding hands as they waited for the bus. One of the first presents he gave Helen was a cassette of songs by the beautiful country star Crystal Gayle, including her signature hit 'Don't It Make My Brown Eyes Blue' and 'Talking in Your Sleep', a plaintiff song of betrayal, which were slower numbers they both enjoyed dancing to when everyone was getting their breath back at the disco.

George's favourite ballad when he was sixteen was the Don McLean version of the Roy Orbison classic ballad, 'Crying'. Surprisingly perhaps, it never featured in George Michael's repertoire, although its melancholic lyric was ideal for his soaring vocal. The sentiment of love and loss is one he would return to many times in his own songwriting.

For the moment he was happy smooching with Helen to the record, which was one of the biggest number ones of 1980. But he never put pressure on her to take their relationship to the next stage, which was one of the things she most liked about him: 'We were still at school and I felt we were still quite innocent. He would put his arm around me and was affectionate, but he wasn't pushy the way some boys of that age were.'

She found herself falling for George in a big way. Even her mother liked him and she was, in Helen's teenage opinion, notoriously hard to please. She ran her own successful import business and had brought Helen and her brother Martin up as a single parent when she divorced. Helen recalls, 'I wasn't sure she would like him because she could be critical, but he just had a very easy manner with her.'

One of the great myths about George was that he had low self-esteem. That was absolutely untrue. If it had been the case, he wouldn't have had the courage to stand up to his father. 'I don't know where that came from,' observes Helen. 'He was always confident.' Unassuming modesty perhaps was being mistaken for a poor self-image.

One indication that Helen really liked George was that she always paid for everything. He never had any money. Now that he was dating as well as rehearsing and going to school, he had little time for taking on the small jobs around the neighbour-hood that would have given him some spending money. Shelling out money for nothing in a Greek-Cypriot household was not the prescribed way, so he was never going to get a handout from his dad. He would have to get a job and earn his own money – something Jack never tired of telling his son.

Helen had a job working as an usherette at the Watford Palace Theatre: 'I always had more money than him and used to pay for the bus fare into town. It wasn't just his parents saying to him, "Why don't you get a job?" My mum used to complain to me, "He hasn't got a job"!'

They went to see a couple of shows at the theatre where she worked, and afterwards they would go to the bar and she'd introduce him to her workmates. Everyone thought the teen-age couple looked good together.

George seemed to like to keep certain areas of his life separate from others. He never invited Helen to any of the band's rehearsals. In his mind, that was strictly for the boys in the way it might have been were they a six-a-side football team. That would never happen, though, because George was not at all sporty.

They did socialise with David Mortimer and sometimes with his cousin Andros, two key people who travelled with George through much of his life. They didn't see much of Andrew, who had his own set of friends from college, so it was rarely a threesome when they went out, as had been the case with his previous girlfriend, Lesley. Helen liked David in particular: 'He was a sweet person. It seemed to me he was very much in awe of George and wasn't as confident or as direct in what he wanted to do as George was.'

She may not have been to rehearsals but Helen did see The Executive perform their 2 Tone set at the Scout Hut: 'It was very kind of stylised. I think people really loved it or didn't like it that much. But even though I liked it, it didn't get to me on an emotional level.' The Executive's showstopper, 'Rude Boy', left her cold: 'I think there were a bunch of beer-drinking guys who thought it was really cool – much more than the girls.'

By coincidence, The Executive was joined for live gigs by Tony Bywaters, elder brother of Lesley and an accomplished guitarist. He used to help out because, other than Jamie Gould, 'none of them could play guitar very well'. His involvement was another indication of the small suburban world of Bushey. He was struck by George and Andrew's 'schoolboy get-up-and-go'. He recalls, 'They both just knew they were going to be famous. They just knew it.'

It hadn't crossed George's mind at this stage that he might need backing singers, so he never suggested that role for

Helen. He did think she had a nice voice when he heard her sing along to things in his room, but she had no desire to perform in public and hated people staring at her. That was a problem for her when she dressed up in the 2 Tone gear George liked her to wear.

They made a striking pair on the number 142. George usually wore a white shirt matched with what his girlfriend thought were old man's trousers. Helen, 5ft 10in tall, in a black-and-white dress, white tights and white stiletto heels, looked amazing but 'felt so stupid'. She recalls, 'I was very self-conscious. I felt it wasn't really me at all.'

George liked it and encouraged Helen to follow a career in modelling. He persuaded Melanie to give her a makeover and went with her to a modelling agency in Central London to find out what the next step might be. But she planned to go to university, not parade up and down a catwalk.

George's interest in how Helen looked and, perhaps more importantly, how they looked together, was the first fascinating indication of his professional interest in being seen with models and using them in his videos when he became George Michael. Helen, for her part, thought George might be just as well-suited to being an actor, especially after she saw him perform as Wazir in the school pantomime. But nothing was ever going to deviate him from his music master plan.

A year can be a big age gap in your teens. A month after George turned seventeen in June 1980, Helen celebrated her eighteenth birthday. On the day, she planned to hold a very grown-up dinner party at home for her closest friends and naturally she wanted her boyfriend to be there. George didn't want to go. Her friends had all sat their A-levels and were now planning the next big step of leaving home for university and he would have felt left out. They never really socialised with Helen's crowd and he had little to do with them at school. 'Sometimes he was shy with people he didn't know,' she observes.

Instead, he came round during the day and gave her the new Roxy Music album *Flesh and Blood* as a present. It contained two of their best-known hits, 'Oh Yeah', and another imaginative song about yearning, 'Over You'. Helen was about to go to Sweden to visit family for the summer, so she was pleased she would have the album with her to remind her of George. At least, she would have done if he hadn't immediately asked her if he could borrow it. 'I loved the album. I said OK, but I wasn't at all happy about it because I had just been given it. It really put me out because I wanted to keep it!'

They had been dating for five months when Helen went off to Sweden for five weeks, but things were not the same between them when she got back. She was looking forward to starting a new chapter in her life at university while George was pressing on with The Executive. George had also reconnected with a girl called Jane who he'd first fancied at the age of twelve when he saw her ice-skating at the Queensway rink in London. She didn't notice him.

Jane, now a buxom teenager, came to one of The Executive gigs in the summer and decided she liked the look of the swarthy singer, with no recollection of their first encounter, five years previously. George would later famously suggest in a song that he two-timed Helen with Jane. That may or may not have been the case, but he told Helen about Jane. Any desire he had to date another girl wasn't the single reason they split up. They went to The King Stag pub in Bournehall Road, Bushey, for a grown-up conversation. Helen was now eighteen so could enjoy a rum and coke legally, while George was seventeen with stubble and looked, as ever, twenty-five.

Helen remembers it vividly: 'I was just saying I'm going to university, you're not. You might want to go out with other people. I might want to go out with other people. I think it was quite realistic and quite mature in that way.'

And that was that, although it was one of those conversations that afterwards made you want to beat your forehead against the wall and wish you hadn't been so bloomin' grown-up about things: 'I knew there were going to be big changes in my life and that our worlds were very different at this point, but I did feel very sad. It was the first break-up of my life. I was very, *very* fond of him. I was in love with him.'

George now had no girlfriend and he was soon to have no band either. The Executive was falling apart. Niggles and ill feeling began to fester. Helen Tye may have thought David Mortimer sweet, but Jamie Gould found him far too cocky and decided to play full-time with his other band.

Michael Burdett continued to attend rehearsals and even help with songwriting duties, before drifting off to pursue his own musical career. He became a well-known composer for television and co-wrote the theme music for both *MasterChef* and *Homes Under the Hammer*. Then Andy Leaver had to leave due to ill health. The Executive soldiered on as a four-piece and even recorded another set of demos that included the Andy Williams hit 'Can't Get Used to Losing You', which would subsequently be recorded by 2 Tone band The Beat.

The Executive's version was not enough to win them any more attention than their original demo. David and Paul were also getting itchy feet. Andrew's brother had matured into a brilliant drummer and was much in demand by other bands. David was considering offers of work abroad.

As a four-piece they played a gig at Cassio College with George on bass guitar but it was not a success. He forgot many of the notes and had to sing them instead. Nobody seemed to mind, but the enthusiasm for 2 Tone was waning.

Andrew had one last try at generating some interest when he came across another regular in his favourite local pub, The Three Crowns on the High Road in Bushey. By coincidence, Mark Dean's mum and dad lived a few doors down from the Ridgeleys in Chiltern Avenue. Their son had made a mercurial start to a career in the music business and had the chat and the sharp suits to show for his initial success. He had quickly become established when he found work with And Son Music Ltd, which handled publishing for The Jam. He had been noticed by the legendary music impresario Bryan Morrison as well as impressing many with his ability to spot talent. Keen to pursue the then fashion for mod revivals, he signed the band Secret Affair, who had a top-twenty hit with a song called 'Time for Action'.

Mark was definitely on the up when the boy from his street thrust a tape of The Executive into his hand. Grudgingly, he listened to it, declared it to be 'rubbish' and dropped it in the bin. It was time for The Executive to pack it in.

6

VISION OF THE FUTURE

George appeared on television for the first time in February 1981, holding centre stage at Le Beat Route in Greek Street. He seemed a little unsure of himself as the camera panned across the dance floor and lingered on him, a strapping seventeen-year-old with a black beard, his trademark bushy hair and wearing a vivid orange suit. They weren't there to film him. He wasn't a celebrity then. The crew from BBC *Nationwide* were preparing a feature on Spandau Ballet and the blossoming New Romantic scene.

George had loved the Soho club ever since the first time he was allowed in and spotted Spandau singer Tony Hadley at the bar and cultural icon Steve Strange playing Space Invaders. A schoolboy from Radlett could catch the bus into London and be mixing with the fashionable and famous who, earlier that day, he might have been reading about in pop papers and glossy magazines in the sixth-form common room.

Friday nights became his favourite time of the week, although he wasn't always allowed in. Sometimes the club owner Ollie O'Donnell thought he and Andrew were just too suburban. Stung by such criticism, they began dressing in more outlandish clothes. Andrew started wearing a single plait in his hair in the manner of Adam Ant, as well as bright red satin trousers. When he wasn't sporting his orange suit, George preferred a green waistcoat and matching hat.

Enforcing a strict door policy was one of the canny ways the clubs created exclusivity and publicity. Club host Steve Strange pulled off a masterstroke when he refused entry to Mick Jagger to Blitz in Covent Garden on the grounds that he was too normal and 'didn't look right'. Steve was a pop star in his own right with the group Visage, whose best-known song was the top-ten hit 'Fade to Grey'. But more importantly, he blended music and fashion together – a trend followed by Spandau Ballet, Duran Duran and Culture Club, whose singer Boy George was once employed at Blitz as the cloakroom attendant. George had never embraced punk, so when he and Andrew tired of 2 Tone, they were in their element in this new cultural movement sweeping through London. As one of his closest friends observes, 'George was a club boy.'

At Le Beat Route, George was able to reconnect with his inner disco. He was still a big fan of Roxy Music, who, along with David Bowie, formed the backdrop for the New Romantics. But he also discovered a funkier sound. In particular he liked 'Burn Rubber on Me (Why You Wanna Hurt Me)' by The Gap Band. It was one of those records that was a minor chart hit but became much more popular in the clubs. While the lyric was another that dealt with lost love – a man being abandoned by a girl – George was more interested in the beat. He liked it so much that, as George Michael, he sampled the track for his single 'Star People 97'.

Andrew first heard it lying in the bath listening to Capital Radio and couldn't believe what a great track it was and an 'absolute breakaway from the rest of the real middle-of-the-road shit'.

Sometimes David Mortimer would join them clubbing, but most nights it would be George, Andrew and his new girl-friend, Shirlie Holliman. George hadn't dated since Helen Tye, but as from those early teenage years with Lesley Bywaters, three was never a crowd for the boys, especially if dancing was involved.

Andrew had met Shirlie on the eve of his eighteenth birth-day in January 1981 in The Three Crowns. She was blonde, bubbly and self-assured. They hit it off straight away.

One of five children, Shirlie was born and raised in Bushey. Like Andrew, Lesley Bywaters and Helen Tye, she had been part of a generation that all went to the same primary and secondary schools. She was a year older than Andrew and had barely noticed him at Bushey Meads. She had spotted Georgios Panayiotou, though, and had been one of the gang who mocked him when he was carrying his violin case around the playground.

When she left school, she was working with horses, training to be a riding instructor and dreaming of being a singer. Andrew certainly gained her attention when he started telling her about his group. She immediately suggested that he should ditch the singer and use her instead. They started dating and, almost at once, she met Andrew's best friend, Yog, when they went over to the house in Radlett. She was immediately struck by how close the two boys were, laughing at the same things, enjoying their music and each other's company.

Although she and Andrew began a serious relationship, George soon became her best friend. She loved the nights they went dancing, not just to Le Beat Route but also other more local clubs around North London, like Bogarts in Harrow.

Shirlie recalled that they would work out their dance routines in George's bedroom before emerging all sweaty, to be met by a raised eyebrow or two from his mum and sisters: 'It was so much fun – they became my world. They were great times but I sometimes felt like a spare part next to George – his talent overawed me. He was the organiser and Andrew had the charisma.' Shirlie always preferred dancing with George because she thought he had better rhythm than her boyfriend: 'Andrew was too bony and hard and George was far softer – he just suited me to dance with.'

George was in his element. He told his friend and fellow club enthusiast, the writer Paul Simper, 'I loved dancing at Le Beat Route. Nobody gave a fuck who I was, so you could throw yourself around. If Shirlie was with me we'd really do that pair dancing. We'd always make a bit of space and really show off.' Shirlie doesn't quite remember it that way. She joked that they only cleared the floor when they were dancing really badly.

His many club nights, aged seventeen, reveal the amount of freedom George enjoyed. As the young man of the family he was never prevented from going out, even though he was supposed to be studying for his A-levels. He didn't tell his family or his friends that one of the places he occasionally slipped into was a gay disco above a pub close to the Manor House Tube station. The human rights campaigner Peter Tatchell met him there long before George became well known and was struck, as many were, by what a good dancer he was, always singing along as he showed off his latest moves: 'He had a good voice and said he was going to be a pop star. There were lots of wannabes in those days, I thought.'

Incredibly, while he was leading an almost secret life as a club boy, George, or more precisely Georgios, had been appointed a prefect at Bushey Meads. It would not be an achievement that featured on his CV. He wasn't the most popular, especially with the orchestra after he took a fellow violinist to see the deputy headmaster after he had told Georgios to 'sod off'.

He sailed through his A-levels before settling to a summer of leisure with his friends. Shirlie had a car, which proved to be a great bonus, ferrying everyone to the swimming pool in Watford, where they splashed away their mornings before adjourning for ice cream, McDonald's and milkshakes in the afternoon.

Andrew had left college with nothing to show for it except two years of fun and freedom. He took a job briefly as a cleaner and then worked in a warehouse before signing on the dole, which he preferred. George sarcastically said it suited his friend because he was a 'lazy bastard'. That was not an option for him because his parents absolutely would not stand for it. Having decided he was not a candidate for further education, George was under increasing pressure from them to settle on a career. They gave him a deadline of six months to get a recording deal or he would be out on his ear. Jack Panos loved his son dearly, but he was becoming increasingly agitated that he was just drifting.

He started a job as a labourer but didn't last long, although he found it a quick way to get fit and toned. He tried a few nights serving drinks in the Angus Pride but he kept getting the orders wrong and it soon became clear to everyone that he was not going to follow in his father's footsteps.

Jack, however, secured him work as a DJ at a busy and popular dinner/dance restaurant in Rickmansworth Road, Northwood called Bel Air, which was owned by Andrew Georgiades, the father of George Georgiades. His old primary-school friend recalls, 'George's dad brought him to my dad and said, "Andrew, can you give him a job? He wants to bloody do music. I want him to build a career and he wants to do this. Can you give him a job doing something until he sorts himself out?" So Dad had him as a DJ. He didn't like the music he had to play. It was The Jacksons, Lionel Ritchie and Abba, but his taste was a bit more funky.'

Georgios, as they called him at the restaurant, was forever trying to slip something more disco into the night's music, usually without success. He was hidden from the diners behind a pillar so they couldn't see the incongruous bearded figure in stylish winklepicker shoes. But they could hear him.

Looking back, George could laugh about it: 'Every night I would have to say, "Good evening, ladies and gentlemen, I hope you have enjoyed your meal. Welcome to Bel Air restaurant, we hope you will partake of a little dancing."' As soon as he started speaking the restaurant would immediately go completely quiet, which he found embarrassing and nerve-racking: 'My hands just used to get clammy and sweaty every night before I had to do this. I was absolutely hopeless at it.'

It was far from the worst job in the world. The hours meant he could take on afternoon shifts as an usher and doorman at the Empire Cinema in Merton Road, Watford. He enjoyed being able to watch the films for free before hopping on a bus down to Northwood.

One evening a melody came into his head just as he was paying the driver: 'It was as I walked on to the bus and was handing the guy the change. I remember getting the melody and going up and sitting at the back of the bus and putting words to it and everything. I used to do a little bit every day, on my way between working at the cinema and as a DJ … every day in my head.'

The melody on the bus became his most famous and popular song, the immortal 'Careless Whisper'. He ran the melody past Andrew back in his room in Radlett and his friend came up with the guitar parts that earned him a songwriting credit on the track, one of only three he shared with George. Andrew was more impressed than his sister Melanie, who cheekily called the song 'Tuneless Whisper'. George was very protective of his songwriting and wouldn't have included Andrew unless he had made a real and important contribution.

For the lyric, George drew inspiration from his split with Helen when he had eyes for another girl. The teenage Georgios Panayiotou was in no way a player. He had just two girlfriends at school and did not sleep with either of them. He was, however, a creative and articulate young man who could put into words feelings of love and loss that would strike a universal nerve. Just six words became one of the great lines of popular music: 'Guilty feet have got no rhythm'. He was still only seventeen.

At a later date, he played a demo of the song to Helen, with whom he remained on good terms. She remembers the occasion clearly. One afternoon when she was back from University

College London (UCL), he rang and asked her to come over because he wanted her to listen to a recording of a new song: 'I went to his house and we went up to his room and we sat on the floor and listened to his cassette. And we listened to "Careless Whisper" and I was completely astounded. I just thought, "This is amazing!" It's such a beautiful song … so professional, so beautiful and I just knew it was going to be incredibly successful. I was really blown away.

'I had absolutely no idea that it had anything to do with me or with him or anything of his feelings. He did not talk in a direct way about his feelings to me, other than his ambitions or his work and his creativity. He didn't say anything about being conflicted about wanting to break up with me or anything like that.'

At this stage, 'Careless Whisper' was a one-off. Andrew and George couldn't project their personality as two fun-loving soul boys through a song which possessed such an old-fashioned quality. They needed something more instant that better showcased them as club boys. They needed some dance tracks.

The two were still dancing at Le Beat Route whenever they could. On one particular night, Andrew was bopping about, showing off, when he started exclaiming exuberantly, 'Wham! Bam! I'm the Man' and doing a rap which George described as 'terrible', although in his defence, Andrew was just trying to be funny. Andrew's performance gave George the idea for a new song. He was looking for energy, dance-ability and humour.

Rap music had yet to take over the world back in 1981. It was still in its embryonic stage of popularity and was the exclusive preserve of black American hip-hop artists. The

Sugarhill Gang crossed the Atlantic with a song that is generally regarded as the first UK chart hit of the new genre. Their 'Rapper's Delight', which combined rap and disco, had been a summer top-three hit in the UK in 1979. The lyric was spoken over a mix of the disco classic 'Good Times' by Chic.

George wanted to create a rap that you could dance to and came up with the lyric to 'Wham Rap! (Enjoy What You Do)', which wasn't designed to be taken too seriously; it was meant to be fun. He saw it as parody of the times, or more precisely, a 'piss-take'. Superficially, it glorified being on the dole with such immortal lines as: 'I'm a soul boy. I'm a dole boy'. On closer inspection, it was almost a rap pitching Andrew against George.

The Andrew character may not have a job but he's having a good time with the boys 'down on the line'. By contrast, George is having to deal with parents or 'folks' who are telling him to get a job or 'get out of this house'. It was early proof that George was a clever and articulate eighteen-year-old.

This was a promising start to their songwriting together, but it became more problematic when Andrew and Shirlie decided to live together and moved into a grotty flat in the basement of her aunt's house in Peckham, Southeast London, which was quite a dramatic move from leafy Bushey. They immediately felt isolated as it was such an effort to keep in touch with friends, particularly George.

Fortunately, neither of them enjoyed the experience very much, especially having to use an outdoor loo. After a few weeks they returned to their respective parents, although they continued their relationship. Now he was back home, it was a time for parties. Usually that would consist of Andrew getting drunk and George making sure he got home safely. The one time it was the other way round was when George made a rare attempt to chat up a girl in a club and was upset at being rebuffed. He decided to drown his sorrows in a bottle of vermouth and had to spend the night at Andrew's house. He was in a dreadful state, on his knees in the kitchen, when Mrs Ridgeley found him; she kindly asked, 'Do you want a bowl, dear?' and thoughtfully provided one for him to be sick into if the need arose. The problem was he kept on falling forward and ending up with his head in the bowl. Eventually he was put to bed to sleep it off and in the morning Andrew's mother, who seemed to know exactly what to do in these situations, brought him up a glass of the aptly named Andrews liver salts.

They found time to write another song together, although really the process involved George using his friend as a sounding board for his musical ideas. He had no intention of making a career as a rap artist: 'Rap was quite funny at first but it got really boring,' he declared.

Instead, he again drew inspiration from Le Beat Route and, specifically, its trademark Caribbean décor. He wrote a lyric about the perfect club where you might meet celebrities, get a perfect suntan and have free drinks. It was poking gentle fun at the Club 18–30 holidays – although George had never been on one.

Andrew was again keen for them to make a new demo and suggested they use his parents' living room, first making sure they were out. They spent £30 hiring a Portastudio for the day. George had wanted one for his birthday but his father had ignored that request and given him a pair of fine antique guns as a financial investment.

They waited until the coast was clear, then set up everything using an old broom as a microphone stand and recorded bits of 'Wham Rap!', 'Club Tropicana' and 'Careless Whisper'. They were little more than snapshots in sound and not completed songs by any means. By the end of the afternoon, they expressed themselves satisfied with what George would later describe as a 'crappy little demo'.

Despite the obvious appeal of the fun dance tracks, they both realised that 'Careless Whisper' was a cut above. Andrew described it as a 'worldwide number one' in waiting. 'Julio Iglesias will be green,' he said. George was so proud of the song that he couldn't stop playing it to people. When Shirlie heard it, she realised for the first time that he was going to be a huge star.

He was allowed to include it in his dinner set at Bel Air and the diners liked it. The manager of the Empire, Shirley-Ann Mallery, who had a soft spot for George, let him play it one evening in the foyer of the cinema and he received a round of applause. Nobody could have foreseen that it would become staple background music for thousands of foyers around the world.

The boys needed a new name. They didn't want to resurrect The Executive and, this time around, believed something fun and boisterous would better fit their new image. Their first thought was Wham Bam! They had always liked the idea of calling a band after a record because one could publicise the other, as it did with 'Hey Hey We're the Monkees' or any number of Wombles tracks. After thinking about it, they shortened it to Wham! as the Bam made it seem too silly, like something out of *Batman*.

'Wham Bam' had also been the name of a forgettable summer hit of the seventies by the American country rock group, Silver. Going further back, the pop pioneer Jack Good produced a show called *Wham!* in 1960 in which DJ Keith Fordyce introduced leading British acts of the time, including Joe Brown, Billy Fury and Johnny Kidd & the Pirates. Perhaps George had come across the 1963 painting 'Whaam!' by Roy Lichtenstein in his art lessons, one of the most iconic of all pop art images.

The suburban soul boys thought Wham! was original and reflective of the fun element they wanted to bring to their music. They later discovered that there was an American band of that name already in existence, which would be a small inconvenience.

The newly named Wham! began another depressing round of record companies in London – many of them had already heard The Executive demos when Michael Burdett was trying to progress the band. They always managed to bluff their way in for an audience, but that was as good as it got. It was a depressing time, when A&R men thought they could spot talent on the basis of listening for ten seconds before they turned off the tape. They would be sent on their way with the word 'crap' ringing in their ears.

The boys were getting nowhere and it wouldn't be long before the six-month time limit set by George's father for a deal to be signed would be up. They decided to approach again Bushey's young music mogul, Mark Dean. Through Andrew's mother, they kept hearing of his mercurial rise. In the world of music things can happen very quickly. He had moved on to an A&R job with Phonogram and been largely responsible for signing two of the biggest charts acts of 1981, Soft Cell and ABC.

Just twenty-one, he had the confidence and the swagger of a young man going places very fast. His ambition was to start his own label and he persuaded the powerful CBS company to back his independent Innervision Records. The deal was not a particularly good one for Mark, and the fine financial margins he had to work with would subsequently have a disastrous effect on his relationship with Wham!

That was in the future. For the moment his mum was pestering him to hear another demo from Andrew Ridgeley and his friend. Finally, he had a quick listen, expecting to once again be unimpressed. But he loved it. Instantly, he could envision success for the boys, who were clearly special: 'I couldn't believe it but I had stumbled on talent on my doorstep.'

He invited them to his new offices in South Molton Street and met George for the first time. He sensed that the duo had an appealing image and that they had a brashness that worked. He explained his philosophy: 'I like good songs. I like songs with style. But if a band has no idea about the image they want to project, if they don't know what to tell the press, then they can forget it. It's all a question of attitude. I believe in arrogance and attitude. An artist should believe in what he's doing.'

He suggested that he finance a proper demo of the songs. While this was beginning to be exciting for the two teenagers, George was still working at Bel Air. The night before the recording, he was the DJ as usual. It would be his last shift with his old friend George Georgiades, who was now at catering college. He remembers, 'I asked him what he was doing tomorrow. And he said, "Well, I'm cutting a demo" and I thought, "Yeah, right." I did wish him good luck but in my head I thought, "Let's see how you do." I never saw him again at my dad's.'

Mark booked Wham! into the Halligan Band Centre in the Holloway Road, not far from the neighbourhood where George's mother grew up. Madness and Spandau Ballet had rehearsed there and it was a well-known, if slightly dark, basement studio in North London. He also arranged for a proper band to back the duo dispensing with the usual drum machines and synthesisers. They re-recorded the demo songs as well as another that would become 'Young Guns' but that didn't yet have a proper lyric. George had to write it in the studio, literally as they went along. He had help. The backing singer hired for the day was Lynda Hayes, who had settled in London after arriving from her native Chicago in the late seventies. Lynda had already earned a reputation as a dependable voice for adverts and studio sessions. She wrote the memorable line: 'Hey shut up chick, that's a friend of mine, just watch your mouth babe, you're out of line'. Lynda loved that she was technically one of the first female rappers. She observed, '"Out of line" wasn't even a phrase heard in England in 1982. I brought it from Chicago.'

Rather like 'Wham Rap!', 'Young Guns (Go for It)' was intended to be a witty social commentary. This time George's target was boys and girls who marry too young and the ensuing drudgery in their lives. He explained, 'It just seemed that the funniest thing relating to that was the way you get the boys up the pub saying, "Where's so and so?" "Oh, he's at home, she's kept him in again." It was tongue-in-cheek sexism.'

He even managed to give himself a name-check in the lyric. The overall effect was exuberant fun. You could imagine it being sung by the cast of *Grease*.

Pride of place in the recordings was reserved for 'Careless Whisper'. George described it in his autobiography as 'one of the most incredible moments of my life', hearing his song, written on the bus, performed properly with a band complete with a real-life saxophone.

While he was glowing with self-satisfaction, Mark phoned to say he was heading over with a contract that Tony Parsons memorably described as a 'premature ejaculation of agreement'. The three of them retired to a 'greasy spoon' café round the corner from the studios. Everyone involved seemed to have a different version of what went on.

George signed a contract with Innervision during this unscheduled tea break. It was completely out of character. He'd been cautious enough to employ a lawyer, Robert Allan, a friend of his father's, to oversee negotiations between Wham! and Mark Dean, but when faced with a concrete offer, he seemed to panic and sign in haste. He didn't take the trouble to ring Robert to check that he was happy and all the amendments had been taken in.

The meeting, if it can be called that, still grated with George more than twenty years later. He claimed that Mark told them that the deal would go away if they didn't sign right then. Mark had also said they wouldn't own the demos. George recalled, 'It was a total threat, a complete and utter threat.'

It's easy to cast Mark Dean as a villain in the scenario that left the boys with an appalling contract, but he too was a novice in such matters and had himself signed a deal with

CBS, which would inevitably put the squeeze on his own company. He later maintained that he put no pressure on them to sign there and then and would happily have waited. According to Mark, Wham! were desperate for him to sign them, although he did admit in retrospect that all parties were very stupid to conduct business in this random fashion.

Everybody seemed in such a rush, swept along by the excitement of finally releasing a record and making sure they were in the next CBS schedule of new releases. In effect, on 24 March 1982, Georgios Panayiotou and Andrew Ridgeley signed their future away for a £500 advance each and the prospect of their name on a hit. They were far more beguiled by thoughts of fame than by the sums of money involved.

Perhaps the most obvious observation in the whole sorry saga is that Wham! did not have a manager to negotiate the deal for them but, as Shirlie pointed out, she had never heard George take advice from anyone. In the future it might have been more difficult to get out of if the contract had not been so laughably bad. The positive news was that they had a deal with someone determined to make them a success. There would be singles to record, an album to make and fans to idolise them.

The first task was to record their debut single, which everyone agreed should be the intoxicatingly catchy 'Wham Rap!' An experienced producer, Bob Carter, who had seen success with Junior and Hazel O'Connor, came on board to oversee the recording at the Maison Rouge Studios in Fulham Broadway.

All was set fair for a June release, except for one ongoing problem: George wasn't happy with his name. The first pressing of the disc had already gone ahead with the credit G Panos/A Ridgeley. He didn't like it. It was too Greek.

One afternoon he was discussing the problem with David Mortimer at his friend's house in Edgware. It was commonplace for pop stars to change their names. Tom Jones, Freddie Mercury and Elton John were just three pop heroes who had found a name that better suited their image. Even David had changed his name to what he thought was the more pop-friendly David Austin. He said his real name reminded him of Meg Mortimer and her son Sandy, who were the lead characters in *Crossroads*, the popular long-running soap which seemed to be on television every night throughout their childhood.

Yog was happy with George. Many people called him that already, so he was used to it. Perhaps he should follow Elton's example and opt for two first names? Michael came into his head because David's dad was Michael Mortimer and he was sitting in his living room. One of his Greek uncles was also called Michael. And then he remembered his old primary-school friend, Michael Salousti. David liked it and so the decision was speedily taken. As with many decisions in his life, George acted quickly and firmly. He didn't dither over it.

He did try it out on Helen Tye to see if she liked it: 'He said his stage name would be George Michael. I said, "Oh, OK. Why?" He explained that it couldn't be this long Greek name that didn't roll off the tongue. He said, "I don't want to be associated with Demis Roussos."'

On the eve of his nineteenth birthday, Georgios Panayiotou prepared to begin an exciting new life as George Michael.

PART TWO

AT THE TOP OF A DREAM

7

HEY SUCKER

The young man who had become George Michael was still an eighteen-year-old club boy at heart who liked nothing better than having one too many drinks at the Camden Palace on the Tuesday and Thursday nights hosted by Steve Strange. He may not have got into so many alcoholic scrapes as Andrew Ridgeley but he wasn't far behind.

It would have been easy to underestimate a teenager who liked a party. Fortunately, music publisher Dick Leahy didn't make that mistake. Mark Dean had at one time worked for his partner Bryan Morrison and asked him to listen to Wham! By coincidence, Dick had also received the demo tape from a friend of a friend of George's parents. He was immediately struck by the difference between 'Wham Rap!' and 'Careless Whisper' and wanted to meet the songwriter who could craft such contrasting songs.

Mark brought George and Andrew in to meet him. From the outset he saw them as a double act with real presence and charisma: 'They walked into the office and almost without hearing the songs you knew they were going to make it.' But he *had* heard the songs and was very keen to sign them to Morrison Leahy Music. He was one of the shrewdest men in the music business with an enviable track record that George couldn't help but admire.

Like Mark, Dick's background was in A&R, working in the late 1960s for Philips Records when Dusty Springfield and The Walker Brothers were among their roster of artists. As managing director of Bell Records in the 1970s, he had dominated the charts with acts including Gary Glitter and David Cassidy. His label had released 'Daydreamer', a huge plus as far as George was concerned.

He seemed to have the knack of discovering teen dreams, as he proved when he signed the Bay City Rollers in 1971. Later, as the boss of GTO Records, he was responsible for many of the best-known disco hits of the seventies, including the Donna Summer classic 'I Feel Love'. He displayed his business acumen by selling GTO Records to CBS and subsequently moving into the lucrative world of music publishing.

When he met Wham!, Dick, who was two years younger than George's father, was in his mid-forties. Tall, suntanned, silver-haired and prosperous-looking, he had a taste for Havana cigars. George may have been impressed but he was not overawed.

Just a few weeks after the deal with Innervision had concluded so swiftly, George took on a major role in negotiations with Morrison Leahy. Dick recalled, 'I found out very early on that he knew what he was talking about.' Despite sometimes getting a poor press for not encouraging his son more, it seemed that Jack Panos had passed on a positive and astute business head. Dick observed, 'He's a very clear thinker.

He has an ability to take information and make a decision, not to shilly-shally around.'

Negotiations were not a case of George trying to extract greedily every last penny he could from the deal. Dick recalled, 'It's the control.' He insisted, for instance, that he had an absolute veto on who could record any future George Michael songs that he didn't want to record himself. He also demanded the right of approval of any secondary usage of his songs, which would cover their use in jingles, for example.

This was his first publishing agreement and he was still just eighteen. Happy with the deal, George would seek Dick's counsel throughout his career but particularly in those early days.

Dick and CBS very much saw Wham! as a club band and so a campaign was launched to create a following for the boys in the clubs of North London and the suburbs. They were learning their trade.

George and Andrew quickly discovered there was a big difference between showing off your Travolta-style moves among friends in Le Beat Route and performing them in public. Personal appearances promoting 'Wham, Rap!' in the clubs and discos of Watford and North London were not easy.

For starters, the mainly drunken male crowd were more interested in the two newly recruited female backing singers and dancers, Shirlie Holliman and Amanda Washbourn. Shirlie was an obvious choice and needed little persuading; she found Amanda, another striking blonde who had also attended Bushey Meads.

Mandy, as they called her, was only sixteen, which was quite young to be facing such a testosterone-filled environment.

George, in particular, was uneasy about how the girls were treated. The band, he said, were like a bunch of strippers, dashing into a club, performing their frantic, all-action number to a backing track and rushing off to the next venue. Sometimes they would have to change into their stage clothes in the toilets but, if all went well, they could be in and out in twenty minutes and on to the next engagement.

It was a hard school, having to fend off the drunks who thought it was perfectly acceptable to join in and be pop stars for three minutes. George hated it: 'The drunks would go up behind the girls. It was an absolute nightmare.'

George had to battle with his chivalrous instincts because the attention the girls received was probably due in no small measure to his meddling in their appearance, another early example of a desire to control his situation. He wanted them to dress sexily, showing off their legs in tight-fitting frocks. He was merely continuing his interest in seeing how he looked alongside women – a habit he had first acquired with Helen Tye. In some ways he saw the image of Wham! as a painting from art class, with each component adding to the appreciation of the canvas as a whole.

These very early personal appearances highlighted a conflict that George would continue to wrestle with for the rest of his career. He disliked being public property, but at the same time was happy to clinically manipulate his image – or in this case Wham!'s – to enhance his chance of success. He lost weight, shaved off his beard and made sure his teeth were as white as Andrew's. The image they presented even at this very early stage was very much a double act, although imperceptibly George was emerging as the driving force.

Amanda Washbourn abruptly left, apparently wanting to begin a career in styling or hairdressing. Some thought George had given her a subtle push because he thought her too young and unworldly for the rigorous demands of promotion. If that were true, it was a further indication of a ruthless streak as far as business was concerned.

One report suggested that she had missed an important PA (personal appearance) in front of CBS executives, which George frowned upon. He considered the musical meeting essential to getting the record company's backing, even though her absence was explained reasonably by her supporting a friend at a court appearance. Shortly afterwards it was left to Shirlie to tell Amanda they would be using another girl in future.

As a replacement, George envisaged a black girl, who would form a neat contrast with blonde Shirlie. He may well have thought black with blonde provided a better overall look for the Wham! girls – their very own 2 Tone backing singers. In the original line-up there was a good chance they could be mistaken for Bucks Fizz, one of the biggest chart acts of the year.

They found a stunning former model from Deptford, Southeast London, called Diane Sealy, who had become a singer under the clever new name of Dee C. Lee, and who at twenty was more worldly and committed than Amanda. She was working as an in-house session singer at EMI Publishing, recording three or four tracks a day for their contracted song-writers. Mark Dean contacted EMI, saying he was looking for a black female singer for his new band, and her name came up. He was impressed that she had done backing vocals for the jazz funk group Central Line and asked her to come and meet the boys. She recalled, 'We just clicked. They were really young and innocent, very sweet and great fun.'

She was originally signed for one single, but they liked her, asked her to stay and started paying her a wage. 'When it suited them, I was a member,' she added, resignedly. Dee C. Lee was on board in time to shoot the original promo for 'Wham Rap!', which had perhaps been the plan.

Despite their best efforts, 'Wham Rap!' proved a huge disappointment when it was released in June 1982 just before George's nineteenth birthday. Because it was backed by CBS, the track received some airplay and managed to sneak into *Record Mirror*'s Club Chart at number 25 but made no impact on the proper chart. The song failed even to break into the top 100 and was officially a flop.

Perhaps the timing was wrong for a song about the DHSS, even one that poked fun. Nobody seemed to get the joke at first and thought it was a bold and defiant statement about the joys of being on the dole. This was the month when the Falklands War was won and Britain was preparing to welcome home the nation's brave soldiers. The World Cup in Spain began that year and Princess Diana gave birth to the boy who would be king, Prince William. A more summery song like 'Club Tropicana' might have better suited the prevailing national mood.

They managed to gather some interest from the music press, however, and had their picture in the *NME* as well as being nominated as a Record of the Week in *Sounds*. In their early interviews Andrew did much of the talking as if, behind the scenes, it had been decided that he should be the face of the band and George the voice.

Originally there was some talk that Wham! were a black rapping band from the US, but this speculation was quickly quashed when their picture appeared in the music press. Bands can survive one poor-performing single but perhaps not two. The follow-up had to do better.

They redoubled their efforts to get noticed. The more appearances they did, the better they became. Dee C. Lee recalled, 'It didn't really feel like work. It was a new and fresh experience and we became more confident with every show.'

Not everything went smoothly. During one appearance at the premier West End nightclub Stringfellows, George misjudged the slipperiness of the glass floor. He was attempting a high kick when he skidded and his shoe went spinning off into the crowd. He kicked the other one off and spent the rest of the song performing in a pair of bright red socks.

More successfully, they appeared at Bolts, a weekend gay night at Lazer's in Haringey, North London, run by Norman Scott, a well-known London-based DJ. The appearance was set up by the marketing department of CBS. In return for a couple of drinks, Wham! mimed as usual to their record. Norman thought they were so good he immediately asked if they could come back.

Sure enough, they popped in to Bolts for the second time, but on this occasion Norman played a trick on them. They arrived late and he had enjoyed a couple of drinks before they arrived. He knew they had live mics, so flipped the record over and played the instrumental backing track. George realised instantly what had happened and they all rallied round to sing live despite having to continue with their energetic dance routines. It was Wham!'s first-ever truly live performance.

Norman said, 'It was a bit cheeky of me but they were so pleased about how it went.'

Afterwards, Caroline Douratsos from CBS Disco Promotions sent Norman a personal note in which she gave him a 'big thank-you' from George and Andrew. She told him, 'Being put on the spot like that gave Wham! the confidence to now see they can handle a live PA … it was just fabulous and the crowd obviously loved it.'

Wham! promised to return to Bolts to showcase their new single when it was released in October. First, they had to finalise the recording of 'Young Guns'. This time there was a crucial difference – George shared production duties with Steve Brown, who had worked with Elton John and Freddie Mercury. They got along well and George thrived in the studio environment. He made an important contribution by dusting off his musical education from his time at Bushey Meads.

The renowned composer and future Oscar winner, Anne Dudley, who the following year formed The Art of Noise, was arranging the brass section on the recording. She witnessed first-hand George's well-developed ear for music when he noticed that she'd changed around a chord. He immediately spotted a difference that would have passed others by.

Delighted with the result, George and Andrew embarked on another round of personal appearances with Shirlie and Dee C. Lee. The signs were not good, however: the song hovered around the top-fifty spot on release. The track started at number 73, went up to 48 and then back down to number 52. Dick Leahy and his team went into action to try and keep the song afloat by ringing contacts and calling in favours to obtain more radio airplay.

Dick always believed that George Michael would become an enormous success whatever the fate of 'Young Guns', but he didn't really want to take that chance and his efforts saw the single crawl back up to 42, which was still a flop.

Another PA at Stringfellows was the first lucky break. A BBC producer was in the club that night and thought Wham! would be perfect for *Saturday Superstore*, a new morning show for children that had taken over the slot previously occupied by *Multi-Coloured Swap Shop*. They were almost cancelled because of their chart position, but after some arm-twisting from Dick, it went ahead.

Shirlie recalled, 'It all escalated from there.' A day or two later she was out shopping in Watford with George when they had the thrill of being recognised for the very first time: 'People were staring and pointing at us.'

Their appearance was enough to put them on the radar of *Top of the Pops*. Unfortunately the premier TV music show had a rule that you only appeared if you were in the top forty. And Wham! remained agonisingly outside. But fate was on their side – an act pulled out at the last minute for the first broadcast of November 1982. They were on. As DJ Paul Gambaccini wryly observed, 'What a break. They should send Christmas cards to whoever that was – I'll tell ya.'

For the occasion, Wham! were more than just the two boys and the two girls. They put together a proper band, with David Austin playing guitar, Paul Ridgeley on drums and a new man on bass, Deon Estus from Detroit. Deon would become a long-standing friend and member of George Michael's musical world. He had settled in Europe after coming over to back Marvin Gaye and was living in Ireland when he took a call from Dick Leahy, telling him about this 'young Greek guy'.

While it was shown on Thursday evenings, *Top of the Pops* was filmed the night before at the TV Centre in White City. Coincidentally, the host Mike Smith was also making his debut: 'It's my first *Top of the Pops*, and it's their first *Top of the Pops* … Wham!'

And there was George miming the memorable first line, 'Hey sucker …' What followed were three of the most exciting minutes in TV pop history. George was on fire. All the moves they had rehearsed so diligently in his home in Radlett, then honed to perfection in the clubs, were completed seamlessly, just as if it was a Hollywood musical and they were professional stars much practised in choreography.

They acted the story: young gun George is horrified to discover his fellow soul boy Andrew is about to ruin his life and get married. He would be a daddy by the time he was twenty-one. The fiancée, played by Shirlie, loathes 'creepy guy' George, but Andrew sticks up for his pal and tells his 'chick' that she is out of line. Both Shirlie and Dee C. Lee were miming to the original studio vocal of Lynda Hayes.

George commanded the stage, bare-chested and toned in a brown leather waistcoat. His athleticism provided a striking contrast with the chart competition at the time. Tony Hadley and Simon Le Bon were far too cool to prance about in this exuberant fashion, while Boy George tended to sway gently.

Andrew was less ostentatious but he was step perfect and performed his dialogue with Shirlie with just the right amount of theatre. He was languid and handsome. Dee C. Lee was elegant and radiant, but the eye was drawn to Shirlie, in a short and sexy white dress.

Afterwards, George, dripping with sweat, turned to David Austin and told him, 'This is it. This is the rest of my life!' And then they all got the bus home.

8

BUTCH CASSIDY AND
THE SUNDANCE KID

The line for the first Wham! concert stretched round the block. The excited teenage girls were not, however, queuing at Earls Court or Wembley but for entry to the main hall at Bushey Meads School. When they offered to play in December 1982, the headmaster, John Earnshaw, was worried that their appearance would cause a riot, but he liked to support music and here was a shining example that you could make it if you went to his school.

They did practically cause a riot – certainly among the girls – but they would soon be facing vast crowds, a hundred times bigger than the 300 lucky students who crammed in to see them in the school auditorium. Their parents went as well, glowing with pride. They didn't have a band with them, so the occasion was little more than a glorified PA, but they received a rapturous reception and there were no drunks to bother them. It was an early Christmas present for everyone.

Both Andrew and George liked spending Christmas at home. They visited each other as usual on the day itself and made sure they looked after Shirlie, who was very drunk and insisted on taking the same wine glass around from house to house, which made everyone laugh. It was a happy time.

Behind the laughter and the seasonal cheer, George was getting frustrated with Andrew, who he really didn't feel was pulling his weight. The one appearance on *Top of the Pops* didn't make George Michael but it probably made Wham! Within days, CBS had 30,000 orders for the track and during the next month it rose to number three in the charts, eventually selling more than 400,000 copies.

That burst of success brought with it enormous pressure. George had to write, produce and sing the lead vocal on their first album. Of course, he didn't *have* to do it, but he was a perfectionist and, as Dick Leahy had identified, he wanted to be in charge of his destiny.

The worst part was having to write a song 'to order' that would be the successor to 'Wham Rap!' and 'Young Guns'. And Andrew wasn't helping, which created frostiness between them that threatened Wham!'s existence just when they were getting started.

George explained, 'The first year, when Andrew and I realised things had to change, there was friction. We'd start getting rude with each other. There was a time I was really pissed off at him, because he'd been late for a photo or recording session. I was saying, "For fuck's sake, I'm doing all the work on this album. The least you can do is take care of your side of things".'

Eventually they had a huge argument about it and Andrew was able to tell George the truth about the reason for his apparently careless attitude and what was really troubling him. George finally understood Andrew's feelings: 'He couldn't bear the unspoken unevenness of it. Once it was out in the open, neither of us had a problem with it.'

Andrew had a point. In The Executive they had been equal partners. They were both leaders of the group and some thought Andrew had the better voice. They wrote songs together, even if George took the major role in that. But when Yog became George Michael, it was as if the floodgates opened and all his natural, overwhelming talent came gushing out. He quite simply took over.

Fortunately, Andrew proved to be a strong and resilient character. The argument, which Andrew has never spoken about, cleared the air and they went back to being the best of friends. That didn't solve the issue of writing the next hit single, however.

He and Andrew were beginning to lead quite separate lives. Now on good terms again, they still laughed and giggled at the same things, but Andrew had his own set of friends, his entourage from his days at Cassio College. They liked a drink or two and would happily join him in the local pubs around Bushey, in which he spent much more time since his split from Shirlie earlier in the year. He remained close to his ex, paying her the compliment of being the only serious girl-friend in his life so far. For nights out in the West End, he and the gang drifted towards the glamorous clubs such as Stringfellows or Xenon, where they could drink champagne and chase women.

George preferred to be lower key. At first it was a novelty to be recognised, but he swiftly tired of it. After a long day at the studios in Fulham, he would slip quietly into one of his favourite clubs, where he could enjoy a late-night cocktail or two. As well as the Camden Palace, he liked the Wag Club in Wardour Street, which Ollie O'Donnell had opened with Chris Sullivan after Le Beat Route closed. In these pre-mobile, pre-internet times he could pop in for a drink without featuring on someone's Instagram account two minutes later.

One side effect of the pressure George was under was that he was smoking far too much. He never smoked at school, but he was more than making up for it by puffing his way through a pack or two a day. His habit did nothing to help his voice that was suffering anyway with so much vocal work at the studio.

As it turned out, he didn't have to do anything extra towards the next single. Innervision simply re-released 'Wham Rap!', which, for economic reasons, was the sensible thing to do. George was disappointed that it didn't sell as well as 'Young Guns', although it still scraped into the top ten. Already his ambitions had become much higher.

Everyone seemed to think he needed another record in the same style of the first two in order to build on their success and reinforce Wham!'s image as two fun-loving buddies. Eventually he came up with 'Bad Boys', a song he loathed and would always cite as the least-favourite composition and video of his career.

George Michael was a slow, painstaking writer of songs. He laboured and agonised over each component until he thought he could do no better. 'Bad Boys' was put together in the studio over what seemed like months, with George liable at any moment to scrap an entire day's recording because he didn't like it. Primarily, he thought the track too 'formularised'. 'I was trying not to disappoint people,' he explained.

He was trying too hard to write a trilogy: 'Wham Rap!', 'Young Guns' and 'Bad Boys'. At least the last name contained the trademark humour of the first two, although some listeners took the line 'I'm handsome tall and strong' to be an indication of arrogance and not of a witty nineteen-year-old being tongue-in-cheek.

Their teenage fans, however, were too busy swooning to worry about his songwriting concerns, and the record rose to number two in the charts in May 1983. Only the classic Police track 'Every Breath You Take' sold more.

His embarrassment with the video focused on the shots towards the end when he and Andrew, in leather jackets, T-shirts and biker boots, sang the final chorus with a group of male dancers behind them. He had a point in that it looked more like an audition for Village People than bad boys dancing in the style of Michael Jackson's famous *Thriller* video. 'We look such a pair of wankers in it,' George later observed.

Andrew liked 'Bad Boys', considering it to be a 'bloody good dance record'. George's verdict was entirely different: 'I hate it. It's like an albatross around my neck.'

He couldn't continue to do everything himself, especially as his relationship with Mark Dean was deteriorating by the day. For instance, they went six weeks without even speaking after an argument in a club one evening became overheated. Now that the debut album was nearly completed, Dick Leahy took George to one side and told him in his quietly persuasive manner that he was jeopardising his future by not having a proper manager.

George and Andrew had already met Jazz Summers, a tough and ambitious ex-army man who ambushed them one afternoon. He had heard the demo of 'Wham Rap!' at a record company and dashed over to Mark Dean's office in South Molton Street to find out if they had management. He was delighted to discover they didn't, even more so when Mark played him another demo – this time of 'Careless Whisper'. By chance, the boys were on their way in for a meeting.

He was dazzled by how handsome they both were, particularly Andrew, but only had time to murmur how 'fucking' awesome he thought their songs were before he overstayed his welcome. Jazz used the F-word a lot.

He had managed a folk singer called Richard Digance and a New Wave band called Blue Zoo, who were in the top twenty the week 'Young Guns' was a top-three record. Things were promising, but he saw Wham! as his ticket to the big time. He engineered a meeting with Dick Leahy and Bryan Morrison, who he vaguely knew, but was sent packing with the words that he was not big enough to manage Wham!, which was true. Jazz needed someone with more standing within the industry, so he went to see Simon Napier-Bell, one of the best-known managers in pop, to ask him to be his partner in looking after Wham! He literally turned up on Simon's doorstep at his house in Bryanston Square, close to Marble Arch.

Simon was premier league. At various times he had managed The Yardbirds and Marc Bolan. He had co-written one of the great anthems of the sixties, 'You Don't Have to Say You Love Me' by Dusty Springfield. Most recently, he had guided the career of Japan, a group from Catford in Southeast London fronted by the charismatic David Sylvian, who was once voted the world's most beautiful man – an accolade that Simon and his publicity team astutely made sure the whole world knew about. The band split in December 1982, prompting Simon to take a break from management – until Jazz Summers knocked on his door four months later.

He was intrigued when Jazz enthused about a new group. Simon had watched Wham! perform 'Bad Boys' on *Top of the Pops*, so knew exactly who they were when Jazz produced a press cutting about them from his pocket. He noted in his entertaining memoir, *I'm Coming to Take You to Lunch*, 'They'd sung and danced with an extraordinary macho exuberance yet there seemed to be a strange intimacy between them.'

Simon was openly gay, suave, witty and a complete contrast to the energetic and belligerent Jazz. They would make a great team. With Simon on board, Dick Leahy and Bryan Morrison were much more amenable to arranging an introduction to the boys. Dick told Simon, 'I think you and George will be just the right combination.'

The meeting took place at Simon's luxurious and impressive home. Both he and Jazz realised almost immediately that the two members of Wham! were completely different. On TV they came across as two soul boys cut from the same fun-loving cloth. In reality, in his George Michael persona, Georgios Panayiotou was serious, sincere and focused. Jazz noted that he seemed completely confident.

Andrew lay on a sofa and turned the pages of a book – a memoir that Simon had written about his musical life in the sixties. Every so often, he looked up to offer a comment: 'Seems like Simon spent most of the sixties either drunk or having sex. He sounds just the right person for us.' George, meanwhile, was conducting a proper interview, perched on the edge of an armchair demanding to know what guarantees their prospective management team could give them. He ignored Andrew when he was discussing business.

George seemed satisfied, although Simon soon learned he could be unpredictable in his response: 'One minute you could be discussing a routine bit of business, the next you were enveloped in burning suspicion.'

George and Andrew signed a contract with Nomis – Simon's name spelt backwards – giving the managers a 12 per cent cut of their earnings. The most pressing matter for the new team was money. Wham! didn't have any, despite three hit records and a blossoming profile as the new big act in British pop. They were existing on a miserly allowance of £40 a week from Innervision. Jazz was to the point when he analysed the situation: 'Wham!'s record deal with Innervision was one of the most notoriously awful, unfair fucking record deals that ever got signed in the whole torrid history of pop music.'

Simon was confident that the contract was so appalling that he and Jazz would be able to overturn it in the courts, especially as they now had Wham!'s new lawyer in their corner. Tony Russell already enjoyed a reputation as one of the smartest legal minds in the entertainment business; George trusted his judgement implicitly. Intriguingly, from the very beginning George had planted the idea in the media that Wham! had a very bad deal, which suggested he understood all along what he was signing. In their very first interview as a top-ten band, he told *NME* about the £500 advance and hinted that they had signed the deal too speedily.

'Club Tropicana' was a much more satisfactory experience. The new track may have seemed a departure from the social commentary of the first three singles, but George had written it at the same time as 'Wham Rap!' and well before 'Young Guns' and 'Bad Boys'.

They decided to shoot a video abroad and not in a club, taking the storyline of the lyric literally and searching for the right Mediterranean location. Simon had stayed at Pikes Hotel on Ibiza and thought it would make an ideal location. As director, they recruited a former BBC documentary maker Duncan Gibbins, who was making a name for himself directing pop videos for Eurythmics and Musical Youth.

He decided that George and Andrew would be packing their Speedos, silk shorts and shades instead of their leather jackets. The video was light and undemanding as George and Andrew tried but failed to get off with Shirlie and Dee C. Lee. They never progressed further than meaningful glances. The original song was a gentle satire, but it had now become something of a celebration of lazy days in the sun.

The hotel's owner, Tony Pike, one of the best-known faces on the island and a great friend of Freddie Mercury, was even given a small role as the barman in one of the scenes. At the end of the video, Andrew and George are revealed as airline pilots while Shirlie and Dee are air hostesses. The result was very silly, completely camp and great fun.

Behind the scenes, however, something far more significant was taking place that would have a profound effect on the rest of George's life. He told Shirlie that he was gay. They had arrived on the island before Andrew and had what she described as an 'intense conversation' at the hotel.

She recalled that he wore a big doe-eyed help-me expression: 'I was quite confused, I guess, because there were girls attracted to him and he still liked girls. So I thought, "He's just had an experience, he's gone off and done this and he needs to talk about it." So I didn't take it that it was that big a conversation actually.'

George didn't tell her what that experience might have been. He asked her not to tell Andrew, who, of course, she told straight away. 'So incapable of keeping that quiet,' he laughed. The three of them had further conversations about what George should do next. His two friends understandably failed to recognise what a big announcement this was for him. 'I think because we were so young and took it so lightly, we just said, "Don't worry about it, forget it",' remembered Shirlie.

Andrew made the specific point that it was a particularly bad idea to inform his father when George said he was think-ing of talking to his parents about it. George explained, 'What I was saying was I thought it was time to tell my mum and dad because if I had told my mum and dad the whole situation would have been different. I wouldn't have been able to stay *in* professionally if I'd told my mum and dad.'

George took a holiday in Cyprus to recharge his batteries and think about what to do. In the end he decided to say nothing and be, as he put it, 'a sex symbol to thousands of virgins'. He realised much later what a momentous decision he had made to live a public lie: 'I was too immature to know I was sacrificing as much as I was.'

In George's defence – if he needs one – this was 1983 and for someone in the world of entertainment to 'come out' was a huge step. And homosexuality had yet to arrive in Bushey or Radlett. Helen, his girlfriend at Bushey Meads, remembers that she and her friends were barely aware of its existence and she certainly didn't speculate on her affectionate boyfriend's preference.

'Relax', the notorious single by Frankie Goes to Hollywood, was not released until October that year and not banned by the BBC until January 1984. The leaders of the group, Holly Johnson and Paul Rutherford, were obviously gay and their openness about their sexuality was part of the commercial strategy of the band. Their audience was an entirely different one to Wham!'s.

The timeless gay elegy, 'Smalltown Boy' by the Bronski Beat portrayed the homophobia of provincial towns but not until a year after 'Club Tropicana' made the charts. Meanwhile, Elton John married German sound engineer Renate Blauel in February 1984 and didn't tell *Rolling Stone* magazine that he was happy being gay until after the marriage was dissolved four years later.

With the clearness of hindsight, it seems ludicrous to think that there was ever ambiguity about the sexual orientation of Freddie Mercury or Boy George, who would become a catty and witty thorn in the other George's side for many years. And Barry Manilow, the perennial heart-throb, was in a relationship with his manager Garry Kief for nearly forty years, marrying him in 2014 and finally coming out as gay in a magazine interview in April 2017. He said at the time that he was worried about upsetting his female fan base.

George Michael was just nineteen and wasn't completely sure at first whether he was gay or bisexual. He did not sleep with his two girlfriends at Bushey Meads but he would try sex with one or two young women in his Wham! days. They were anonymous, joyless encounters.

George never admitted taking account of commercial considerations in his decision not to come out, even though Wham! would soon be embarking on their first tour and there were tickets to be sold. He decided to remain in the closet, the rather hackneyed expression that describes a secret gay life. He didn't shut the door, though.

It hadn't occurred to Simon that George was gay until someone phoned him shortly after he became his manager and said, 'That new singer of yours, a friend of mine says he's gay.' He dismissed it: 'You're mistaken. George is as straight as a die.' Simon's job was to exploit Wham!'s image to make them as successful and rich as possible. He observed, 'If George was aware he was gay and was covering it up, he was doing the right thing. The image of Wham! was an image of male friendship – the image that Hollywood has played on in endless films – two straight guys whose friendship with each other transcends all other things.'

Simon saw his charges as Butch Cassidy and the Sundance Kid. He thought George and Andrew needed to play their roles as straight as the characters in the movie. He added, 'The world wanted a heterosexual duo.'

George was pragmatic enough at this stage to play his role. He dutifully turned up to a ghastly piece of PR, a blind date with the stunning Keren Woodward from all-girl group Bananarama. The idea was that the magazine *No. 1*, a new *Smash Hits* spin-off, would set up two young stars together on a blind date and write a feature about it. It was excruciating: 'Take a lonely girl from Bananarama, Take a fast rapping boy from Wham! Mix them together, add a cocktail or two and a No.1 reporter and the result – Whamarama.'

George, who hadn't yet passed his driving test, took a taxi from Radlett to the rendezvous – lunch at the South of the Border restaurant near the magazine's offices in Waterloo. He was very late and Keren and the reporter, Paul Simper, had already downed a couple of vodka and tonics and started their lunch when he eventually showed. He was clearly more interested in whatever he was listening to on his Walkman.

They chatted dully about shared experiences, including recent appearances on *American Bandstand* and *Solid Gold*, two dated but extremely popular US television shows. George had been particularly unimpressed with the male dancers, who were wearing white flared trousers.

Both Keren and George acted very professionally, but there was zero chemistry between them, although they remained friendly whenever they bumped into one another later. Keren recalled, 'I remember thinking, "Oh God, why couldn't it have been with Andrew?"' Ironically, a few years later she and Andrew began a long-standing relationship.

After their lunch, George walked back with Paul to the IPC magazine offices in King's Reach Tower so he could play him the track he had just been working on in the studio. It was the just-finished mix of one called 'Bassline' and George was very excited about it. By the time the first album was released, he had retitled it 'A Ray of Sunshine', a track with a hint of Earth, Wind & Fire that would have been a favourite during disco nights at Le Beat Route.

George was a great one for playing his new work to people, constantly enthusiastic and, it seemed, seeking a pat on the back. He lived and breathed his music.

Away from the recording studio, he began to spend more time in gay clubs and could often be seen wearing his favourite leather jacket while enjoying a drink at Heaven in Charing Cross, then the most famous, primarily gay nightspot in London. He also liked Bolts at weekends because he wasn't bothered there. He never came out to the DJ Norman Scott, who assumed it was kept quiet because of Wham!'s success. Norman observed, 'People asked me about him. They even asked if I thought he and Andrew were having an affair, but Andrew only came down when they were performing. George came just because he enjoyed it. I didn't know he was gay. He never let on to me. I thought there was a chance that perhaps he was.'

More than two years after George decided not to come out to his parents – or the world – Rock Hudson died from AIDS-related complications in October 1985. He was the first major celebrity to be struck down by the virus and it sent shock waves through society.

In George's mind the grim spectre of AIDS deprived him of the choice of coming out to his mum, who he feared would be worried for his safety. In the future, HIV was to feature distressingly in his story.

9

FANTASTIC REACTION

George's frustration with Innervision boiled over after he'd finished recording the first Wham! album. He took the master tapes home to Radlett and told his bemused mother to guard them. When he informed Dick Leahy what he had done, his wise advisor told him calmly to hand them straight back to Mark Dean.

In George's defence, he had been up for forty-eight consecutive hours at the studios, putting the finishing touches to the modestly named *Fantastic*, and wasn't thinking too clearly. Dick told him he would have a much better case in court if he was arguing his legal position with a number one album in his back pocket.

Fantastic duly topped the charts when it was released in July 1983, eventually selling nearly 900,000 copies. As well as their families, George and Andrew included David and Andros alongside Shirlie and Dee in their thank yous. Poignantly, they dedicated the album to Andrew Leaver and Paul Atkins, both of whom had died since they had left Bushey Meads. Their former bandmate Andy had finally succumbed to cancer at the age of twenty. Just a few months later, Paul, another class-mate, was killed in a car accident. George and Andrew attended both funerals, keenly aware, and a little embarrassed, that they were the centre of attention because of their new fame as pop stars.

The reviews for *Fantastic* were mixed and not every critic praised George Michael. *Rolling Stone* magazine thought his 'earnest whine' was synthetic. The reviewer said: 'Probably the biggest problem with Wham! is that the group lacks a really distinctive vocalist.'

The *NME* was more complimentary, praising in particular the 'touching sensitivity' of 'Nothing Looks the Same in the Light', which surely would have reached number one had it been released as a single. The rhythmic ballad, on which George played all the instruments, told of the emptiness of a misguided one-night stand. George never said if he was speaking from experience, but the words were a touch more mature than 'Careless Whisper' and the forerunner of his heartfelt and introspective songs of the future. Intriguingly, both contained the sentiment, 'Please stay'.

'Careless Whisper' was not included on the album. The song was always going to be George's ticket to solo stardom and the start of the credibility he craved. George protected the song as if it was a precious diamond that he kept locked away in a safe. Every so often, he would take it out, polish it a bit, admire its sparkle and hide the jewel away again.

He took the diamond with him when he flew to the US that summer to record as George Michael for the first time. Simon Napier-Bell had arranged for him to work on the song with Jerry Wexler, the renowned producer of Aretha Franklin,

Dusty Springfield and Ray Charles, at the Muscle Shoals Sound Studios in Alabama, about sixty miles from Nashville. Jerry was at the very top of the tree and, for once, George was slightly overawed by his surroundings and, temporarily, let others take over and hand him the finished product.

At first George seemed pleased that he was flying home with such a classy, slick and expensive sound. It was as if Kenny G had teamed up with Hall & Oates. But in reality he was just putting on a brave face when he told people that they would 'get used to it'. As the weeks went by, however, he became less confident that this version was the very best he could do. Jazz Summers didn't like it and nor did Dick Leahy. Even Simon acknowledged, 'It had no kick to it; no balls.'

More pressingly, Wham! needed to find a new sidekick for Shirlie after Dee, who'd been feeling increasingly marginalised in the group, left abruptly. She felt undervalued, which she probably was. She explained, 'I left because George kept saying in interviews that he was going to "kick the girls out" and that we were "only for show" and that wasn't doing me any favours.'

George wasn't the only one with ambition. Dee was writing songs and wanted to be appreciated as an artist in her own right. 'They kept me so tied up with dance classes and working out Wham! routines for *Top of the Pops*, I used to get worn into the ground. I'd ring up my mother and say, "I've got to come home, Mum, I'm just so tired."'

Dee released various singles without much success until her own composition, 'See the Day', became her biggest hit in 1985. She was better known as a vocalist with Paul Weller's band The Style Council, eventually marrying the former leader of The Jam in 1987 and having two children before their divorce ten years later.

George was keen to find another black girl so that the look of the group remained the same with the live tour coming up. He was very fastidious about that. A replacement was quickly found: some friends of Simon's recommended a young singer called Helen DeMacque, who everyone called 'Pepsi'. She went along to the manager's home in Bryanston Square, now also Wham! HQ, where he hired her on the spot – provided the others approved. Shirlie picked her up from the station in Radlett to take her to George's house. On the way she listened to Helen's demo cassette in the car. She was impressed by her voice, which reminded her of Shirley Bassey, and discovered they both liked the Welsh diva's voice.

Pepsi had the distinct impression that it was really up to Shirlie whether she joined the group: 'I got in the car and we clicked right away.' Shrewdly, she did not try and join in when the other three started cracking in-jokes but took her time to get to know them.

Shirlie observed that the two of them were very compatible: 'It would have been embarrassing if none of us liked her. But I really did, because, although she looked quite tomboyish, she had this strong feminine streak.'

Since she'd split with Andrew, Shirlie had been dating Martin Kemp from Spandau Ballet. He'd seen her performing with Wham! on *Top of the Pops* and, rather sweetly, fallen 'completely in love with her'. A few weeks later, they bumped into each other at the aftershow party for the opening night of *Yakety Yak*, a rock and roll show starring the McGann brothers and the group Darts, which had transferred to the Astoria Theatre in Charing Cross Road.

Martin went over to chat to her and gave her his number. A couple of weeks later she rang and they arranged to meet at the Camden Palace. He recalled their first date: 'As I am walking towards the Palace I could see Shirlie standing on the pavement and next to her I realised the worst thing that could happen – she had brought a wingman. And nobody wants that on a date, do they? Nobody wants the girl to bring her mate. But her mate was George. And I have to say, George was one of the nicest people you could want to meet.'

George gave Martin his seal of approval, a relief for Shirlie, who valued his opinion highly. She was one of a few women with whom over the years he had a long-standing, close, platonic relationship. He loved Shirlie and genuinely liked Martin.

Spandau Ballet were for a while rivals of Wham!, but Martin and George liked nothing better than talking for hours about life and the world. With Shirlie and Martin, he could be Georgios again – as if he were chatting to his mum in the kitchen at Oakridge Avenue. They remained his friends for life.

Shirlie was in love but she had to concentrate on Wham!'s first tour. She and Pepsi were a united front against the thousands of young girls intent on getting a message to George or Andrew by handing Pepsi and Shirlie pieces of their underwear with their phone numbers on them. The ploy never worked.

When the *Club Fantastic* Disco Evening began at the Capital Centre in Aberdeen in October 1982, underwear became an unexpected hazard. Andrew and George were scarcely Tom Jones, but so many bras and knickers were tossed on stage that they needed to assign a roadie to sweep them up so they didn't trip during one of the dance routines.

Pepsi and Shirlie were listed as 'tour crew'. George was careful not to promote the girls as being part of Wham! They were strictly members of the backing band – just as Dion Estus was on bass guitar. *Record Mirror* in its review of the show at the Playhouse Theatre in Edinburgh described them as 'two pretty dancing accessories'. Dee C. Lee would probably have punched the writer, Jim Reid. On a positive note, he loved the show: 'Wham! are a success because they come across as the cocky smile 'n' wink pair their songs portray. They ham it, they milk it and the crowd love it.'

The theme of the shows was a night at a club. The Capital Radio DJ Gary Crowley played a succession of dancing hits to get everyone in the mood and the audience of mainly sixteen-year-old girls screamed every time they thought they caught a glimpse of George and Andrew about to come on.

They had to wait an hour before George launched into 'Hey sucker!' Their managers had struck a £50,000 deal with Fila sportswear to wear the label's clothing throughout the show, so there was a costume change that basically consisted of wearing different-coloured shorts. They ensured maximum publicity by thrusting shuttlecocks down their pants before hitting them into the audience. In private, George hated the stunt, telling Simon it was 'tacky crap' and that he and Andrew came across as 'two silly schoolboys'. More importantly, in the long run, 'Careless Whisper' was finally unveiled as the big song they had been talking up for weeks.

At half-time, everyone took a breather and a specially filmed video was shown which featured their parents, and most noticeably, George's father behind the wheel of his Rolls-Royce ferrying his hungover son in his pyjamas over to Andrew's house. For some reason, the media and the fans decided to ignore the obvious contrast between the bad boys singing about the DHSS and the wealthy teenage life of George Michael. During the next decade, they would focus interminably on Posh Spice and the fact that her nouveau-riche father drove a Roller. But they never gave George a tough time about it, preferring instead to pose the same tired question about his sexuality.

George's dad was happy to be part of his new world, bristling with pride at watching his son on TV or on stage. 'I couldn't believe I was seeing my son,' he said. Jack had been considerably happier to see some money coming in after Wham!'s managers, Simon and Jazz, successfully negotiated a fee of £110,000 for the tour from leading promoter Harvey Goldsmith. As George observed, 'He is very financial.' In fact, everyone was feeling more optimistic about money, although most of the earnings were being used to fund the legal action against Innervision.

Not everything went well throughout the tour. Strenuous singing and too many cigarettes took their toll on George's voice and they had to cancel and reschedule some gigs. He was clearly in charge of the tour. Already, he alone made most of the decisions, insisting on quality above money-saving. He didn't enjoy the touring experience and, as a result, had a lack of enthusiasm for being on the road that would stay with him.

After the last date at the Hammersmith Odeon at the end of November, it was time to finally sort out the festering legal headache with Mark Dean and Innervision. The company, perhaps sensing doom, had released the 'Club Tropicana Megamix', basically a rework of the existing material. More seriously, the label wanted to release the Jerry Wexler-produced version of 'Careless Whisper'. Fortunately, Dick Leahy was able to stop that.

Eventually, in March 1984, CBS decided to settle the case without going to court. George had won. The giant label did not want to see a major new act not making any money for them because of a disagreement with a very minor subsidiary. Innervision ended up declaring bankruptcy while Simon and Jazz negotiated a new deal for Wham! with Epic Records, another subsidiary of CBS. The signing-on fee, according to Simon, was £250,000. At last, some real money.

George was very much his mother's son and the pursuit of money was no more a factor in his life at this time than it ever had been before. Following her lead, he cared little for that side of things. George was primarily motivated by injustice. He hated the feeling that he was being ripped off.

Now that there was some cash in the till, Simon and Jazz could start to build a team around Wham! The unforgettable Connie Filippello became their publicist. She already worked for Nomis and had endeared herself to Andrew and George by referring to them as her 'wonderful sex-gods'. Connie, a beguiling mix of Australian and Italian, used the word 'dahlink' in a way that would have had Zsa Zsa Gabor purring with pride. She could get anything in the paper, whether it bore any relation to the truth or not.

The day-to-day running of Wham!'s affairs was taken over by the unassuming and capable Siobhan Bailey. George was still living at home so his mother was always there for him, keeping him fed and doing his washing. She was a normal voice in the madness of stardom. In the big world, Siobhan took over many of the maternal duties, although these tended to be more organisational, including booking George's driving lessons. He liked cars and was particularly keen to obtain a licence. Most of all, though, Siobhan was another cheerleader, who was immensely proud every time he had a hit. That was important to George. He thrived on being appreciated and liked to bask in the glory of something well done.

The third member of what would become Team George was the energetic Gary Farrow, who Nomis brought in as an independent plugger and general consultant with the brief to turn Wham! into a 'scream' band. He had worked his way up by the sheer force of his personality from being a runner at Elton John's Rocket Records and achieved just what Jazz and Simon asked him to.

George trusted these three implicitly because they put his interests first. He valued their loyalty and returned it. By this stage, it really was the George show and they understood that. He was in control. All three would remain close to him for many years. The music journalist Rick Sky observes, 'George had the ability to suss out who he could trust and who he couldn't. It was a sign of his incredible maturity. He wouldn't surround himself with anybody who would divulge secrets. Sometimes he might make a mistake but they were got rid of very quickly.'

George became godfather to Gary's daughter Lauren – just as he would do with Shirlie and Martin Kemp's children. Every Christmas he would turn into Santa Claus, call in and bring an armful of presents. He took his role very seriously.

The two closest to him remained David Austin and Andros Georgiou. His cousin had largely been absent during George's teenage years, simply because he lived in South London. They picked up their friendship again when Andros started joining him for nights out in clubland. He soon became one of his most trusted companions and a constant fixture on trips abroad, practically at George's side every day, much more so than Andrew.

Occasionally, a crossover took place and someone from his gay world would become a public companion. Pat Fernandes, a voluptuous black woman with a dazzling smile, became the centre of attention when she appeared to be his date at various events. She was just a close friend and nothing more, although that didn't stop media speculation that they were a couple.

Pat had first been noticed alongside George as a dancer on the video for Wham!'s comeback single 'Wake Me Up Before You Go-Go'. They hadn't released anything new during the months of legal action, but here was an instant classic, one of the best feel-good tracks of modern pop and totally different to anything George had written before. Jazz Summers told him, 'I think this is a smash.'

He had been inspired one day when he popped round to Andrew's house and discovered that his mate was still nursing a hangover in bed. He had pinned a note for his parents to the door that should have read 'Wake Me Up Before You Go', except that, slightly the worse for wear, he had two attempts at writing 'go'. The note therefore read 'Wake Me Up Before

You Go Go', which became the catchiest of choruses for George's new song.

In the video Pat is one of the dancers that included Pepsi and Shirlie, and she certainly seemed to have some airtime, which would have been with George's approval. The video, directed by Duncan Giddings, was frothy, but most noticeable for the famous 'Choose Life' T-shirt that George and Andrew wore. It was designed by Katharine Hamnett and was nothing to do with the anti-abortion community who later hijacked the slogan, much to her annoyance. Her inspiration was Buddhism and advocated the right of individuals to choose their own destiny whatever their gender or sexuality. George liked the concept. He would also have approved of another Hamnett creation: 'Use a Condom,' it proclaimed.

George liked dancing with 'Patty', as she was known in clubland. She was happy to drive him around as he had yet to pass his test. She had many gay friends, particularly in Boy George's circle, whose flat in Camden she once lived in. The Culture Club singer had no problem calling her a fag hag and referred to her as his sidekick.

The feud between the two Georges began after the media suggested Patty and George Michael were lovers. Boy George laughed when the papers ran a headline, 'How Pat Broke My Heart', suggesting that it should have read 'How Pat Broke My Hoover'. He was always fast with a witty quip.

Georgios Panayiotou was a warm and funny man. The George Michael image he created took life much more seriously, or as Boy George observed, 'He's got no sense of hummus.' Boy George would later admit that it was 'cheap and cruel' to poke fun at George's sexuality. A touch of professional jealousy may also have played its part. Clearly they were rivals and Wham! were in the process of brushing Culture Club aside as the most successful British band of the eighties.

The two Georges were never close, although Bananarama, once tried to act as peacemakers by inviting them both to a dinner party and not telling either one who would be there. They passed a pleasant enough evening but neither was invited into the other's circle of friends.

George continued to fret about his personal appearance. He was bored with what he considered to be an overplayed narrative of him portrayed as the ugly duckling transformed into a swan by his association with Andrew Ridgeley. But that didn't stop him wanting to present the best possible image to the public. Or the best side of his face.

He got into the habit of turning the right side of his face away from the camera because he only wanted to present the left. His insecurity stretched to social gatherings and, in company, he would invariably sit with what he considered to be his good side facing his assembled friends.

His hair, the symbol of his adolescent insecurities, remained his principal obsession. His sister Melanie, who he called 'Mel', was in charge of making sure he was happy with his hair and makeup for all photography and videos. She received a special thank you on the *Fantastic* album for her efforts.

Melanie was also a key player in the saga of the 'Careless Whisper' video. She was not involved at the beginning. George flew alone to Barbados to lie in the sun for a couple of days before a film crew joined him for the shoot. The weather was disappointing so he didn't stay long and jetted off to Miami, causing chaos.

Duncan Gibbins, who had again been brought in to direct, recalled, 'One hour before we're all due to fly off with the film crew and all the equipment, I suddenly get this frantic call from George, telling me to meet him in Miami instead. We ended up renting boats and choppers all over Miami over the course of two very long, hot and humid days.'

It had been a nightmare as they struggled to find the right locations. Duncan had suggested a storyline in the style of a 'fairly hard-edged *Miami Vice* story', but George, who had complete control, decided he wanted something more like a glossy teen romance.

After two days, everyone was delighted with the footage when they reviewed it – except George. He hated his hair. He told his manager, Simon Napier-Bell, that he considered it 'too long, too posy and too poofy'. All the humidity had made it 'frizzy'. Duncan continued, 'He said we'd have to do the entire thing again.'

An SOS call was made to Melanie, who literally took the first flight out of London so that she could attend to her brother's hair. She was the only one he would trust, so popping down to the local barber's was never an option. Her trim became one of the most expensive cut and blow-drys of all time because the entire video had to be reshot, which doubled the budget by more than $60,000.

George hadn't finished, though. After all the footage had been shipped back to London and edited, he went back into the studio to re-record the track yet again, which caused all his singing on the video to be out of sync. As a result, Duncan had to re-film him on a 'moody soundstage' in London that forms the beginning of the video and then cut to George singing over what was little more than a travel guide to Miami.

The city, looking particularly warm and inviting, becomes the backdrop for his anguish. He thinks of the beautiful girl he rejected as he gazes at the Freedom Tower – aptly named considering the title of a new song he was working on. The video ends with his walking, crestfallen, into the penthouse of the Grove Towers condominiums.

Despite all the hiccups, the video for 'Careless Whisper' would become one of the most famous – and most watched – of all time. On YouTube, it has been viewed more than 275 million times and still rising fast, second only to 'Last Christmas' in George Michael's career.

'Wake Me Up Before You Go-Go' had already raced to number one when it was finally decided it was time to put a toe into more mature waters and release 'Careless Whisper' in August 1984. This single too climbed effortlessly to the top of the charts, a vindication of all the faith that George had placed in the song. By this time, he had already told Andrew and his two managers his future plans. They were all in New York to whip up some enthusiasm for launching Wham! in the US when he announced one evening that sometime soon they would have to start thinking about him going solo. The success of 'Careless Whisper' meant that particular clock was already ticking.

10

MAKING IT BIG

George liked to keep a tune with him. He might just have a few notes in his head, but from there he would painstakingly build up a song. The practice had served him well with 'Careless Whisper' and he was hoping it would do the same for a few notes he had thought of while watching television with Andrew.

They were sprawled out in front of *Match of the Day* in the lounge at Oakridge Avenue. Football was not his favourite viewing but he was happy to join his friend, who had entertained ambitions of becoming a professional in his younger days. George's mind was wandering and suddenly he yelled out and ran upstairs.

When the game had finished, Andrew ambled up to George's room to see what was up. There was George singing into a tape recorder, worried that if he didn't do it there and then he might have lost the song that became 'Last Christmas'.

He took the woefully unfinished melody with him when they went to the South of France, where he planned to write and record the second Wham! album. He was finding it difficult. Jazz Summers was so concerned that he took Andrew aside and asked him if he could help because George was under so much pressure. Andrew told him, 'George writes the songs. The trick is to let him get on with it.'

They were staying for the summer of 1984 at the Château Miraval, near the small town of Brignoles in Provence. The studios there were owned by the acclaimed French pianist and composer Jacques Loussier, whose trio had been frequent guests on British television shows in the seventies.

There was an idyllic setting of manicured lawns, an obligatory swimming pool, all-day sun and good wine. Andrew loved it. Even George seemed to relax, although he didn't spend every day lounging around. There was too much work to do and, in any case, he thrived on being in the studio. When a magazine competition winner called Debbie Jones came to spend the weekend with them, George happily played her the tracks he had already recorded while Andrew had a lie-in. She was the first fan to hear the new single, which would be called 'Freedom'. He told her it was about a situation where a girl tells her boyfriend he can see other people because she's going to. But he doesn't want to because he only wants her. He told Debbie that it was 'sort of' written from experience.

One can imagine that in his head he had drawn on his experience in The King Stag, Bushey, when he and Helen Tye had a grown-up conversation about meeting new people. They were not advocating fooling around, but it could easily have been embellished to give an effective lyric.

Debbie noticed that he was humming a song repeatedly and so she asked him what it was. He turned to her and he sang, 'Last Christmas, I gave you my heart …'. She remembered, 'He was the kindest man and so talented.'

Another guest at the château arrived by helicopter one afternoon: Elton John flew in to record an advertisement. George was thrilled to meet one of his childhood heroes for the first time. Elton paid George the compliment of taking him seriously and putting him at ease. The younger man could only dream at this stage of matching Elton's status as a critically acclaimed superstar. He had conquered America in the seventies, achieving six number ones in the *Billboard* chart.

Elton had dragged himself up from a modest start in life in the London suburb of Pinner by the sheer force of his personality and his musical talent. He had created an image of a flamboyant and outrageous pop star that allowed his abilities to flourish. George was never going to wear outrageous spectacles or funny hats but he understood the power of presentation.

Simon Napier-Bell could see how influential Elton would be: 'He provided the perfect model for George to follow in his new career as a solo artist – in charge of his own business and his own life – able to make every decision for himself, good or bad. Once George had seen it close up, it had to be what he aspired to from now on.'

Elton invited him over to dinner at his sumptuous villa near St Tropez and George quickly decided that he wanted one for himself. The two men established an easy friendship based on mutual respect and their paths were to cross both professionally and privately for many years.

Elton was enthusiastic about giving time and money to charity and encouraged George to do the same. Wham! had already played a concert in aid of Capital Radio's Help a London Child appeal and both he and Andrew had been disconcerted when an item on the station subsequently suggested they should do something.

George Michael wasn't allowed to be the sensible or intelligent man he was. He had ideals and views on many subjects. He should have featured on everyone's list of who you'd like to sit beside at a dinner party. The mainstream media and music press decided early on that he was a frothy popster who had no business having a view on anything serious.

He knew the problem was Wham!'s image, which he had done so much to promote initially. Now, he complained, 'We are at the height of our popularity but in the pits as far as credibility goes.' His allusion to mining would prove unwittingly apt when he told his managers that he wanted to be more involved in a good cause.

Jazz Summers had been asked by the National Union of Mineworkers if Wham! would appear at a show called Five Nights for the Miners at the Royal Festival Hall in September 1984 to raise money for the families of the striking miners who were struggling to even buy food. George felt a genuine sympathy with the plight of the beleaguered pitmen and agreed to perform on the last night.

A parade of left-leaning acts featured, including The Style Council, led by Paul Weller, and jazz–dance band Working Week, as well as representatives from the new wave of comedians that included Ben Elton and Nigel Planer. Wham! seemed an incongruous presence, sandwiched between Rik Mayall and Alexei Sayle. They were roundly booed by certain sections of the audience, who seemed to resent their presence at such a serious and worthy event.

The band's reception wasn't helped by their decision to use a backing track instead of singing live, because, as George explained, they were concerned at not being able to use their own sound crew. A glitch meant that at one stage he announced the wrong song and the track had to be rewound. The press gleefully referred to their performance as a 'Mimers' Benefit'. For some reason the media have always been outraged by anyone miming, failing to realise a show is first and foremost an entertainment. *Melody Maker* waded in; 'Dressed in white and posturing farcically, Wham! greatly pleased the three rows of young girls at the back of the hall and left everybody else stone-faced and baffled.'

George was genuinely hurt by the criticism: 'What are we supposed to do? Go on in grey overcoats and say, "This is our single 'Wake Me Up Before You Go-Go'; we're really sorry it's been number one but listen to it anyway."' He was not going to apologise: 'We were there to do people some good and all we got were insults. It's so pathetic.'

Afterwards, he was introduced backstage to the miners' leader, Arthur Scargill. He wasn't impressed, believing that Scargill was enjoying the industrial action too much: 'I didn't like him at all. You couldn't get two worse people involved in an argument than Thatcher and Scargill – between the two of them they are capable of bringing this country to a halt.' When the strike came to an end in March 1985, George reflected, 'When we did the benefit I really thought there was some kind of hope. I thought it was really sad when it came to an end because they really hadn't got anything out of it.'

George didn't shy away from good deeds after the debacle of the miners' benefit and there was no bigger celebrity cause than the famine in Ethiopia. He readily accepted an invitation from Bob Geldof to go to the Sarm West Studios in Ladbroke Grove, West London, and be one of close to forty acts taking part in the recording of the Band Aid song 'Do They Know It's Christmas?'

The best-known charity record of them all was devised by Bob, then better known as lead singer of The Boomtown Rats, after he had watched a news report on the BBC depicting starving children, and vowed that something had to be done.

George sang the third line, after Paul Young and Boy George, 'But say a prayer; Pray for the other ones; At Christmas time …', before Simon Le Bon took over the lyric. When Boy George heard the finished record he couldn't resist having a bitchy dig, asking who the girl singing after him was. After being told it was George Michael, he said, 'He sounds really camp. But he is though, isn't he?'

George didn't want to be outed by his namesake but, for the most part, gritted his teeth at this provocation. He was not so gracious when Paul Weller came up to have a go at him in front of everyone. The 'modfather', as he was called, was apparently outraged by George's remarks about Arthur Scargill. George told him, 'Don't be a wanker all your life. Give yourself a day off.' One can imagine that if the leader of The Style Council had been 'King of the Wall' at Bushey Meads School, he would have been speedily despatched to the ground by young Georgios.

During the recording, George wasn't made to feel particularly comfortable and, for once, Andrew wasn't there to offer his laid-back support. He didn't really have a designated role on the day and never showed, making tame excuses that he had overslept.

Wham! were arguably the most successful British band of the year so, inevitably, there was plenty of jealousy mixed with a general lack of respect. *Make It Big* topped the charts in mid-November 1984. The three singles from the album released so far – 'Wake Me Up Before You Go-Go', 'Careless Whisper' and 'Freedom' – had already reached number one.

George was never reticent about including songs by other artists that he liked and which suited his voice – he enjoyed singing classic numbers. On this album he covered the track 'If You Were There' by The Isley Brothers and perfectly matched the smooth soul of the original.

Rolling Stone was for the most part complimentary: '*Make It Big* is an almost flawless pop record, a record that does exactly what it wants to and has a great deal of fun doing it.' The magazine thought 'Freedom' was 'truly irresistible', but did think some of the lesser-known tracks sounded a little thin. 'Last Christmas' was not on the album but was about to be released as a seasonal single.

The much-played film of the Band Aid recording session has so far had more than 296 million views on YouTube. The official snowy video for 'Last Christmas', which Band Aid kept off the top of the seasonal charts, has been watched, astonishingly, by very nearly as many.

The video, which was filmed in the Swiss Alps resort of Saas-Fee, turned into one big holiday for George and Andrew's friends. George insisted that their mates and family should travel with them – and always first class. He was very generous and picked up the bill. He loved being able to do this.

'It was a riot,' remembers one of the inner circle on the trip. 'Andy couldn't be filmed because his eyes were so swollen through laughter and booze. During the dinner party scenes, they wanted it to look post-meal, so the booze had to be consumed – and it was.'

As usual, Pat Fernandes was part of the gang helping to keep George company. They all liked her and thought her great fun. This was one of the few occasions when everyone joined them but, increasingly, George and Andrew were spending time with different sets of friends.

The drunken partying infuriated the film crew, who were trying to work to a schedule. The director, Andy Morahan, who was just starting out on a glittering career as one of the world's premier video directors, was tolerant at first. Everyone thought he was a 'top bloke', but in the end he had to send the revellers home except for George and Kathy Hill, the stunning brunette who had given his heart away for Christmas.

Of the modern seasonal songs, perhaps only Mariah Carey's 'All I Want for Christmas Is You' or 'Fairytale of New York' by The Pogues, featuring Kirsty MacColl, can rival 'Last Christmas' for enduring popularity. Year after year the song sounds new and fresh, resonating with the public because of its universal message of sadness and loss – the special qualities that George could bring even to a Christmas song. One writer called it 'the bitterest Christmas tune we've got'.

George was proud that it was the biggest-selling number-two record of all time, with sales of 1.8 million. All their royalties from the song for one year went to Bob Geldof's Ethiopian appeal, a donation that Wham! could afford but which, even so, was an unusually generous gesture in those days. The total benefit to the charity was estimated at more than £250,000. George said that all it had cost the stars who'd taken part on the Band Aid disc was a day of their time. He explained why he wanted to do more: 'People were singing "Feed the World" and saying it was the most worthwhile thing they had ever done and I thought, "Did you actually do anything else about it?" I'll bet most of the people there didn't even go and buy the record.'

His gesture almost fell flat when publishers Dick James Music launched a legal action claiming the song infringed their copyright of 'Can't Smile Without You', a 1978 hit for Barry Manilow. The company claimed the melodies were very similar and all the royalties were frozen while legal proceedings took place. Eventually, the action was withdrawn. George commented sarcastically, 'If they had won, would they have asked the starving to give back the food?'

After Christmas, the single was immediately flipped, on the advice of Gary Farrow, the band's consultant, and one of George's most critically acclaimed songs, 'Everything She Wants', became the A-side. He was proud of the track, often declaring it to be his favourite Wham! song and continuing to perform it in his future solo concerts. For once, the song didn't emerge from a snatch of melody in his head but from a distinctive drum beat.

The lyric wasn't based on personal experience but describes a man trapped in a marriage that isn't going well: 'He's faced with the "happy" news of an arriving baby, so he's in that situation where he can't back out.' The sentiment was light years away from the frothy 'Wake Me Up Before You Go-Go', although it was the next track on *Make It Big*.

George knew young men – presumably from Bushey Meads – who had found themselves in this situation and it's one he would have hated. He would be asked in interviews from time to time if he was looking forward to having a family, and he was not enthusiastic. He did, however, tell Tony Parsons that he could see himself with a young son, and that he felt a pang of jealousy when he saw lads of his age out with their little boy. Perhaps he wanted to enjoy the things he felt he missed out on when his dad was at work.

'Everything She Wants' was a highlight of the *Big Tour*, which would eventually take them all over the world: to Japan, Australia, the USA and, most famously, to China. They began in December 1984 in the less grandiose surroundings of the Whitley Bay Ice Rink. All tickets were standing and cost £6.50. Approximately 8,000 girls took advantage of the deal even though they were all very cold.

In the short space of time since their first tour, the dynamic had changed. Now, George was very much to the fore, receiving the loudest screams, particularly when he launched into 'Careless Whisper'. In the minds of his teenage audience, it seemed to have morphed into a love song, which he sung just for them.

They played three shows in Whitley as well as travelling to Glasgow, Edinburgh and Dublin before landing back at Wembley Arena in time for Christmas. George hated the whole experience. He complained to his mum and dad that he was trapped in his room all day, just waiting around, and it was 'driving him mad.' In Leeds, he hurt his back showing off some Madonna dance moves backstage and had to cancel a concert and go back to Radlett to see a physiotherapist and be fussed over by his mother.

George was at home for Christmas, choosing to spend New Year's Eve on the town with Pat Fernandes. They started out at the Camden Palace but quickly moved on to Bolts in Haringey. DJ Norman Scott was surprised to see him that night but George explained why they had moved on: 'I couldn't even go to the toilet without being pestered. I don't mind but there is a limit, so we came here.'

He and Pat could enjoy a dance at Bolts without being bothered. It was an unspoken rule in a gay club. The quickest way of getting George onto the floor – something his friends found very amusing – was to put one of his own records on the turntable. He would be up like a shot, especially after a glass or two of his favourite French white wine.

Joking apart, the novelty of fans and public recognition had completely worn off. His thoughts were turning to the future and the sort of life he wanted. He told the pop writer, Chris Heath, 'I'm trying to decide whether my ambition is likely to make me very unhappy.' He was expressing his concern that he would have to continue to sell his songs in the same way. Touring to promote a record would become the norm and he didn't want that. He had longed to be a famous pop star since he was a boy, but now he was unsure exactly what would be best for him moving forward.

In the short term, his ambition to be taken seriously achieved fruition when he was named Songwriter of the Year at the annual Ivor Novello Awards in March 1985. A few weeks earlier, Wham! had won Best Group at the BRITs, but this latter award meant so much more to him. Elton John made the presentation at the Grosvenor House Hotel in Park Lane and said, 'George is the greatest songwriter of his generation. He deserves to win this award and I would like to work with him in the future.' It was a wish that would come true many times over.

George Michael walked up onto the stage to receive the statuette. For a fleeting moment he forgot the distinction between his public and private persona. He became Georgios Panayiotou once more and wiped away a tear.

11

THE TRIP OF A LIFETIME

George wanted to do something that hadn't been done before, which would literally go down in the history books. Simon Napier-Bell and Jazz Summers had suggested, almost casually, over dinner at the Bombay Brasserie in Kensington that they should organise a trip by Wham! to China. His eyes lit up at the idea of being the first band to ever play in the communist country. 'Fix it,' he told them.

His managers thought shrewdly that Wham! could maximise publicity for such a momentous musical event and use it as a springboard for becoming a superstar group in the US. While he appreciated that business motive, George was not shy to admit he was more driven by ego. He would be achieving something that heroes including Queen and Elton John wanted to do.

He gave the go-ahead straight away. Simon took up negotiating duties while Jazz concentrated on organising an American stadium tour. For the next eighteen months, Simon would fly back and forth to China, trying to persuade officials there that Wham! were exactly the clean-cut, wholesome band that could only benefit the country's image to the outside world.

Jazz and Simon decided that a film of the trip would help to finance it. George was not especially keen to have film crews following him around all the time. The project, which seemed so promising on paper, would prove to be an unhappy one for everyone.

Lindsay Anderson was a bizarre choice to direct the film of the tour. He was sixty-two and old enough to be their grandfather. His best-known film, *If ...*, a provocative satire of English public-school life, had been released sixteen years before. He had directed many acclaimed theatre productions and enjoyed a distinguished, although not exactly mainstream, reputation: the sort of figure who would have been profiled on *The South Bank Show*. He didn't get Wham! at all and loathed George Michael.

In his diary he wrote: 'How on earth have two (lower) middle class boys from Watford managed to transform themselves into these vibrant figures of pop myth ...? It's a complete mystery.' The boys remained an enigma to him even after they had lunch together: 'I have really nothing to say to them: confident, bright, uninteresting, respectable, of the Eighties ... I get the impression they will be reasonably cooperative. Certainly not inspiring.'

A small Wham! army travelled to Hong Kong a few weeks later for two warm-up gigs before flying on to Beijing, where the main event would be held at the beginning of April 1985. As well as both sets of parents, George's sisters, Connie Filippello, lawyer Tony Russell and his wife, personal assistants, journalists and photographers, and all the musicians, Lindsay insisted on a thirty-five-strong film crew. Jazz Summers took along the vivacious singer Yazz, who would later become his wife and record one of the most memorable anthems of the eighties, 'The Only Way Is Up'. In total, close to one hundred personnel made the trip.

George was sensible enough not to play the big-time pop singer in front of his hosts. He spoke all the right, government-approved words at the first of many banquets held in their honour by the Chinese Youth Federation: 'Andrew and I are extremely flattered and honoured to be here today. We just hope our performance will represent a cultural introduction between young people here and in the West and help them see what goes on in the rest of the world. I think I speak for everyone when I say this may be a small step for Wham! but a great step for the youth of the world.'

A politician would have been proud of the gracious speech, but it didn't take long for everyone involved to become thoroughly disheartened. George had no idea at first just how empty those words would sound ten days later.

He understood that he had to play the game during the trip to make it a success and he made sure he smiled often and widely when a photographer shoved a camera under his nose. He had a special hollow grin on these occasions – all flashing white teeth but without his eyes being in the room. He and Andrew dutifully posed for pictures with locals at The Great Wall while Lindsay Anderson's film crews followed their every move. Lindsay fell off the wall, twisting his ankle badly and straining a ligament, which confined him to a wheelchair, although he was still able to bark instructions. As Simon Napier-Bell observed, it seemed to be Lindsay versus the world: 'From the moment he arrived in China, Lindsay had turned into a tyrant.'

George did not appreciate his every move being shadowed by the crew and it soon became apparent that he and Lindsay were not getting on. Andrew seemed to be more comfortable on film, happy to give a running commentary as they were shown around the country. He soon tired of it though and mooched about most of the time in dark sunglasses.

George's mood was not improved before the Beijing concert when the *Daily Mirror* ran a story that he was cracking up and had collapsed with the stress of it all. The scoop was obviously untrue and only deepened his suspicion of the tabloid press. He reacted poorly to what he interpreted as being bullied by Fleet Street. 'I never envisaged that when we started,' he complained bitterly.

Perhaps his discomfort at being in such proximity with four leading reporters from the national press may well have been exacerbated by a fear that his secret sexuality might be exposed; he was very careful to spend most of his time on the China trip in the company of his parents and sisters. The pop columnist from the *Daily Star*, Rick Sky, was well aware of the gay rumours surrounding George. He had even heard that he had been seen cottaging – anonymous sex between men in a public lavatory – at the end of the Northern Line. An amusing side effect of unsubstantiated stories about him was that the papers could link him with any random female in the knowledge that he was most unlikely to complain.

The concert was in front of a crowd of 15,000 at the People's Gymnasium. Unintentionally hilarious were the cassette tapes given out to every concertgoer at the entrance.

On one side were Wham! originals sung by George. On the other, the same songs in Chinese performed by Cheng Fangyuan, a female pop star. She sang a doctored set of lyrics: 'Wake Me Up Before You Go-Go' had no hint of 'Take Me Dancing Tonight'. Instead the not quite so catchy lines were:

> Wake me up before you go-go
> Men fight to be first to reach the peak
> Wake me up before you go-go
> Women are on the same journey
> and will not fall behind.

They were introduced on stage by Kan Lijun, now a well-known Chinese television presenter. She recalled, 'No one had ever seen anything like it before. The singers were all moving a lot and it was very loud. We were used to people who stood still when they performed. All the young people were amazed and everyone was tapping their feet. Of course the police weren't happy and they were scared there would be riots.'

Many in the audience were not the excited young people the group were hoping to reach; they could not afford the tickets. Instead they were given away by officials to friends and family, who had no idea about Wham! whatsoever. George was taken aback when he saw the polite yet sad faces watching him and he began the first song hesitantly. One real fan said afterwards that he had been too scared to sing along because nobody else was. A loudspeaker announcement in Chinese had been made before the boys took to the stage: 'Dancing is not allowed', which infuriated George when he found out.

Foot tapping was not what he had envisaged and he felt they had been 'stitched up' over that. His mood darkened further when a young man was arrested and beaten for getting up and dancing.

George became less cooperative as the tour continued; Andrew was equally unimpressed, describing the trip as a 'pain in the arse'. Both of them found the country oppressive with no incentive for the population to do well and improve their situation in life. He observed, 'All the joys of life we take for granted, they've simply been taken away from them.'

He also had some harsh words for the Chinese authorities who 'were the biggest bunch of capitalists and mercenaries we've ever come across. They extorted money out of us left, right and centre.'

Shirlie hated the whole experience. She complained, 'I just think what we are doing here is bad. I just don't think it's right. People here are sad, they want freedom but they're not allowed to have it and, in a way, we're giving them a taste of something they can't really have.'

Even worse was the flight between shows from Beijing to Guangzhou (Canton). Shirlie and Pepsi were sat next to the band's trumpet player when he suddenly had a delusional fit, thought he was the devil and started stabbing himself with a small knife. The girls were terrified and had to cling to each other while standing on the window seat, allowing Wham!'s two bodyguards to restrain him. The pilot had to turn the plane round so that the musician could be treated by doctors. George and Andrew were travelling separately, so missed the nerve-jangling episode, although it was practically the last straw for Shirlie, who cried, 'I just want to go home.'

Things did improve in Guangzhou, although George's back was still troublesome. It didn't help matters when he joined in a football game – the Wham! band against the Wham! Chinese road crew. Andrew, resplendent in a QPR strip, scored twice as the visitors romped to an 8–2 victory. George decided not to join a bowling competition, a sport he had never tried.

The Guangzhou concert at the Sun Yat-sen Memorial Hall was much jollier than the edgy night in Beijing, with the smaller 5,000-strong audience more aware of Wham! and their music, thanks to imports readily available from Hong Kong. Simon thought it like a concert in one of the provincial arenas in the UK.

While George and Andrew may both have been disgruntled at the way events turned out in China, there was no denying one element had been an astounding success. For two weeks, Wham! had been the most talked-about group in the world and the hoped-for stadium tour in the US was about to become a reality. Even Dick Leahy admitted that it was a great coup and a magnificent piece of promotion by Simon.

Rick Sky agrees: 'The amount of coverage was phenomenal. It was a huge deal because it meant they didn't have to tour all those thankless places in states like Alabama and Wisconsin. America can be quite stressful and China changed that for them.'

Afterwards, they could look forward to the movie. Lindsay showed the first cut to George, Andrew, Simon and Jazz at a small preview theatre in Wardour Street. George was twenty-five minutes late, which left the director red-faced with anger, but they all settled down to watch the rough cut full of optimism.

Simon recalled, 'He had made the film so achingly boring we could scarcely sit through it. He had been trying to make political commentary, which wouldn't have mattered if he'd managed to capture Wham!'s spirit and personality. But because their happy-go-lucky attitude was everything Lindsay hated in life, he'd got nowhere near them.'

George told him some of it was OK but the rest was boring. Andrew even called it 'bloody boring'. Lindsay went away to re-edit but George liked the second version even less than the first, declaring, 'It looks like Lindsay's being scornful of us.' The director was promptly fired. One insider on the film sarcastically remarked, 'Lindsay seemed more interested in filming Chinese people doing Tai Chi than in getting shots of Wham! performing.'

They brought in video directors Strath Hamilton and Andy Morahan, who George liked and trusted, to bring a more contemporary feel to the project. It was soon discovered that there was not enough suitable footage of the band in concert. They needed more material than the four songs Lindsay had filmed, so, quietly and rather ludicrously, every one slipped into Shepperton Studios to film Wham! pretending to perform in China.

Lindsay was furious at what he considered to be the butchering of his 'beautiful' film. After he died, his archive passed to the University of Stirling, where his diary revealed the extent of his ill feeling towards George, who he described as 'a young millionaire with an inflated ego'. He called him 'a shivering aspirant plucked out of the street, who turns into a tyrant of fabulous wealth, whose every command his minions must dash to execute.' He concluded in withering fashion, 'I was struck by his total disinterest in China. His vision only extends to the top 10.'

Lindsay had indeed been scornful of Wham! – and George, in particular. As many others did, he underestimated the focus and professional ruthlessness of the twenty-one-year-old George Michael. George had been a little in awe of Jerry Wexler but generally he was unimpressed by reputation.

After the trip, George described succinctly the China adventure to *The Face* magazine: 'I just thought the whole thing was a shambles.'

12

THE FINAL

George Michael was twenty-one and a multimillionaire. He didn't know what to do with his fortune. Sometimes he might splash out as much as £1,000 on a new jacket but forget to wear it, eventually discovering it scrunched up and ruined at the bottom of a suitcase. He had arrived on a gravy train to a greater degree than his father ever did, even if the two men shared a similar work ethic. On his return from China he moved out of his parents' house and rented a two-storey flat in Knightsbridge, the first home of his own. He didn't have time to furnish it properly and his mother took his washing away when she popped in to make sure he was looking after himself.

He had yet to pass his driving test, so it made sense to have a more central location for both business and pleasure. But it wasn't very private. He could walk to his favourite restaurants, like Le Caprice and Langan's Brasserie, but Pat Fernandes would drive him or he would take a cab if he didn't want to be recognised. Sometimes he ordered a chauffeur-driven limousine but this would always attract attention. He couldn't take a stroll to the shops without being mobbed. He quickly decided that he needed to buy a place with more privacy.

Even the house in Oakridge Avenue was becoming less of a sanctuary and he didn't enjoy inflicting his fame on his loyal parents. He realised how much his life had changed when he was visiting one afternoon and spent some time in the garden alone, gazing out to the field and farmland beyond. The view hadn't really changed in the decade his family had lived there. He reflected, 'I was thinking of all the things that have happened over the past five years and how it didn't really matter, how small it was in relation to all this – the insignificance of man next to nature. It just felt nice how I could just stand there and nothing really had changed.'

As George stood quietly contemplating his life, he heard some tittering coming from behind the bushes in his neighbour's garden: 'I looked over and there were all these kids there with cameras, all trying to take my picture. I just thought, "Don't kid yourself" and went back inside.'

George was so busy he had no time to house hunt yet. He'd barely had the chance to draw breath in London when he was jetting off to New York for a Motown Gala at the Harlem Apollo. Before he walked on stage to perform 'Careless Whisper', Simon asked him if he was feeling nervous. 'Not a bit,' George replied. He even had the confidence to stop the song when the musicians lost their place, telling the audience that he would have to start again. They gave him a round of applause. On the night, he sang with Stevie Wonder and Smokey Robinson. George had discovered he loved duets, and they would form a significant part of his recording output in the future.

An even more notable collaboration took place on 13 July 1985 when he performed at the Live Aid concert, one of the legendary days of popular music. More than 70,000 people flooded into Wembley Stadium on a gloriously sunny day and clear warm evening to listen to a who's who of pop that included Paul McCartney, David Bowie, The Who, Queen and Elton John. George came on during Elton's set to sing a solo version of the timeless power ballad 'Don't Let the Sun Go Down on Me'.

Elton was in a jovial mood and introduced George to the crowd as a 'friend of mine' who he admired 'very much for his musical talent, more than anything else'. While it was just one number, the performance was a showcase for George as a serious solo artist. He looked more mature for starters, bearded and wearing a leather jacket, white T-shirt and blue jeans, and fashionable sunglasses, of course.

He walked on with Andrew, who was delighted to be part of the event and happily went to the back to share a microphone with the singer Kiki Dee. George stayed centre stage. He said afterwards that his pitch was slightly off in the first couple of verses but, overall, it was, the critics thought, a towering performance and one of the most memorable of the night. He stood next to Elton when they were introduced backstage to Diana, Princess of Wales.

His performance at Live Aid demonstrated how George was edging closer towards going solo. For the moment he needed to concentrate on Wham! and their prestigious stadium tour in the US, which would be a further shop window for his talents.

George may not have enjoyed the touring but he liked the

US, not least because he didn't feel under siege concerning his sexuality the whole time. In the UK it was almost a national pastime. One national newspaper conducted a survey entitled 'The British Showbiz Personality Most Likely To Be Gay' and George had been the clear winner. As he succinctly put it, 'There's a section of Fleet Street who are desperate to know who I am fucking.' He refused to confirm or deny the inevitable question about the gay rumours that seemed to slip into every interview. He liked the ambiguity, claiming that sort of thing had done no harm to the careers of David Bowie or Mick Jagger.

George was a great subject for interview, always approaching every discussion in an intelligent fashion. 'I don't think anyone should have to answer a "gay or straight" question,' he said. But he kept being asked.

He continued to reinforce the image of Wham! as two heterosexual boys having fun. Andrew helped by occupying the newspapers with tales of drunkenness and sex. The ridiculous nature of the predicament that George found himself in was perfectly captured in his 'relationship' with the young American actress Brooke Shields.

The American tour opened with a couple of nights at the Poplar Creek Music Theater in the suburbs of Chicago. The whole world seemed to know of his date with Brooke in the rooftop restaurant at the Mayfair Regent hotel, where they were both staying. After the meal, George politely escorted her back to her room. Brooke, who famously remained a virgin for two more years until she was twenty-two, recalled in her memoir, 'He left without even trying to kiss me. I was so touched by what a real gentleman he was.'

George was happy to keep the photo opportunity going for a little longer when the Wham! circus moved on to New York. They had dinner together at a restaurant in Manhattan and Brooke observed, 'I thought he was a remarkable, respectful and patient gentleman who was obviously aware of my hesitance regarding sex.'

One of George's inner circle puts the experience in a more realistic light: 'They cleared the entire restaurant. There was security everywhere. Brooke Shields was the most eligible female on the planet. I think maybe her mum put it together. Of course he was giggling about it and we were giggling with him. George was never going back to hers.'

The unlikely couple had one more date, at a birthday party for the inimitable Grace Jones at the trendy Palladium nightclub in New York. Boy George was there with the fleeting pop star Marilyn. They mischievously went up to Brooke and whispered in her ear, 'He's a poof. He's a poof.' According to Boy George, 'She didn't know what it was, but looked worried.'

After the party, George gently told her that they needed to take a break because he wanted to concentrate on his career. Looking back on their brief connection, Brooke remembered, 'Nobody had ever been willing to move so slowly. It must be love.' It wasn't. George was polite about the episode, telling *Rolling Stone* that Brooke was probably the most beautiful woman he had ever met. He hated the attention when they went to the party, saying, 'It was absolutely hellish.'

Simon Napier-Bell welcomed the publicity but recalled that the idea was more to stop any careless gay whispers at a time when George was breaking America. The problem was that Brooke Shields was the star they always wheeled out on these occasions. He observed, 'She was obviously a bit of a fag hag. So it seemed to confirm rather than contradict it.'

Intriguingly, George never had a famous girlfriend or boyfriend. The pretend relationship with Brooke Shields was the nearest he ever came to being part of a celebrity couple. While it was completely true that he was too busy to start a proper relationship with anyone, a more likely explanation for his dropping of Brooke was that he was finding it increasingly difficult to live the lie of Wham! He was growing up.

No woman has ever come forward claiming a night of passion with George, as they have done with Andrew. Close friends, however, do confirm that he enjoyed the company of 'pretty girls' when on tour in the US, although he hated the fact that they were sleeping with him because he was George Michael the star, rather than Georgios Panayiotou. He felt used.

George's perspective was gradually changing as he realised he was exclusively gay. He seemed to be able to accept that more easily away from the UK. In Los Angeles in September 1985 he met Bradford Branson, a very handsome fashion and portrait photographer.

Brad, as his friends called him, was the son of a petroleum engineer and a legal secretary and grew up in West Los Angeles. As a boy he would join his friends to play on the backlot of the old MGM Studios and from an early age was drawn to celebrity and the world of Hollywood. As a young man, he worked briefly for screen legends Gloria Swanson and Kathryn Grayson, who would tell him wonderful stories from the golden age of movie-making. He turned to photography, originally as a means of getting into movies, before realising that it was his vocation.

The influential California-based photographer Paul Jasmin took him under his wing and taught him the value of style. Brad decided that music was the best medium for him, and his early work, including photographs of Eurythmics, began to appear in Andy Warhol's *Interview* magazine. When he met George he had recently completed shooting the pictures for *Vanity Fair* to accompany a feature on the underground club scene in Los Angeles written by Bret Easton Ellis, who would go on to write *American Psycho*.

George had wandered into the achingly trendy Dirtbox, one of the 'floating clubs' – an idea originating in London – that would pop up anywhere and were essentially illegal then because they served alcohol late into the night. Brad was with a friend, a British journalist called Fiona Russell Powell, who for a short time performed with the group ABC under the name Eden.

Fiona, who worked principally for *The Face* magazine, was very much part of the nightclub scene in London and well aware of George's preferences but she'd decided early on not to tell the wider world. She followed a code of loyalty and silence among the gay society whose company she so much enjoyed. Even Boy George was not in the business of outing people. He only made an exception in George Michael's case because he was living such a blatant lie and he liked winding up his pop rival.

According to Fiona, Brad was very gay and took 'a lot of drugs, including heroin'. He instantly found George very attractive when he came over to chat to Fiona, who politely introduced them. Brad was clearly star-struck and 'uncool' about the whole thing. Fiona didn't notice any knowing glances between them, but when George left to go back to the Mondrian Hotel in West Hollywood, Brad followed a few minutes later.

Fiona had told Brad that George liked men but that she didn't expect anything to come of it. She was astonished, therefore, to get a call from Brad, who was in George's hotel suite. He spent three days and two nights there. Brad told her, 'Promise not to tell anyone about this. He's really worried.' She gave him her word and kept to it for more than ten years.

George obviously enjoyed his hassle-free time in Los Angeles and stayed on for two weeks after the band had left. He singled out the Dirtbox as a place he really liked, mostly because it wasn't legal. He observed, 'I've always liked illegal places. Although I'm a fairly cautious person I love any area where you can feel danger – as long as it doesn't mean I'm going to get my head kicked in. Places with danger and sex are good fun.'

George never spoke about his relationship with Brad, which seemed to be ongoing in a casual yet close manner for a number of years. The photographer once suggested that he was the inspiration for one of the greatest of all George Michael songs, 'A Different Corner'. The lyric was intensely personal and far more agonising than his first solo single, 'Careless Whisper'. He subsequently talked about it in terms of emotional development. He had an intense two-week relationship with someone that he said did not develop into something more because he was George Michael and the other person was intimidated by the circumstances of his fame.

George described the song dramatically as 'the sound of a man whose heart has been broken'.

The timing of the writing of the song strongly suggests that it was about Brad Branson, although George has never revealed the identity. For his part, Brad did once let slip that it was about him, in a 2006 interview in which he recalled George playing him the demo of the beautiful song.

Brad became one of the most acclaimed portrait photographers of the eighties and nineties and he was a familiar face in George's entourage, both personally and professionally. He moved to Amsterdam in the late eighties and worked on photo shoots for George for many years. He was also unwittingly instrumental in the rest of the gang discovering what Andrew and Shirlie had known since George was nineteen.

This was a group of friends who would not be propping up the bar at Heaven or the Wag Club every night so had no real idea that George was gay – whatever rumours they might have heard. Coincidentally, everyone was staying on Ibiza again, enjoying a party break. On one evening, the lads had been out on the town and returned to their hotel to continue drinking in their suite. Suddenly, two of the gang came flying through the door and exclaimed that they had just seen George 'making out' with Brad Branson. By 'making out', they did not mean having a cup of tea. Everyone was wide-eyed with surprise, except Andrew, who was laughing his head off.

Brad would go on to take one of the most iconic pictures of George Michael, the moody cover shot on his third solo album, *Older*, where half his face is dramatically in shade. They had remained close friends when Brad returned to Los Angeles in the early nineties and gave up photography at the end of the decade, saying he was disillusioned with his art. Brad, who was the same age as George, died suddenly from cancer in 2012, aged forty-nine.

After the eight-date stadium tour, everyone was on a high – except George. He alone realised that the final date at the Pontiac Silverdome in Detroit would be Wham!'s last-ever concert in the US. He informed Andrew, Jazz Summers and Simon Napier-Bell that he would be a solo artist in the future and that plans should be put in place for winding up the group. This would not include another album, he said, although he would produce more material, perhaps for a final EP. More importantly, he wanted one big last concert in London.

The fans had no idea that the biggest band of the eighties would be history within a year. A new single 'I'm Your Man' followed seamlessly the Motown style of 'Wake Me Up Before You Go-Go' and 'Freedom' and reached number one. George maintained the lyric was a more grown-up and sexual one because he had just had very good sex. He always had a soft spot for the song and was still performing it live more than twenty years later.

Faced with a large tax bill, Andrew had moved to Monte Carlo with his new girlfriend, a stunning model called Donya Fiorentino who had been the girlfriend of *Miami Vice* star Don Johnson. He wanted to be a racing driver and this was an ideal location in which to make a fresh start.

George, however, was not doing so well. The steel he showed moving forward professionally vanished from his personal life. He shoved a photographer up against the wall outside Stringfellows when he didn't want to end a night out with Shirlie by having his picture taken. On another occasion, he and his best friend, David Austin, had a drunken fight outside the club.

He clearly needed to get away and so went back to California to collect himself and work on material for his first solo album. He felt safer in Beverly Hills with no photographers camped on his doorstep. He didn't feel under scrutiny the whole time. Now that he was spending more time there, he drifted away from some of the old guard in London, including Pat Fernandes. She vanished from his entourage.

George had become increasingly uneasy about being asked questions about Pat. He did divulge inadvertently in one interview that she was his friend *and* assistant, which suggested that she might have had a paid position within his organisation. Pat has seldom spoken about her association with George. She was once quoted as saying that they had rowed about a question involving Andy Pandy during a game of Trivial Pursuit, which was hardly 'kiss and tell'. She apparently ended up in Dubai, where she was tracked down and offered a large sum of money by a national newspaper to reveal all about their relationship, but she declined. She may well have signed a confidentiality agreement.

George became close to another woman, who he met in Los Angeles. She, too, would be referred to by an eager media as his 'girlfriend', although she may have been just a very good friend. Kathy Jeung was a member of the arty, almost bohemian set that Brad Branson was part of in LA. She was a Chinese-American woman, who was completely unfazed by George's fame. She worked as a part-time DJ, makeup artist and model. George liked her because she treated him as an ordinary guy, not a superstar. For a while she was his muse, someone to awaken his creative side. She had her own life in LA but she would make time for him. Analysing his relationships with the opposite sex and, in particular, those with his teenage girlfriends, a psychiatrist might wonder if George was less likely to sleep with a woman he liked.

His regular lunchtime companion was Rob Kahane, who was Wham!'s efficient US agent. He had worked his way up from sorting letters in a mailroom and delivering coffee to Barbra Streisand. George always respected someone who had done well through their own efforts. One day Rob brought along the latest edition of entertainment newspaper the *Hollywood Reporter* to show him the front-page headline: 'Wham! Sold to Sun City'.

Jazz and Simon had negotiated to sell Nomis to a company whose principal shareholder was Sol Kerzner. He had developed the notorious casino complex known as Sun City in the poverty-stricken South African homeland of Bophuthatswana, which, understandably, was a target for anti-apartheid supporters and not something George wanted to be associated with at all.

He was furious that he knew nothing about it. Rob Kahane revealed, 'This is the first time I saw George Michael lose it because he is pretty together. He was so angry and pissed off and he kept saying, "How could they do this? How could they sell me to something they know I don't believe in?"'

In their defence, Jazz and Simon thought they were negotiating with the promoter Harvey Goldsmith and had not appreciated that Kerzner was his parent company's major shareholder. Their efforts to appease George got nowhere. In his mind they had crossed a line. Jazz described their situation memorably to Simon as 'a horrible fucking feeling we're fucking fucked'.

He was right. George flew back to London for the BRITs, at which Wham! received an Outstanding Achievement award alongside Elton John, who seemed to pop up everywhere in his professional life. They were given the accolade jointly for taking British pop music to China and, in Elton's case, Russia. They walked up on stage to the sound of Elton's latest hit, the exquisite ballad 'Nikita', which was a good choice because George had recorded the backing vocals and can distinctly be heard towards the end of the song.

Bizarrely, they were presented with their awards by the politician Norman Tebbit, who told the audience that he knew nothing about pop music. George, dressed in a cowboy hat, silk jacket and no shirt, managed to avoid talking to Jazz and Simon even though they joined him on stage. Within days he released a statement saying he had parted company with Nomis. The takeover deal fell through without their biggest asset and soon afterwards Jazz and Simon went their separate ways, too. In fairness they had done an impeccable job with Wham!, although neither was particularly close to George.

George may have been planning new management for his solo career in any case, but this turn of events forced his hand. He took Connie Fileppello and Siobhan Bailey with him and appointed Rob Kahane and his business partner Michael Lippman as his managers. Michael, a former lawyer, had at one time been David Bowie's manager. They would have special responsibility for launching George's solo career in the US.

George made the official announcement that Wham! were splitting up at the end of February 1986 on the talk show *Aspel & Company*. Three months later *The Final* album was released; it was more of a greatest hits compilation, with a few tracks that hadn't featured on the first two albums. These included 'Last Christmas' and 'A Different Corner', which had been his second solo UK number one in April. The album has grown in stature over the years, especially when it was re-released in 2008. Ian Wade for BBC Online described it as the duo's 'epitaph, with the brand dying young and leaving a fantastic Greatest Hits. Amazing.'

In the build-up to their farewell, Wham! did a number of reflective interviews. Andrew had put up with some ghastly media that heroically took the spotlight away from George during the previous couple of years. He hated the relentless abuse from the media and their fixation with stories about his drinking and pursuit of women – not forgetting his notorious nose job.

When all was concluded, however, Andrew would be a millionaire, living in a tax haven with a very beautiful eighteen-year-old girlfriend. He recognised early on that George had the talent and ambition to sustain the group, so he'd put away his ego and let his friend get on with it. He had been the image of Wham! but gradually the personality of George Michael took over. Jazz Summers described him as a 'cool guy'. When George was asked what would happen to his friend after their goodbye concert, he replied simply, 'Andrew will be all right,' which would turn out to be true.

Wham! The Final took place at Wembley Stadium in front of 72,000 fans on the hottest Saturday of summer, 28 June

1986, three days after George's twenty-third birthday. He'd celebrated with a warm-up concert at the Brixton Academy before joining friends, including Kathy, for drinks and dancing at the Café de Paris in Piccadilly.

Next day it was Wham!'s last *Top of the Pops* recording, singing their final number one single, 'The Edge of Heaven', another expert slice of pop music. The lyrics were quite explicitly sexual – sort of *Fifty Shades of Grey* in a three-minute pop song. George said he wrote them on purpose because he didn't think anyone would notice the undertone, which was probably true. Elton John had returned the 'Nikita' favour by playing piano on the track.

The Final concert itself was even noisier than Live Aid, with thousands of young female Wham! fans screaming every time their heroes strutted down the walkways. Beforehand, they had premiered scenes from the China film, now called *Foreign Skies*, which one critic found 'terribly tedious, just lots of footage of Wham! having their photos taken with Chinese people.'

The concert itself began at 7.30pm with 'Everything She Wants'. Pepsi and Shirlie were there and so was David Austin. Elton John provided one of the highlights, coming on stage dressed in a clown costume that made him appear the spitting image of Ronald McDonald. He played piano during 'The Edge of Heaven' and joined George to sing his own classic, 'Candle in the Wind'.

The occasion was a mixture of joy and sadness. It seemed as if all 72,000 sang along to 'Last Christmas' and 'Careless Whisper'. George ran around a lot in his fringed leather jacket, pretending to be an airplane before launching into 'Wake Me

Up Before You Go-Go'. Elton was there again for the last-ever Wham! song, a version of 'I'm Your Man' that saw Simon Le Bon join them as well. *Smash Hits* observed: 'thousands of fans sniffle into their hankies'. And that was it … after just four short years, the end of Wham!

George could look back with satisfaction on his creation of a band that was 'built on a careless, upbeat image of fair-haired sun-tanned boys singing about love without pain'. He already knew the principal difficulty he would face as a solo artist: 'The test is now to come across much more as a real person.'

13

GOING SOLO

Shortly after Wham! The Final, George quietly drove himself and his father to the launch of a campaign by Haringey Council in North London to promote awareness of genetic blood disorders. He had become aware of the good work of the UK Thalassaemia Society (UKTS) when the organisation had provided help and care to a member of his family who suffered from the condition.

Cypriots are particularly susceptible to carrying the faulty gene that can lead to a raft of debilitating symptoms including chronic anaemia. George never revealed which member of his family had the inherited disease but he quietly gave the society a substantial amount of money over many years. In 2002, he became its patron and continued to be its biggest benefactor. His annual donation was made with the strict condition that it remained private.

George was reserved during the function at the Wood Green Civic Centre, preferring as ever to engage in one-on-one conversation. Driving to the event, however, did allow him to get behind the wheel of his new car, a black Mercedes

Sports, which he bought to celebrate passing his driving test at the first attempt after an intensive course of lessons. His father, who appreciated the status of an expensive car, beamed proudly in the passenger seat as they waved goodbye. Everyone was eager to cheer them off. George slightly ruined the grand getaway by stalling twice as he lurched down the street.

Worryingly, there was a family crisis when his sister Yioda slipped over and cracked her head. She was very ill. George explained, 'For two weeks she was in absolute agony and it was horrible. There was absolutely nothing I could do and I remember thinking I would give absolutely everything up just so long as she was OK. Then luckily she was. It turned out the pain wasn't actually from a head injury but from a trapped nerve at the top of her spine.'

The frightening episode, he admitted, gave George a whole new perspective on what was important in his life. Perhaps he was taking his career – being George Michael – far too seriously. Prophetically, he told Paul Simper, the music journalist who had become a friend, that he was much more afraid of those he loved dying than of dying himself: 'I have a strange feeling that I'm not going to live to a very old age. I've always had that.'

George retreated back to Los Angeles and his new circle of friends. These included Kathy Jeung, Brad Branson and his cousin Andros Georgios, who was often at his side and had his own ambitions in the music business. Meanwhile, Andrew was living a life of luxury in Monte Carlo while Pepsi and Shirlie were embarking on their pop careers as a duo.

David Austin remained close, but in the late eighties was furthering his own career. George had co-written and produced David's debut single, 'Turn to Gold', two years before, in the summer of 1984. George even sang backing vocals and, perhaps unsurprisingly, the track sounded like a cut from a Wham! album. He was always loyal to his friend and did his best to help him. He even went on children's game show *Cheggers Plays Pop* to give David a big introduction, but the song languished in the charts and didn't make the top fifty.

Many observers have wondered why George and David never formed another musical partnership after their busking days. According to George, they would have argued too much. He'd needed the laid-back approach of Andrew when he was finding the right image for himself in Wham!

Over the years, David had developed as an accomplished musician and songwriter in his own right and at one stage moved to Nashville to work with leading country musicians. George's friends enjoyed David's company when he visited Los Angeles. One recalls, 'David would come to LA every so often and was fantastic value. He could just pick up an acoustic guitar and play a song by anybody you wanted – from Elvis to the Eagles.'

Despite having his friends around him, George felt isolated and down. He was sinking under the responsibility of being a solo star and he hadn't even started yet. He admitted, 'I'm not very good at being a pop star in broad daylight.' He'd heard that the *News of the World* had an exclusive story about him, which he assumed was a gay revelation. He had become more of a target now that Andrew wasn't there to take most of the media attention.

He was drinking far too much and taking ecstasy for the first time. Periods of drug-induced highs, days when he felt wonderful, were mixed with terrible lows when he would be awake in the small hours of the morning, believing his whole life was a mess. His state of mind was an early indication that he was a man susceptible to bouts of depression. Yet still he kept his true sexuality hidden from the world.

George described what turned out to be an unplanned year off as a 'very long, quiet wobbler'. He was always prone to self-analysis, so understood how he was feeling – he was looking at everything in a negative and self-pitying way.

Andrew saved the day when he flew in from Monaco. He was alarmed to see how dreadful George looked. He had piled on the pounds through boozing and sitting around the house in Beverly Hills where he had set up home. The two friends stayed up late into the night, drinking good wine and putting the world to rights. It was just like the old days, except the wine was of a much higher quality.

George felt much better for seeing his old pal and being able to reveal how he was feeling to someone who was so non-judgemental about things. He pulled himself together and decided to start again by putting all his energy into his solo career and doing everything properly. It began in spectacular fashion with a duet alongside the incomparable Aretha Franklin. 'I Knew You Were Waiting (For Me)' was an instant dance classic when it was released in January 1987, although George had actually travelled to the historic ghetto area of Detroit to record with the Queen of Soul before Wham!'s final hurrah the year before.

He had accepted immediately when Clive Davis, the

legendary boss of Arista Records, first suggested he get together with Aretha. It was her track and one of the songs released on her album, *Aretha*, two months earlier. As the invited guest, George had absolutely nothing to do with writing or producing. He was in awe of Aretha's voice: 'As much as I love a lot of other female artists, no one touches her really.'

Aretha arrived at the United Sound Systems Studio clutching a large box that contained a rack of lamb ribs. She offered George some but he declined because he was going through a temporary stage of not eating meat.

They sang their verses and ad libs separately before sharing a microphone for the chorus, a very unusual occurrence in a recording but it was the way Aretha preferred to do things. While George sang his part in the vocal booth, he watched Aretha the other side of the glass chomp her way through the entire box of ribs. When she had finished each one she would toss it across the room into a bin. Every time it was a slam dunk. 'Boy, could she hit that bucket,' observed George, admiringly. 'She could have worked in a fairground.'

George found it strange not being the producer, but was impressed with Narada Michael Walden, who had been responsible for some of Aretha's best-known tracks, including 'Who's Zoomin' Who'. He created an easy atmosphere in the studio that allowed George to stay relaxed. Sensibly, George didn't try and compete with Aretha and she in turn was complimentary: 'He had a very unique sound, very different to anything out there.'

George felt much more confident putting across his point of view in the video that Andy Morahan flew in to direct with a budget of £150,000. Aretha recalled, 'We had a super time.

George was calling the shots – how he wants this, how he wanted that. He was very friendly, personable and easy to talk to.' George was very much setting the tone for his solo image – leather waistcoat, white T-shirt and jeans, aviator shades and designer stubble. Unusually, he didn't sport an earring – probably because Aretha was wearing two giant gold loops.

They never recorded together again, which is a pity. 'I Knew You Were Waiting (For Me)' remains Aretha's only number one in the UK, where it prevented the debut record of Pepsi & Shirlie, 'Heartache', from reaching that position. As a forerunner for George Michael's solo career it could scarcely have performed any better, especially as it also topped the *Billboard* chart in the US in March.

George was back to doing everything for his own solo album, for which he wrote, arranged, produced, sang and played most of the instruments. Much of the final production work was done at the popular Puk Recording Studios near Randers in Denmark, where Elton John finished many recordings. Chris Porter was once again brought in to act as engineer. He had worked on the very first single, 'Wham Rap!', and had been a constant presence since he helped George and Andrew record the B-side to 'Club Tropicana'. They booked the Good Earth Studios in Soho for eleven hours and left with a track called 'Blue (Armed with Love)', which George had written from scratch.

Chris had realised there was much more depth to George than he thought. George seemed to write most of his songs in a studio, arriving, as he had always done, with just the germ of the idea, meaning Chris was by his side through many hours of recording. They ended up working on five albums together

Georgios Panayiotou was a sweet little boy who everybody called Yogi.

Showing off that cheeky grin, aged five, when his family were living in North London.

His hair already had a mind of its own when he was eight. He was never happy with it.

At least he didn't have to wear those glasses all the time as a teenager. He had swapped them for contact lenses by the time he was on holiday in Cyprus, aged sixteen.

Taken on the stairs of the family home in Radlett, this picture was sent to record companies by George's first group, The Executive. From top: Andy Leaver, Jamie Gould, Andrew Ridgeley, George, his best friend David Austin and Paul Ridgeley, Andrew's younger brother.

Shirlie Holliman loved dancing with George. She thought they were well suited because he had the best rhythm.

A very rare picture of The Executive rehearsing. George is on keyboards, local musician Noel Castelle is playing the saxophone and Andrew Ridgeley is the singer!

George and Andrew were always in tune with one another. At a press call for the Wham! album *Make It Big* in November 1984, Andrew makes sure he has the chance to get a word in.

Meeting childhood heroes was a bonus of fame. In April 1985, George shares a table with David Cassidy and his wife Meryl Tanz, while his constant companion Pat Fernandes smiles happily to his left.

In the early days, his cousin Andros Georgiou was often by his side. His father Jack and Andros's girlfriend Kay join in the applause at the 1986 Ivor Novello Awards.

It was 'Fantastic' while it lasted. Wham! were one-hit wonders when Andrew and George had their photo taken on New Year's Day, 1983.

Sometimes an ice cream is just more interesting than a Western pop group posing on the Great Wall of China.

Wham! The Final at Wembley Stadium in June 1986 was the last time George and Andrew would perform alongside their famous backing singers, Pepsi and Shirlie.

And then it was all over: the boys reflect on the day backstage with Elton John in baby-pink boxer shorts.

Above: His proud parents Jack and Lesley were with him to celebrate his thirtieth birthday at Newmarket Racecourse.

Left: George always enjoyed posing with models – especially if they were supermodels. Top row: Shana Zadrick, Linda Evangelista and Nadja Auermann; bottom row: Tyra Banks, Estelle Lefébure and Beverly Peele.

Kathy Jeung, who featured in the notorious 'I Want Your Sex' video, travelled with him when the *Faith World Tour* began in Japan in February 1988.

George met his great love Anselmo Feleppa and best friend Lucia Guanabara when he played the Rock in Rio Festival in January, 1991. His life would never be the same.

George never lost the joy of singing. On stage with long-standing backing singer Shirley Lewis during the Australian leg of the *Faith World Tour*.

Joining Liza Minnelli when she sings 'We Are the Champions', the finale of the Freddie Mercury Tribute Concert for AIDS Awareness at Wembley Stadium in April 1992.

Producing a barnstorming version of 'Living for the City' with the song's composer, Stevie Wonder, at the annual VH1 Honors benefit at the Universal Amphitheatre, Los Angeles, in April 1997.

George made a surprise appearance at Live 8 London in July 2005 to sing 'Drive My Car' with the incomparable Paul McCartney.

George was the best company. He was a good friend to Princess Diana, who felt relaxed in his company. They sat beside each other at the Concert of Hope, Wembley, for World AIDS Day in December 1994.

He was very fond of Geri Halliwell and they made an elegant couple at a tribute to Elizabeth Taylor at the Dorchester Hotel in May 2000.

Sharing a private moment with his partner Kenny Goss at Versace's Paris show in July 2002.

Having a great night out with his old friends from Bananarama, Keren Woodward and Sara Dallin, who squeezes onto his lap as they share a taxi after dinner at The Ivy.

George Michael . . .
the public legend.

Georgios Panayiotou . . .
the private man.

and Chris is proud to report that they never had a cross word.

One of the songs that needed work on the first solo album was the title track, 'Faith', and, in particular, its famous guitar intro. George knew what he wanted – a very stark and dry sound.

Chris recalled, 'The only acoustic guitar lying around was this horrible aluminium-body guitar that The Damned had left there.' They rang out for another, better guitar to be delivered to the studio, but by the time it arrived the track had already been recorded and George was happy: 'So that's what you hear and it became the signature sound of the record.'

The first track to be released as a single proved to be one of the most controversial of his career, probably more for its title than anything else. One American DJ even refused to introduce it as 'I Want Your Sex', preferring instead to just announce George Michael's new record. The S-word was as frowned upon as if it had been the F-word.

George told *Spin* magazine, 'It's the worst reaction I've had on a record for years. Black radio would not play "I Want Your Sex". For them it was too dirty. Don't ask me why that is, when every good black song on the charts is full of innuendos.'

Much of its notoriety came from the glossy video, which featured some erotic interaction between George and a bewitching Kathy Jeung. George was suitably outraged when it was blacklisted by both the BBC and IBA, but releasing the song as the first track from the album was a deliberate exercise in stirring up publicity. That worked a treat in the US and delighted his management team. Michael Lippman said it 'snowballed beyond our wildest dreams'.

The strategy slightly backfired in the UK, where nobody could see the video, which, as George acknowledged, was pretty tame. He commented, 'If I was rubbing oil into my girlfriend's arse there might be something to talk about.'

Those who were able to watch it did see flesh at one point, when George, revealing himself to be left-handed, uses a red lipstick to write 'Explore' on Kathy's thigh and 'Monogamy' on her naked back. That was about as exciting as it got. The *Washington Post* described it as 'vacuous'.

Commercially, the performance of the song was greatly improved in the US when it featured on the soundtrack of the Eddie Murphy movie, *Beverly Hills Cop II*. Disappointingly perhaps, the single only reached number three in the UK and two in the US. As a publicity tool, however, it more than served its purpose. Interviewers were lining up to talk about the adult George, who was promoting a much sexier image. He explained, 'Some of my new music is more abrasive and sexual, much more real.'

In amongst the clichéd and rather obvious coverage, George did air some thoughtful views on sex in society; he believed that children should be allowed to see sex in terms of caring and love as opposed to pornography.

George took advantage of being back in the UK to promote the record to buy his first home. He paid an estimated £2 million to purchase a house called Weeping Ash in a quiet cul-de-sac close to Hampstead village in North London. The location was unassuming with none of the trimmings that would suggest it was where a famous and wealthy person lived.

The journalist and television host Jane Moore once visited him and described what she found: 'There are no security gates, no imposing entrance pillars, and not so much as a CCTV camera or concrete lion in sight. The man even answers his own front door, for God's sake.'

He described it as a 'Scandinavian house in the middle of North London – all pine and glass'. The house was named after a beautiful tree in the small, lush, well-planted garden. He was nearly in tears when the Great Storm of October 1987 wrecked the outdoors and ruined the tree.

George could easily have afforded a housekeeper, but he preferred to live alone. Instead, his loyal mum would come round every week to clean and vacuum the place. Sometimes Yioda would pop in to organise his laundry but, mostly, it was just Lesley who made sure her son was all right. Despite belonging to a close family growing up, George seemed to have little problem with living by himself: 'I love to come home, close the door and there's no one there and not a sound. I love the feeling of solitude.'

He bought the property fully furnished and added little to stamp his own personality on it. His chief luxury was having four television sets scattered around the house – in his bedroom, kitchen, upstairs living room and downstairs lounge.

George preferred to eat out with friends when he was in London and would turn on the TV while he was getting ready. His favourite was *Blind Date*, the popular dating show with Cilla Black: 'You watch and see who the three people are and if one of them is really ugly or funny you'll watch it but if not, you'll go off and do something else until the next bunch comes up.'

As a child George read a lot of books, but as an adult with a dwindling attention span he preferred to watch television.

Much of his later philanthropy would be inspired by something he viewed.

George was interested in investing his money wisely, and took advice from his father that property was a good bet. He was not prone to outrageous bursts of personal extravagance and had no desire to copy the spending sprees of Elton John. He enjoyed being generous to friends and family and would rather spend money on others than himself. One afternoon he had been to visit Oakridge Avenue and, as he left, realised that his family had four new cars, including a Rolls-Royce, gleaming in the driveway. He had bought the lot.

Back in Los Angeles, he also treated Kathy Yeung to a new convertible as a thank you for her loving friendship. She spent much of the time at his villa in Beverly Hills, which was in a prestigious street on a hillside north of Sunset Boulevard. She kept her own apartment, however, and never showed any desire to move to London.

Plans were already in place to promote George's new album, *Faith*, with a huge world tour, so he would have little time to enjoy his homes. The publicity generated by 'I Want Your Sex' was followed up by the release of the title track as a single just before the album became available in October 1987. Both reached number one in the US before Christmas. The *Washington Post* called George 'the closest thing to a pop genius since Elton John'.

The ballads 'Father Figure' and 'One More Try' drew most of the favourable attention. They appeared timeless whereas the more funk-orientated material was very much a product of the eighties. Connie Johnson in the *LA Times* called 'Father Figure' one of the 'gentlest, most romantic songs George

Michael's ever written'. George, less elegantly, called it 'bonkworthy'.

'Father Figure' was the next US number one, although the first George Michael single in the UK not to reach the top ten. The accompanying video became one of his most acclaimed and he and Andy Morahan shared the MTV Award for Best Direction in 1988. In fairness, they could have been joined on stage by Tony Scott, the acclaimed British director of *Beverly Hills Cop II*, who had filmed the love scenes. His current girl-friend, the stunning raven-haired actress and model Tania Coleridge, had been cast as George's love interest: 'At the time, I had been with Tony Scott for some five years. He wasn't sure if he liked the idea of me being in a love scene if he wasn't involved – so he shot the love scene. Just he and George and I were there. You can notice in the way the film rolls.'

Tania had a very upper-class start in life as the daughter of the fifth Baron Coleridge and could list the poet Coleridge as an ancestor on her father's side. As a punk with a dodgy Mohican she was spotted walking down the King's Road by the renowned model agent, Sarah Doukas. Her life was trans-formed as if it were a screenplay for a movie, and she modelled in Milan before becoming a muse for the renowned fashion photographer, Helmut Newton. She posed for 'quite a lot of racy stuff' before 'Father Figure'.

Newton's distinctive black-and-white stills were clearly the inspiration for the iconic video, although Tania hated it at the time, largely due to having her outfits stolen and the shoot dragging on for four days in downtown LA.

George had an ongoing fascination with models, their beauty and physicality and, most importantly, how they made him look when they were next to him. In the story he played the driver of a yellow cab in New York who picks up the stunning Tania, who is wearing a distinctive long white coat and black stilettos.

George's favourite imagery invariably involved light and shade, black-and-white, two-tone, and urban streets at night lit by atmospheric lamplight. For 'A Different Corner' he had been filmed completely in white except for his hair and beard. Even the telephone is white. In 'Father Figure' he is in black with a white T-shirt. Tania begins in the white coat but wears black for modelling down a catwalk, and in black bra and suspenders for their love scenes.

She was in no doubt that George was gay: 'Getting to know him over those few days, he was clearly gay to me. I think he probably had to dig pretty deep to get through those love scenes. I remember it being quite tricky for him but we got through it. We had to kiss again and again.' Many years later, she could laugh about it: 'I had to say, "George, just kiss me properly so we can get out of here!"'

The video was played repeatedly in what was arguably the golden age of MTV and one that helped change the public perception of George Michael from lightweight to serious solo artist. Tania found herself being recognised as the girl in 'Father Figure' wherever she went. She did a lot of press with George for the rest of the year and the media assumed they were an item, even going so far as producing a fake picture of them together on a beach. That took some explaining to her dad, who couldn't understand why she hadn't told him that George Michael was her boyfriend.

George thought 'One More Try' was, at that point, the best song he had written. Unusually for him, he wrote the whole thing from start to finish in eight hours. Chris Porter was 'completely knocked out' by a vocal that demonstrated what a good soul singer George was becoming. He thought the track was the principal reason why the album crossed over so successfully into the R&B charts and was so well received by a black audience. Elton John heard it and paid George the ultimate compliment: 'I don't get jealous of many songs, but I'm jealous of this song. I'd love to have written this.'

George was busy on the exhausting *Faith World Tour* by the time it reached number one in the US in April 1988. Kathy Jeung accompanied him when the tour began in Japan and Australia; she would go back to the hotel with him, but his American publicist Phil Lobel recalled that they had adjoining rooms.

Phil was very skilful at getting him the maximum press attention with the minimum cooperation. George refused to do any interviews for the tour, so Phil said he didn't have to and didn't ask him why he objected to them. In the end he did just three American sit-downs: *Interview* magazine, *Rolling Stone* – and the *Detroit Free Press*, because of his regard for all things Motown.

The publicist, who was with him for a very important year in his career, managed to turn a nine-word aside to *Entertainment Tonight* into a clip that went round the world. George was about to take to the stage in Detroit with Aretha Franklin as his guest. He turned to the cameras set up at the side and said simply, 'I know this will be a really great show.'

In those pre-internet times, Phil converted a two-hour special George did for VH-1, in which he talked about each song on *Faith*, into 127 separate interviews. He simply told journalists that George was on tour but he would fax them the answers to any questions they had. He would then go through his transcription of the VH-1 show, crafting the right response from what George had already said. There was no Google to discover that a paper in Chicago was carrying the same replies as one in Atlanta.

On the tour, George led a lonely existence when Kathy returned home to Los Angeles. At home he could choose his own company; on the road he was a prisoner of his hotel room. Phil never had a conversation with George about his sexuality. He explained, 'It wasn't my place to ask.' Even his manager, Rob Kahane, never spoke to him about it. In effect, George spent eighteen months guarding his secret. 'He would basically retreat to the privacy of his own world and be alone,' added Phil.

As George Michael, the star, he took control of every aspect of the mammoth 137-date tour. He oversaw the design of the giant stage that was shaped like a cage, the state-of-the-art lighting and, especially, the photographs.

Phil recalled when he presented a new set of one hundred publicity photos for George's approval in advance of his three sold-out nights at The Forum in Los Angeles. He carefully laid them out on a tray and waited patiently. In the end George selected just two and instructed his publicist to destroy the ones he had rejected: 'He was very particular about the light and angle and what he wanted.'

George was personable, funny and friendly with the road crew during the day, but after the show he would disappear:

'The music would still be going and they would put the bath-robe on George as he left the stage. He would go straight to the hotel or the Learjet. By the time the lights came up, he was already gone. It was called a hit and run.'

George was acutely aware that he was paying the wages of a great many people who, because of that, couldn't necessarily be honest with him: 'The idea of dishonesty frightens me – being around people who can't tell you to fuck off. Whereas the people I spend time with in my personal life tell me to fuck off on a very regular basis.'

The tour more than fulfilled its purpose. Thanks to *Faith*, George was the top-selling artist of 1988 in the US. He was only the second act to top both the year-end *Billboard* album and singles charts in the modern era. Simon & Garfunkel had been the first in 1970 with 'Bridge Over Troubled Water'. The total worldwide sales of the album topped 25 million.

George told *Blitz* magazine that he was Mr Clean on the tour, hardly ever drank and definitely didn't indulge in cocaine, which he didn't like and didn't do. He joked about being on the road: 'I get offered a lot of drugs and women at home. I don't have to go on tour for that.'

The strain of such a long tour began to tell on his voice and after weeks of complaining of pain when he sang, he was finally diagnosed with a large cyst at the bottom of his throat. After five nights at Earls Court in London he had to take a month off for an operation and subsequent rest. He was fit enough to begin the first of his forty-six American dates at the Capital Centre in Washington in August 1988. One critic praised his 'powerful vocal presence', so the surgery had clearly worked.

The *Faith World Tour* was eighteen months of his life that he loathed: 'I hate touring, fucking ligging, the whole groupie bit. I want to take this album round the world, do a good job. I don't want to be fucked up while I'm out there.'

George fulfilled his obligation and earned millions, but he didn't want to undertake something of this magnitude again: 'The touring isn't real, that's why I don't actually get involved in it. I tend to keep myself to myself. When I'm not touring, it's real. It's still my real life. This isn't real.'

George Michael was at the top of the world. He would accept the screams and the standing ovations, go back to his hotel, shut the door to his room and become Georgios Panayiotou again. He would later confess that he felt a fraud.

PART THREE

YOU HAVE BEEN LOVED

14

NO PICTURES

The man who created George Michael wanted the world to know that was not his name. He was Georgios Kyriacos Panayiotou. He tried hard to reveal his true self in his auto-biographical book, *Bare*, published when he was twenty-seven.

He could have been basking in the triumph of winning the Grammy Award in 1989 for Best Album or being named by *Forbes* magazine as one of the five biggest earners in entertainment but, instead, he wanted to explain why he needed to take off the cloak of George Michael and hang it in the basement.

The book, written by the future best-selling novelist Tony Parsons, is immensely readable and does include fascinating insight into the singer and how he became a superstar. Tony had first interviewed him for *The Face* in the mid-eighties and they had become good friends, enjoying late-night discussions over a bottle of wine at George's Hampstead home. In a typical gesture of friendship and fairness, George split the £430,000 publishing advance with him.

The irony for a book entitled *Bare* is that it didn't reveal George's sexuality. He did not discuss frankly 'all aspects of his life' as the jacket blurb declared. The only mention, for instance, of Brad Branson was in the picture credits for taking the front-cover photograph. George was, however, completely open about his feelings after the slog of the tour. He had become disillusioned with the image he'd created and wanted to refocus purely on his music.

George went back to Beverly Hills where, for a while, he lived the life of a privileged Californian. He topped up his tan, swam in his pool and took tennis lessons. He even treated his friends to a skiing break in the fashionable resort of Aspen in Colorado. He was also going through a very creative period, happy in his work writing the songs for the follow-up to *Faith*. This was much better than touring.

He decided a 'holiday investment' property would be a good idea and found a stunning house ninety miles to the north on a mountainside overlooking the ultra-exclusive Santa Barbara Riviera. He paid $3 million for this taste of paradise. The three-bedroom home, designed by West Coast architect Cliff Hickman, had been built in 1985 in a hexagonal shape that looked like something out of a sci-fi movie. Along with the usual millionaire trappings of beautiful gardens, pool and tennis court, there were also sixteen glass walls that afforded magnificent panoramic views of mountain, city and coast – all at the same time.

The first thing George did was to install a new gate, chain-link fencing and an elaborate security system in complete contrast to the more relaxed feel of his London home. He described it as 'very big and very showbiz'. It was also perfect for throwing extravagant parties when he would invite his LA friends up for the weekend.

These now included Andrew Ridgeley, who had tired of Monte Carlo and dumped his fledging racing driver career in favour of the good life in Encino, Los Angeles, less than a mile from Michael Jackson's house. Andrew's crew moved over with him and most days they could be seen roaring down the immaculate streets on their Japanese race-tuned motorbikes. They became the motorcycling dance club crew of fashionable LA, embracing ecstasy as George had done and turning all-nighters into weekenders. The cult series *Entourage* could have been based on Ridgers and his mates.

Often they would scream past Jacko's limo and flip him or his famous sister Janet the V-sign or some other witty British heckle. They were the best of times, although Andrew's relationship with Donya Fiorentino, which by all accounts had been fractious, petered out and she went back to Don Johnson. Later she would marry director David Fincher and subsequently the actor Gary Oldman, who she met at a Beverly Hills AA meeting. They divorced acrimoniously.

Belatedly, Andrew decided on a solo pop career. He was still being managed by Rob Kahane and Michael Lippman and they negotiated a very favourable deal with Columbia Records for the album, which was called *Son of Albert*, a neat reference to himself. George helped a little, singing backing vocals on the opening track, 'Red Dress'. David Austin collaborated on two songs, 'Shake' and 'Flame'. Some familiar musicians from Wham! days, including Deon Estus, contributed. Another, Hugh Burns, had played guitar on many of the group's hits and was married to Connie Filippello, so it was very much a reunion record for Andrew. He co-wrote eight of the tracks.

The album was a complete flop, peaking at an embarrassing chart position of 130. Andrew was hugely disappointed. Perhaps Wham! fans weren't prepared for their hero to move on to the more rock sound he was pursuing. In some ways its reception highlighted the significant role Andrew had in Wham! He may have left the songwriting and music to George but the fashion and style were largely down to him, and that image was too ingrained for the fans to accept a change.

Andrew had coped well with the uncomplimentary coverage he endured in Wham! He adjusted manfully to the split from George, which he knew was inevitable. A friend observes, 'He took that with good grace. But the failure of the album hit him hard.'

Andrew decided to leave the music once more entirely to George. He was very comfortably placed financially and royalties from 'Careless Whisper' alone would always be his pension. He admitted he had taken 'a beating' over his album and decided to drop out of the limelight. Andrew would appear with George only once more on stage. He would soon return to England because he'd fallen in love with Keren Woodward and they wanted a quieter life.

George, meanwhile, had the difficult task of following up one of the most successful albums of all time. The clue that this was a more serious project than *Faith* came in the title, *Listen Without Prejudice Vol. 1*. He flew into London to finish the production with engineer Chris Porter, where he enjoyed spending time with his family and also catching up with David Austin, who was back from the US and dividing his time between London, where he had a flat near Regent's Park, and a gorgeous apartment in the trendy Saint-Germain-des-Près area of Paris. David was enjoying a golden period in his own career, not least because he had co-written 'Look at your Hands', one of the most underrated tracks on *Faith*. The lyric spoke of an abusive domestic relationship, which was not often the subject matter of a pop song and neither he nor George had first-hand experience of one.

George enjoyed visiting the French capital when he could and had written 'A Different Corner' there a few years before. Musicians would often drop in to see David and on any given afternoon, you might find him enjoying a jam session with Paul Young, Alison Moyet and Maxi Priest.

David had a long-term girlfriend, the fashion designer Rebecca Davies, who at the time was a model booker for the Elite agency in London and Paris. She loved George's company and described him affectionately as 'a gentle soul'. She loved evenings out with her two men. They used to go to the ultra-fashionable club Les Bains Douches and would 'laugh their heads off' when people came up and said George looked just like George Michael. Occasionally, Rebecca would have to pretend that she was George's girlfriend and not David's to deflect any unwelcome gay gossip about him.

One night in Paris, the three of them went to a fabulous French restaurant, where the popular band Gypsy Kings were playing. Just as they were getting up to leave, the band realised George Michael was there and started up their best-known hit 'Bamboléo'. They insisted on playing the entire song, which left the three friends caught halfway between staying and leaving. George solved the dilemma by leading the other two in an impromptu dance that glided them out of the door.

Dancing around the tables of the Angus Pride had not been forgotten after all.

Rebecca played a key role in putting together one of the best-known George Michael videos for his classic song 'Freedom! '90'. Despite their great nights out, George would often prefer to stay in and enjoy his favourite roast and a bottle of red wine. He had come round for dinner at the London flat and they were looking at the iconic issue of *Vogue* that featured a photograph of five supermodels on the cover. George had a light-bulb moment and suggested it would be fantastic if they could get the girls to lip-synch the lyrics.

The very next day, George took Rebecca to lunch at Le Caprice and insisted that she try and organise it. She managed to secure the famous five for a fee of $15,000 each per half a day: Naomi Campbell, Christy Turlington, Cindy Crawford, Tatjana Patitz and Linda Evangelista.

In the very small world of show business, David Fincher, already much in demand for directing many Madonna videos, agreed to film the video for 'Freedom! '90'. All the girls had practised hard to hone their lip-synching skills and couldn't afford any mistakes with George looking on. When Cindy slipped into the bath for one of the most memorable scenes, George couldn't help but joke that he would have paid double if he'd known that was going to happen. The director shot him a look and he had to slink off to the naughty step.

The final cut is a sexy and very cool triumph and, at a cost of £300,000, the culmination of George's fascination with models. Linda Evangelista, who was sporting her new cropped blonde haircut, commented that she is best remembered for that video and not for any of the magazine covers from her glittering career.

George doesn't appear in it. Instead, symbolically, the leather biker's jacket he wore for 'Faith' goes up in flames and the guitar is blown up. The imagery was an unsubtle way of telling the world he was moving on. He was also telling his record company that he meant it when he said he was going to let the music speak for itself and release the new album without promoting it personally or undertaking a concert tour.

His record company, CBS, and its subsidiary, Epic, were now owned by the giant Sony Corporation. None of the bosses were happy at his decision to take himself out of the picture. They received unexpected backing from Frank Sinatra who, for some reason, decided to write a stinging letter to the *Los Angeles Times* after he read an interview in the newspaper in which George revealed his intentions.

Frank wrote that George should 'loosen up' and 'should thank the Lord every morning when he wakes up to have all that he has'. He continued, 'And no more talk about the "tragedy of fame". The tragedy of fame is when no one shows up and you're singing to the cleaning lady in some empty joint that hasn't seen a paying customer since St Swithin's Day.'

Frank had no idea that George was fighting a crisis of confidence brought about by acting a character practically every time he went out of his front door. Rebecca Davies had listened to a sensitive Yog reveal his insecurities: 'I was amazed over a cup of tea when George would voice his concerns that he wasn't really as talented as his fans thought he was.'

Part of his problem with Sony was that he thought the company unsympathetic to his unhappiness: 'I was unhappy because I just didn't spend enough time doing what I had originally wanted to do, which was making and writing music.' He no longer wanted to use the image of George Michael to promote his songs.

Since the early days when he relied on Andrew to project the right image, he had become the centre of attention – a man who magazines had dubbed 'Mr Sex'. He explained how he felt: 'I lost all my confidence. I realised that bi-sexuality was no longer a reality for me and I felt like a fake. So the whole thing turned me into someone who really thought the camera was my enemy.' This was perhaps the real reason why George wanted to take himself out of the picture.

The first, the ballad 'Praying for Time,' had a less glamorous video that consisted of a blank screen, containing just the lyrics of the song. George had given his permission for the record company to release it in a slightly bizarre stand-off between the two. In a way, the video suited the bleak message of the song, a despairing and downbeat look at the lack of compassion in our society. George wanted to avoid writing about the dominant themes of popular music – sex and love – and present an adult reflection on human nature. He explained, 'No particular event inspired the song. It's my way of trying to figure out why it's so hard for people to be good to each other.'

He blamed the media for warping our fundamental humanity: 'We're taught that you have to grab what you can before it's gone. It's almost as if there isn't time for compassion.' In George's song, we should all be praying for that time. He was always prepared to find the time to make a difference.

In 'Praying for Time', he sings, 'Charity is a cloak you wear twice a year.' George had decided he was going to wear it all the time. He set up The Platinum Trust in 1990 to support children and adults with disabilities. His sister Yioda took on the role of running the Trust, which gave secret donations amounting to millions of pounds to some of the UK's leading disabled people's organisations.

The only condition George insisted on was that his financial support was not publicised. He was happy to lend the name of George Michael to his public acts of charity, the high-profile concerts that would benefit most from his superstar support. His more private donations were the personal gift of Georgios Panayiotou and didn't need shouting from the rooftops.

Yioda would quietly visit disabled activists and gather information about applications for grants and then review them with George and other trustees. Among those that only stayed afloat thanks to his generosity was the LGBTQ disabled person's organisation, Regard. Treasurer Julie Newman confirmed, 'There would be no Regard today without The Platinum Trust. He wanted it done quietly and discretely. The way it was handled, it was so gentle. We didn't have to jump through hoops.'

Both George and Yioda were strong advocates for 'inclusion' as a basic human right; society should embrace all people regardless of gender, race or disability. In particular, those living with a disability should be freely and openly accommodated without restrictions or limitations of any kind.

The song 'Praying for Time' was an indication of George's social conscience and very representative of his most serious album to date. *The Boston Globe* praised his sincerity: 'He sings about the homeless, about greed, war, love and above all his shifting lifestyle from his mid-80s days with Wham!'.

The single became his ninth number one in the US *Billboard* charts but only reached number six in the UK. The album, however, went straight to number one in Britain, selling 300,000 copies in its first week. Overall, worldwide sales of 7 million would have been a triumph had that figure not been dwarfed by the success of 'Faith'. Both George and his record company blamed each other.

Despite what he said earlier, George did eventually agree to a tour, but the *Cover to Cover* concerts weren't a conventional series of promotional gigs. He avoided the songs on *Listen Without Prejudice Vol. 1* in favour of some of his favourite numbers by other artists, including 'Fame' by David Bowie and two from Elton John: 'Don't Let the Sun Go Down on Me' and the emotional ballad 'Tonight'. He did offer a few of his own songs, including 'Father Figure', 'Everything She Wants', 'I'm Your Man' and 'Careless Whisper', closing the show with 'Freedom! '90'.

After opening with two nights at the Genting Arena in Birmingham in January 1991, he flew to Brazil to perform at the Rock in Rio II festival at the Maracanã Stadium. Arguments with his record company may have been the most important thing in the professional world of the star, George Michael, but something far more important was going to happen in the life of Georgios Panayiotou. He was about to fall deeply in love for the first time.

15

SOMEBODY TO LOVE

George looked fantastic. He was in the prime of his life. He took to the stage in Rio with a new clipped haircut, large gold hooped earring, designer five o'clock shadow and a dark grey Beatles suit that John Lennon might have worn back in the sixties.

For a man who hated the drudgery and loneliness of touring, he put on a show to remember. He shared top billing at the 1991 Rock in Rio festival with Prince, INXS and Guns N' Roses. He was the headline act on two nights, including the last one, when he was supported by the superb soul singer Lisa Stansfield.

A crowd of 130,000 packed into one of the world's largest football stadiums to listen to George launch into 'Killer' by British acid-house producer Adamski. He had none of the vocal worries that had troubled him during the *Faith World Tour*. Aretha wasn't there this time and he had to finish the concert singing 'I Knew You Were Waiting (For Me)' by himself – although his backing singers were exceptional.

The lights were down as George introduced the encore: 'This song was written ten years ago with a very good friend

of mine – would you please welcome Mr Andrew Ridgeley.'
Looking as immaculate as ever, Andrew calmly walked on
stage to play 'Careless Whisper' followed by 'I'm Your Man',
which had seldom sounded better, with a virtuoso bass introduction by Dion Estus. They concluded with 'Freedom! '90',
the only song from George's new album that he performed.

This time it really was farewell and the two boys from
Wham! would never perform together again. They were paid
handsomely for this last appearance, a sum rumoured to be
$500,000 each. At least George had guaranteed this would be
a fun trip – by inviting thirty of his closest friends and family
along to watch his shows.

He was hugely popular in Brazil and many of his fans had
bought tickets for both nights. One of them, Anselmo Feleppa,
had flown in from New York to see the concerts in the hope
of meeting his idol. Part of a fashionable and cosmopolitan
world in which it was no secret that George Michael was gay
and a desirable pin-up, Anselmo was very handsome with a
smile that could light up any room. He certainly lit up the
lobby of the Copacabana Palace hotel where George and his
party had taken over two floors.

His family came from Petropolis, a picturesque resort in the
mountains, fifty miles from Rio de Janeiro. It was a town where
the well-to-do holidayed to escape the stultifying summer heat
in Brazil's most famous city. His father was the wealthy owner
of a clothing factory and, as a well-educated, outgoing teenager, Anselmo was able to mix with the cream of society visiting his home surroundings. At fifteen, he met the beautiful
Lucia Guanabara, who would become one of Brazil's best-
known socialites and, more importantly, his best friend.

As is traditional in Brazil, his mother Alice stayed at home to raise the family and doted on her son, just as Lesley Panayiotou did on her boy back in England. And like Lesley, Anselmo's mother was popular with all her son's friends. 'She was adorable,' says Lucia. His parents encouraged him to realise his ambitions in the world of fashion and paid for him to travel to Europe, where he spent a year learning French and studying design in Paris.

For six months he shared a smart apartment near the Parc Monceau with Lucia. She met her husband Philippe there. Lucia invited him round to the apartment for dinner, which was slightly problematic because she couldn't cook. Fortunately, Anselmo was an excellent chef. He prepared a delicious meal and then slipped out before her guest arrived so that Lucia could pretend it was all her own work. 'He was a true friend and very loyal,' she observes. 'He was a fantastic person, full of the joy of living. I loved him very much as a brother.'

After Paris, Anselmo settled in New York during the heyday of the Studio 54 club when every night was party time. It was a crazy world and Anselmo was very popular: 'Everybody loved him,' recalls Lucia. 'He never had like a real relationship. He was very flirtatious though.'

Every year Anselmo would return to Brazil to see his family. By this time in the early nineties, he was designing a clothing collection for his father to produce in his factory. Like George, his life was just lacking that special person.

Anselmo knew enough important people in Rio society to hear that George had changed hotels; his first hotel had proved too noisy, so he was checked into the Copacabana Palace. Anselmo hurried over, hoping to see him. He told Lucia that it didn't work out as he'd hoped: 'He didn't actually meet him. He tried to speak to him and I think George saw him. But that's all. They never met that day.' George had noticed him, if only fleetingly, and would later reflect that he knew at first sight that their destinies would come together.

The next day George and his entourage left for a break in Armação dos Búzios, a beach resort about 100 miles along the coast from Rio. 'It's a bit like St Tropez,' explains Lucia. 'Everybody has a house there.' Lucia was there with her children when Anselmo showed up, determined to go to the private island where George was staying and partying.

He told Lucia, 'I have to go there because I want to see George.' 'I said, "You are crazy. What do you think you are doing?" And he said, "You have to go with me. I cannot go by myself." So I went with him to this place.'

By a lucky coincidence, the island was owned by a business partner of his father so he could get in without any trouble. 'He was dancing and showing off for George's benefit. George reacted but again he didn't speak to him.'

Anselmo didn't give up and tried yet again the following day, hoping it would be third time lucky. He heard that there was another party for George in Búzios. This time they cordoned off a roof terrace at a fashionable restaurant. Lucia recalls, 'There were security people so we had to sneak in. Anselmo was dancing again and I think George noticed him because of the day before. This time they finally spoke and that's when it all started.'

George was quickly enamoured of the good-looking Brazilian. They decided to start dating, both looking for more than just a casual encounter. For the first time, George embraced properly being a gay man: 'It's very hard to be proud of your sexuality when it hasn't given you any joy. I was shagging around but I had so little experience of men that my sex life was so ridiculously inadequate for me, right until I met Anselmo.'

Amusingly, Anselmo lied to George about his age. He was born in August 1956 and was nearly seven years older than his new boyfriend. He told George he was three years younger than he actually was, although, as Lucia observes, 'He looked very young and didn't look older than George at all. George laughed so much when he found his passport!'

George had a whole month to spend with Anselmo before the *Cover to Cover* tour resumed in Japan. His Brazilian lover made him laugh more than he had done for years: 'Anselmo loved telling jokes and having fun,' observes Lucia, fondly. George found himself becoming more outgoing, enjoying outdoor pursuits such as hang gliding and scuba diving that the old Yog would never have tried. One of George's close friends who met Anselmo for the first time in Búzios liked him immediately: 'He was always a very happy guy. He had a great smile and was always smiling. It was joyous to hang around with him.'

George slipped back to London to receive the BRIT Award for Best British Album from Robin Gibb of the Bee Gees. *Listen Without Prejudice Vol. 1* had been received more favourably by the UK public than in the US. He thanked Rob Kahane, who had taken over sole managerial responsibility, and acknowledged that he 'was not the easiest person to manage'. He also mentioned PA Siobhan Bailey and Chris Porter before dedicating the award to Ronnie Fischer, the product manager for Epic. He'd done such a sterling job pushing George's records right from the start of Wham! and had died the previous October.

When he left Brazil, George invited Anselmo and Lucia to join him in London, where he was playing four nights at Wembley Arena. Lucia recalls, 'We were so excited, although I remember getting upset because we always had to leave during the last song, "Freedom". We had to go backstage and get in the limousine so that George could join us as soon as he left the stage. At the time, I'd never lived the superstar life, so it was amazing for both of us.

'We used to go back to the hotel and have fun – partying but not drugs; nothing like that. Anselmo was not a drug person, not at all. He was not that kind of person. He liked to party and all that, as well as being international in his outlook, but he came from a good family and had nice values. And I think George could relate to that.'

On the last night, Elton John memorably came on stage for a duet of 'Don't Let the Sun Go Down on Me'. Lucia remembers being enthralled: 'It was very beautiful and such a happy time. George and Elton were very good friends.'

George had never been happier and was showing himself to be a hopeless romantic where Anselmo was concerned. They shared secret jokes that only lovers can enjoy. Both were very tactile people but they couldn't hold hands in public, sadly. It would have caused a huge scandal at the time.

In the coming months, George would take Anselmo around the world with him. He didn't hide him away. They holidayed, often with Lucia, in Greece and Cyprus, as well as visiting George's various homes. He also found an apartment in the exclusive Lagoa area of Rio for Anselmo to use when he wanted to visit Brazil.

Best of all, they spent time living together at the house in Santa Barbara. When he first went there, an excited Anselmo rang Lucia: 'He said to me, "I can't believe I am sitting here and George Michael is playing the piano for me!" And he put the phone near so that I could listen. I knew right from the start that this wasn't just an affair. It was a love story they lived and very beautiful.'

Anselmo came from a traditional and conservative Catholic family and never told his family about his relationship with another man – although his mother certainly knew. George faced a similar predicament. He was fine about introducing Anselmo to his sister Melanie but, at this point in his life, it was a step too far to come out to his father and mother.

Anselmo met Andros on that first trip to Rio. The cousin was a fixture in George's entourage, especially now he lived in Los Angeles. He thought Anselmo was a 'truly wonderful person' and said that everyone in George's world took to him at once: 'He just had IT.' George was best man at his cousin Andros's wedding in Las Vegas to his long-term partner, an actress and model called Jackie Crevitas, who, as Jackie Georgiou, would become a familiar face on American television.

When autumn ushered in the end of their first summer together, Anselmo told George the dreadful news – he had tested positive for HIV. He had known for a couple of months but hadn't wanted to tell George at first. 'He was ashamed,' explains Lucia, heartbreakingly.

George was well aware that the fear of AIDS dominated the gay agenda in the late eighties and early nineties. It had been the principal reason why he hadn't talked about his sexuality with his mother. But now he was facing the reality himself. Anselmo begged George not to tell his friends about his plight and he reluctantly agreed. George was distraught: 'Try to imagine that you've finally found a real love and, six months in, it's devastated. In 1991, it was really terrifying news.'

George had faced an agonising wait before a test confirmed that he was not HIV positive, too. Faced with the enormity of the situation, he quietly decided to do as much as he could to raise money and public awareness about the condition. He did not want to be one of those people who thought in fifteen years' time, 'Fuck, I could have done something.'

He was fulfilling concert dates on the American leg of *Cover to Cover* when he spoke out against the Governor of California Pete Wilson's veto of a gay rights bill, which would have outlawed discrimination against homosexuals. During the concert at the Forum in Inglewood in 1991, George drew attention to the protest rally that had taken place in Santa Monica earlier in the day: 'I know some of you were out marching today. For all those protesting up there, I'd like to add my voice to theirs.' It was a bold move and not one that would endear him to the establishment.

The concerts themselves received a mixed reaction in the US. *The Washington Post* called the gig at the Capital Centre an 'enjoyable self-indulgence' and one that seemed like the 'fulfilment of an adolescent wish'. *The Boston Globe*, less admiringly, thought the idea didn't work and was 'one man's all-out attempt to earn the rights to the soul he sincerely wishes he'd been born with'. After completing the seventeen dates in America, which netted him nearly $5 million, George Michael would not tour again for fifteen years.

To bring home the true sadness of the situation surrounding AIDS back in 1991, Freddie Mercury died on 24 November from complications arising from the condition. He was forty-five and the first major pop star to fall victim. Clearly, he had been slowly deteriorating in the public gaze for some time, but he only confirmed he had the virus the day before his death. He had been a childhood hero to George and now he was gone.

George had persuaded Elton John that they should release their duet of 'Don't Let the Sun Go Down on Me' and the track went to number one before Christmas in the UK and a couple of months later in the US. It would be his tenth and final American number one. All the proceeds, amounting to hundreds of thousands of pounds, went to good causes, including two AIDS agencies – the San Francisco AIDS Foundation and Project Open Hand.

Elton went on to establish the Elton John AIDS Foundation in New York in 1992 and the non-profit organisation has raised more than $200 million in support of HIV projects, including those working on prevention, education and support for those living with the virus. George was keen to be involved and became one of the charity's patrons.

George didn't limit his charitable work to AIDS, although these donations were obviously high profile. The other charities to benefit in the US were the Los Angeles Children's Museum, the Boys & Girls Club of Chicago, the United Negro College Fund, the Hospital for Sick Children in Toronto, and the Jimmy Fund in Boston, which raised money to help fight against cancer. In the UK, profits went to the London Lighthouse hospice, the Rainbow Trust Children's Charity and the Terrence Higgins Trust.

George spent Christmas at home with his family in Radlett, pretending it was not a sombre affair for him and trying to join in while his thoughts were with the man he loved. 'I couldn't go through it with my family,' he explained. 'My parents didn't even know I was gay.'

Nobody knew his personal distress when he took part in The Freddie Mercury Tribute Concert for AIDS Awareness at Wembley Stadium. George sang his heart out with the surviving members of Queen but felt that he was the loneliest man in the world: 'I'm standing on stage, paying tribute to one of my childhood idols who died of that condition. The isolation was just crazy.'

George took the event very seriously, attending every rehearsal to ensure he performed on the night to the best of his ability. On stage, he told the 72,000-strong crowd, 'For God's sake and for Freddie's sake, please be careful.' He sang three Queen songs: '39'– one he used to perform as a busker at Green Park Tube station – 'These Are the Days of Our Lives' with Lisa Stansfield and, most movingly, 'Somebody to Love'.

The last named is one of Freddie's best and most challenging vocals. *Rolling Stone* described George's interpretation as a 'masterful show' and said he 'lived up to the "tribute" promise', his voice soaring where Mercury's did. He brought back memories of the late vocalist's unforgettable appearance at Live Aid: 'His all-in performance lit up the Wembley crowd in a way that recalled the man of honour's show-stopping performance seven years prior.'

David Bowie and Seal applauded from the side of the stage. Brian May, Queen's evergreen guitarist, declared simply, 'George Michael was the best. There's a certain note in his voice when he did "Somebody to Love" that was pure Freddie.' On the first anniversary of the concert, George released the *Five Live* EP that contained his three performances. All the profits from the single, which reached number one in the UK, went to the Mercury Phoenix Trust, the AIDS charity that had been set up in the singer's name.

He abandoned plans to record *Living Without Prejudice Vol. 2* in favour of donating some of the songs he had already written to an AIDS fundraising album, *Red, Hot & Dance*, which also featured Madonna and Seal. The best-known 'Too Funky' was released as a single and was not the success it was expected to be, reaching number four in the UK but only just scraping into the top ten in the US. George was disappointed with the support he was getting from the record company and it would prove to be the last single release under his contract with Sony.

The song revealed George's clever use of sampling, including the famous line from Mrs Robinson in *The Graduate*, 'I am not trying to seduce you', as well as ending on a clip from *Hancock's Half Hour*, 'Will you stop playing with that radio of yours? I'm trying to get to sleep.' Both could easily have been lines from George's own life.

The accompanying video was also an anticlimax after the triumph of 'Freedom! '90'. Linda Evangelista was involved again, along with a host of models and the creative input of French fashion designer Thierry Mugler, but the whole thing felt flat and disjointed. George and Thierry fell out over the way the video was progressing, which didn't help. The final version was George's, although Thierry maintained that his edit was 'more touching'.

Proceeds from the sale of *Red, Hot & Dance* supported the American Foundation for AIDS Research, Gay Men's Health Crisis and the Physicians Against AIDS Coalition. George also donated all his royalties from the 'Too Funky' single.

The album itself sold poorly and George was adamant Sony should have done more: 'It should have been of some importance, I would have thought, to Sony Worldwide simply because it included new material from one of their artists.' Again, he proclaimed his support for AIDS sufferers: 'The many people around the world who will benefit from the *Red, Hot & Dance* project need all the support we can give them.'

His relationship with his record label continued to deteriorate until he decided to take legal steps to try and end his contract. He would later claim in court that the chairman of the Sony subsidiary Columbia Records, Don Ienner, had tried to interfere in the creative process of 'Too Funky' and had walked out of one of his concerts halfway through. Famously, the executive was accused of referring to George as 'that faggot client of yours' in a conversation with Rob Kahane. Don strenuously denied ever making the alleged insult, telling *Billboard* magazine, 'It's a silly accusation, and it's untrue.' But Rob maintained, 'That was the trigger that set George off.' It's easy to imagine that if George believed it to be true – whether the insult was actually made or not – it would cause lasting and irreversible damage to the relationship between artist and employer.

The DJ and broadcaster Paul Gambaccini discussed the battle over George's contract in the 2004 documentary *A*

Different Story: 'Let's not forget that there was a personal problem … That a leading executive of his American record company insulted him dismissively and profoundly – the type of dismissal which would make it impossible to be friends – let's put it that way.'

George's lawyers filed a High Court writ in October 1992, claiming restraint of trade and inequality of earnings and bargaining power. Sony countered by saying that it would contest the action and would insist on the six further albums under the present contract. George acknowledged that if he lost, he might never record again.

He was certainly not going to adopt a lower profile regarding his support for AIDS charities to placate his record company. Rob Kahane observed, 'He was stubborn, but that's also why he performed at so many benefits. He had principles.'

He agreed to appear with Elton again at another fundraiser, this time in support of the Elizabeth Taylor AIDS Foundation show at Madison Square Garden in October 1992. Elton was the principal performer but various stars joined him on stage, including George, Bruce Hornsby and Whoopi Goldberg. George, who had a particular affinity with Elton John's classic ballads, performed 'Candle in the Wind', 'Don't Let the Sun Go Down on Me' and the lesser-known, elegiac song 'Ticking', which had been the closing track on Elton's 1974 album *Caribou*.

Anselmo Feleppa was not hiding away during this time. He was based in LA when George was recording the unreleased album *Trojan Souls*, a project he devised with his cousin Andros. George couldn't actually sing on the album because of his contractual difficulties but had assembled a guest list that included Elton, Sade, Aretha Franklin and Janet Jackson to record a set of new songs.

Andros filmed the recording at Chapel Studios and captured the very rare sight of Anselmo and George arriving together in a Mercedes convertible. At one stage, Anselmo puts his hand on George's shoulder, the nearest they ever came to showing any kind of intimacy in public. In the end the project never came to fruition as tragic events intervened.

After the New Year in 1993, George and Anselmo went on holiday to the Caribbean. Lucia Guanabara joined them for a weekend and remembers what a beautiful house they had found for this time together. George then went back to Los Angeles while his partner travelled to Brazil to stay at the apartment in Rio and visit his family.

There, he started feeling ill. His mother Alice was with him and called an ambulance. Lucia recalls, 'He came here on vacation and he never went back. It was very fast. It was horrible. He didn't want George to know how bad it was. Anselmo was a very proud man.'

Anselmo died on 26 March 1993 from a brain haemorrhage, an unexpected complication from the onset of AIDS. George did not see him in the hospital to say goodbye. Instead he was given the terrible news in a tearful phone call from Lucia.

The next day, George sat down and wrote his parents an emotional letter in which he explained that he was gay and had just lost the man he loved. His father, who many thought would find the admission hard to take because of his traditional Greek-Cypriot outlook, found it difficult at first but then gave his son his complete reassurance and love. He never displayed any disappointment or homophobia and George was hugely grateful to him for that. His mother was devastated at the realisation that he had gone through it all without their support. George never disclosed the contents of the letter but he would later describe his feelings for Anselmo: 'He was the first person I had ever loved and I discovered he loved me, too.'

George didn't go to the funeral so as not to be the centre of media attention when Anselmo's family were saying good-bye. Instead he flew in unobtrusively a few days later and stayed with Lucia. He introduced himself to Anselmo's mother Alice and they visited her son's grave in a Catholic cemetery in Petropolis. They wept together.

16

A BEAUTIFUL REMINDER

George stopped working. He couldn't face it while he was grieving. His manager Rob Kahane was so concerned for his wellbeing that he made sure George wasn't alone in the house in Beverly Hills: 'When he lost Anselmo, I thought he was going to do something bad to himself. I had people stay with him.'

George's prediction a few years before that he would deal badly with bereavement proved to be true. He wasn't just down, he was in a black hole of despair. He realised later that he was clinically depressed but, more than that, he was consumed by anger that the person he loved had been taken from him.

He blamed the Catholic faith for instilling so much guilt in Anselmo for what was happening to him that he wouldn't let George help him as much as he could have done, especially in the last days. He would never forget the upsetting scene one afternoon when he went into his room and Anselmo was sitting in bed with his prayer cards: 'I just thought to myself, "Please don't tell me you think you're going to hell." It makes me so angry and I sincerely hope he didn't fear that.'

In private, he turned to a cocktail of cannabis and ecstasy to get him through the bad days. Some days Rob's sister would pop in to read his tarot cards. He continued to believe, according to his manager, that he would die young.

In public, he was still George Michael, fulfilling his obligations to promote the *Five Live EP* by giving an interview with MTV in which he continued to preach a firm message about AIDS: 'The important thing for the kids, whether they be straight, bisexual, gay, whatever, is to be aware there's a definite threat. They are all going to come into contact with people who are afflicted by the condition. There are plenty of people who will die because they felt it was something that was never going to happen to them.'

Occasionally, his grief overcame him. He had to call a halt to an interview with Radio 1 DJ Simon Bates when he was asked how he was coping with his friend's death – not mentioning Anselmo by name. George choked up and needed time to compose himself and Simon sympathetically agreed not to include his distress in the subsequent broadcast.

He began counselling to help him through and continued to keep in touch with Anselmo's mother. He made plans to visit again – this time taking his sister Melanie with him. She too would love Alice and made sure she stayed in contact with her. She was included as part of the family, as George's mother-in-law.

Almost three months to the day after Anselmo's death, George marked his thirtieth birthday with a party weekend. He might not have felt like celebrating but his family and closest friends thought it would do him good. He absolutely did not want any media coverage of the event, so everyone was picked up from various locations around Watford and bussed to a secret location, which turned out to be a marquee at Newmarket Racecourse.

George's father had developed a passion for horses and George had helped him buy two racehorses as well as a substantial investment in a 100-acre stud farm near Cheshunt in Hertfordshire. The two horses, Nakita and Mr Devious, were both running in the same maiden two-year-old race and finished a respectable third and fourth. Within two weeks both had won races – the latter ridden to victory at Haydock by Frankie Dettori.

In the evening, everyone returned to the farm for a party with the theme 'Heavy Seventies Vibe'. George entered into the spirit of the night by sporting an Afro wig, jumping on stage with Andros and David Austin and giving a knockout performance of the disco hit 'Car Wash'. He had a reputation for throwing an expensive and extravagant bash and this was no exception, with champagne and his favourite caviar in plentiful supply.

Shirlie was there with her husband Martin Kemp, and other pop friends celebrating with him included Pepsi, Neil Tennant, Paul Young and presenter Paula Yates. Andrew and Keren travelled up from their new home in Cornwall, where Andrew had bought a farm near Wadebridge and was settling into a surfing life completely removed from the musical world.

George spent some quiet time at home in Hampstead, speaking to lawyers, working on the court case against Sony and walking his golden Labrador, Hippy. He doted on the dog, which had been a gift from Gary Farrow, now his PR consultant, who proved a great support to him during his legal battle.

Melanie looked after Hippy when George was travelling abroad and, so legend has it, the dog would bound over to the radio to listen attentively whenever a George Michael record was played.

George needed to stay in London for the foreseeable future preparing for the court case. He was able to channel his anger about the death of Anselmo towards his record company in a battle that he would wage for the next three years. He was exasperated that Sony showed him, as he saw it, such little patience or consideration: 'It was obvious that I was going through something personal that meant I couldn't face the world. I didn't know when I would be happy enough to write another song.'

He didn't mention his state of mind when proceedings began in the High Court in London in October 1993. Georgios Panayiotou v Sony Music Entertainment promised to be an ongoing drama. George's claim was based on his contract being an unreasonable restraint of trade. He thought that since being taken over by Sony in 1988, his record company had 'become a small part of the production line for a giant electronics corporation which, frankly, has no understanding of the creative process', which sounded a little bit more pompous than he intended. *The Economist* pointed out that Sony could not really *win* even if it won the case: 'There is no way the music company can force Mr Michael to churn out records.'

George began his day with a rigorous session on the treadmill at home before travelling to the High Court with his parents, who were there to support their son throughout, watching proceedings from the public gallery. The case would continue for a long-winded 178 days. After seventeen, it was his turn to give evidence and be cross-examined.

During three days on the stand, he explained why he wanted an image change and elaborated on his view that Sony had not supported that. He refused to say out loud in court how much he was worth but wrote a figure on a piece of paper to be handed to the judge. Reports at the time had estimated his wealth at £80 million but it may have been higher. It emerged that he had earned close to £100 million for Sony and been paid a royalty of 7.4 per cent. The company had taken 52.5 per cent.

Sony suggested that the case had been brought to conceal the fact that George had writer's block, which to a certain extent was true. He hadn't felt like achieving anything creative since Anselmo's death. When his legal team pointed out they were in possession of a recorded conversation in which Don Ienner allegedly referred to George in an insulting manner, the company admitted that its relationship with the singer had deteriorated.

The only professional engagement George undertook during the court case was to take part in World AIDS Day. He was the headline act at the Concert for Hope, which was a fundraiser for Princess Diana's National AIDS Trust. She had personally asked for George to appear. He wasn't aware of it then, but she was a huge fan and his music could often be heard blaring out of Kensington Palace through an open window.

The show at Wembley Arena at the beginning of December 1993 was hosted by David Bowie in a very stylish suit. He led the crowd in a round of enthusiastic applause for Diana but, disappointingly, didn't perform himself. He introduced the Canadian singer k.d. lang, who George had personally suggested for the concert. She gave a moving rendition of her hit 'Crying', a cover of the Roy Orbison classic which had been such a favourite of the younger George.

Mick Hucknall was on next, before George closed the show. On the night, he performed six numbers, beginning with 'Father Figure' and ending with 'Everything She Wants'. Unusually, he performed both of his songs called 'Freedom'.

Diana and George shared a common bond in that they had both lost someone to AIDS. Two years earlier, the Princess's close friend, art dealer Adrian Ward-Jackson, had died in St Mary's Hospital, London. She had spent his last three days at his bedside comforting him and his family. When an aide asked the Princess when she planned to leave, she answered, 'How can I leave him now, when he needs me most?'

George appreciated, more than anyone realised, how important she was in changing public opinion at a time when fear of AIDS was rife. In 1987, Diana had shaken the hand of a stricken patient in Middlesex Hospital without wearing gloves – a simple gesture but an image that went around the world. She observed, 'It's the stigma, the ignorance and the prejudice attached to AIDS which is so terrible.'

Backstage at the concert, she clearly took a fancy to George, smiling happily and genuinely delighted to chat to him. Subsequently, she invited him to lunch at Kensington Palace many times, but at this stage all his energy was taken up with the legal battle. He realised he could not handle the sort of publicity that might result from them becoming friends.

The case would drag on until June 1994 when Judge Jonathan Parker concluded he was satisfied the contract was 'reasonable and fair' and that Sony behaved properly. In

270 pages, he dismissed all of George's claims, which he said had no substance.

One of the main stumbling blocks for George was that he had renegotiated terms more than once and been paid further cash advances, which in effect confirmed the 1988 contract at the centre of the dispute. Also, he had full and proper legal advice and had entered into the contracts knowingly.

George held a news conference afterwards – not something he relished. He said he would appeal: 'I am convinced that the English legal system will not support Mr Justice Parker's decision, or uphold what is effectively professional slavery.' That was a well-chosen phrase and one that would resonate long after the details of the case had been forgotten.

Sony, unsurprisingly, welcomed the ruling: 'We have great respect for George Michael and his artistry, and look forward to continuing our relationship with him.' There seemed little chance of that happening. George's legal bill, which he was funding entirely himself, was estimated at £6 million and rising.

Now that the case was over, at least for the present, he parted company with Rob Kahane, who the judge singled out for stern criticism. He described his manager as 'a thoroughly unreliable and untrustworthy witness, whose evidence was coloured by an intense dislike of Sony'. The press statement announcing the split simply said that Rob was leaving to 'start his own record label'.

George decided to spend more money on legal fees by lodging an appeal against the court's verdict in August 1994, although it might be two years before it was heard. Even though he had lost the case, the decision seemed to ease a weight from his shoulders, and he finally agreed to accept an invitation from the Princess of Wales.

They clicked instantly in a way that he described as 'a little bit intangible'. He thought Diana was 'like a lot of women who have been attracted to me in my life because they see something non-threatening'. The Princess was a woman he wanted to put his arm around and protect, which was the feeling he always had with the sisters he loved so much.

According to George, there was definitely a spark between them: 'There were certain things that happened that made it clear she was very attracted to me.' He enjoyed Diana's company because she made him feel like an 'ordinary person', not a superstar. Her former chef, Darren McGrady, observed, 'Some people would meet her and they'd be bowing, curtsying and nervous, whereas with George it was like meeting his sister. He didn't care what came out of his mouth.'

She enjoyed the occasions George came to lunch because he would always make her laugh. He also shared her enthusiasm for television soaps and they could swap opinions on the latest plot lines, although Diana's favourite was *Brookside* while George enjoyed *Coronation Street* and *EastEnders* more. Darren recalled, 'She loved his sense of humour. She felt relaxed with him. He was someone she could be comfortable and relaxed with and say anything to. She would tease him. She loved teasing. He would laugh and give as much back.'

Sometimes he would bring Elton John and another mutual friend, the fashion designer Gianni Versace, over with him. 'She would come alive when they were here. She used to laugh like crazy.'

Clearly, these were happier times for George, but he was keeping hidden a growing reliance on cannabis. He admitted to being a 'pothead' while writing his next album. The drug helped him cope with stress and find the right words to describe his feelings over the death of Anselmo. He needed the grass to function as a songwriter. He would later reveal to Tony Parsons that he was smoking as many as twenty-five joints a day in order to cope with his private despair after Anselmo's death – although he never revealed where he was obtaining such a large quantity of the drug.

His dependence did not prevent him from regaining his creativity and his passion for music. Inspired by his feelings for Anselmo he wrote the hauntingly beautiful and melancholic ballad 'Jesus to a Child' in the autumn of 1994 as a tribute to the man he loved. George had been drawn to songs about loss all his life and this encapsulated those feelings perfectly. He wrote the outline of the song in a couple of hours and had completed it within five days. He played all the instruments on the recording, except the guitar part for which he once more used the skilful Hugh Burns.

He unveiled the song for the first time at the inaugural MTV European Music Awards (the EMAs), which were held in front of the Brandenburg Gate in Berlin, five years after the fall of the Berlin Wall. He gave an interpretation full of genuine emotion, backed by a string section and a lone acoustic guitar that picked a rhythm reminiscent of a seductive Brazilian bossa nova. This was a grown-up performance from an artist who had moved on from gazing doe-eyed into the camera while singing the teenage ballad 'Careless Whisper'.

The global television audience was estimated at 250 million, so the occasion could not have been a better showcase for a new song. *The Independent* newspaper described it as 'a slow flow of sad words about lost love and death, slipping by as a guitar weeps and drums patter mournfully behind'. There was no immediate prospect of the seven-minute track being released, but it would not be long before a deal was put together to rescue George Michael as a recording artist.

The man responsible for sorting out his future was the music billionaire and record label boss, David Geffen, who was on friendly terms with George and hated the idea of such a talented and valuable artist remaining dormant. He took the trouble to speak to Michael Schulhof, head of the Sony operation in the US, and tell him that the case could be turned around from a position in which everyone loses to one where everyone wins. For that to be a possibility Sony agreed that George and his loyal solicitor Tony Russell could open discussions with other record companies for a buy-out deal.

While it would have been a commercial masterstroke to release 'Jesus to a Child' in time for Christmas 1994, negotiations dragged on until the following spring when provisional terms were finally agreed. In the US, he would record for DreamWorks SKG, a new company that David Geffen had started with Steven Spielberg and Jeffrey Katzenberg, the former chairman of Walt Disney Studios and a significant philanthropist. Virgin Records secured his music for the rest of the world. Sony were paid $40 million; George was to receive $10 million and a much better royalty rate – a tangible gesture of belief in an artist who had not released an album for five years. He also agreed to promote a greatest hits' package in 1997.

While it could be argued that George had just swapped one conglomerate for another, it was unlikely that David Geffen, who was openly gay, was ever going to refer to him as a 'faggot client'. He eventually signed in July 1995 and three days later left with a party of friends to celebrate his freedom in style at his £1.8 million cliff-top villa overlooking the ocean in the village of Ramatuelle near St Tropez. He had called it 'Chez Nobby', after a childhood nickname he never properly explained. The six-bedroom property had a pool and a gym and was perfect for sitting in the sun and gazing at the Mediterranean.

The reaction to 'Jesus to a Child' was encouraging. The record had been broadcast for the first time in April as part of Capital Radio's fundraising initiative 'Help a London Child'. Listeners bid £20,000 to hear it, a mobile phone company then matched it with another £20,000 before George added a further £30,000 of his own money.

Less publicly, he arranged for Esther Rantzen's charity Childline to benefit from sales of the record when it was eventually released. He made it absolutely clear to Esther that he did not want anyone to know that he was helping. Over the years he gave millions of pounds to her charity. She later explained, 'He has helped hundreds of thousands of children.'

Tony Parsons thought 'Jesus to a Child' was the best thing he had ever done. George told him, 'It's a song about bereavement, but also a song about hope. I didn't want it to be all "woe is me, woe is me".'

The song was finally released in January 1996 when in the post-Christmas lull it was almost guaranteed to reach number one. That duly happened, but only for a solitary week. It was enough though to prove that George was back. The same month, 'Careless Whisper' topped a Capital Radio poll to find London's favourite song.

After the melancholia of 'Jesus to a Child', the next single was 'Fastlove', released just before the album *Older* in May 1996. It was the only up-tempo track but in no way a lightweight disco hit. The lyric was a slightly bleak celebration of one-night stands or, more accurately, an encounter much briefer than that. At the time, nobody particularly picked up that 'Fastlove' might be about cruising for sex to ease the pain of missing a lover.

The song made number one in the UK but only reached number eight in the US, where it would be his last top-ten hit on the *Billboard* chart. 'Fastlove' was one of those classic records forever played in clubs and at parties.

As musical advertisements for the new album, both 'Fastlove' and 'Jesus to a Child' fulfilled their role. *Older* went straight to number one in the UK, shifting an impressive 281,000 copies in the first week, one of the fastest-selling of all time. While it eventually sold a million copies in the US, a peak chart position of number six was disappointing. The performance across the Atlantic suggested that the American public was falling out of love with George.

On the album sleeve was a simple tribute: 'This album is dedicated to Antônio Carlos Jobim who changed the way I look at music and to Anselmo Feleppa who changed the way I look at my life … may they rest in peace.'

Jobim, who died in December 1994, was the great Brazilian composer and the pioneer of bossa nova music. His best-known songs included 'Corcovado', 'Desafinado' and 'The Girl from Ipanema' – all performed with grace and style by the sublime Astrud Gilberto. When George first passed his driving test, these were the mellow sounds that he listened to on the stereo of his sports car and their influence was apparent throughout *Older*.

Reviews were mixed; some were very hostile, others warm and enthusiastic. *The Mail on Sunday* judged it 'uncommonly dreary' and concluded, 'This is the most gruffly self-pitying LP that it has been my displeasure to hear for some very long time.' *Newsweek*, on the other hand, observed, 'It's gorgeous and romantic, ambitious and revelatory, feather-light and exquisitely listenable.'

The Irish Times had a thoughtful and understanding appreciation, highlighting the 'naked expressions of need' that were an antidote to the 'macho ranting' that made up so much of music in the mid-nineties. 'This song cycle is all the more glorious because of that. In essence, what we have here is a feminine sensibility fearless in the ascendant as he does get older; George Michael is coming of age.'

The idea that *Older* represented a song cycle is best illustrated by the first and last tracks. George began with 'Jesus to a Child' and ended the album with the saddest of songs, 'You Have Been Loved', co-written with David Austin. In the lyric, he describes the loss felt by Anselmo's mother Alice and his feelings when he visits the grave with her to lay flowers. He also apologises for being weak, admitting that he was 'terrified' when Anselmo was dying. He questions the comfort given by

God before ending the song and the album with Anselmo's words to him, 'Take care my love, he said. You have been loved.' They are a beautiful farewell.

George thought the album was his best work. Eleven years later, on *Desert Island Discs*, he told presenter Kirsty Young that it always would be so and spoke movingly of the man who inspired it: 'I think the album is a beautiful reminder of him. I wouldn't go through it again to make a great album. This man's life was much more important to me than entertaining people. I never want to feel that loss. I never want to feel that depth of emotion again. I hope he's very, very proud of it somewhere.'

The release of *Older* turned a page in George's life, at least for the moment. He was doing his best to move on. In the summer of 1996, he flew to California to arrange the sale of the home in Santa Barbara that reminded him so much of happier times with Anselmo. He started looking for a new home in Los Angeles, where he would spend more time in the future. On a visit one summer afternoon to an exclusive spa, George began a new chapter in his life.

17

WALTZ AWAY DREAMING

Kenny Goss had a sexy Texan drawl that drew people in. He was fit, tanned and handsome and George felt the instant attraction that he had experienced only once before when he first caught sight of Anselmo. They started chatting at the exclusive Beverly Hot Springs, a posh spa between Hollywood and Downtown LA.

At first they would tell people they met in the queue at the trendy restaurant at the Fred Segal store off Melrose Avenue in West Hollywood. Kenny, who was four years older than George, explained, 'It's a very straight above-board spa but if we tell people we met in a spa they always get the wrong idea.'

Kenny was born in the small Texas town of Brownwood, but his family moved to the Dallas suburbs when he was a small boy. He could never please his dad, who was a hard-working man, a Korean and Second World War veteran. He sold fire protection equipment for buildings while his mother stayed home, raising their two sons. Kenny would later describe them as 'alcoholic, dysfunctional parents'.

George could sympathise with his difficult upbringing, which was far harsher than his own. Kenny battled to look after his younger brother, Tim, who has always spoken of his elder sibling in glowing terms: 'I shudder to think how I might have turned out had I not had one good parent, and that parent was Kenny. He was there at every turn to protect me, but the sad thing is, Kenny had no one to protect him. He was out there all by himself.'

Kenny followed the traditional American path, attending the University of North Texas, where he studied education and political science. At college he was a successful gymnast, fraternity brother and, most notably, a cheer-leader. He was popular with the opposite sex and dated a string of desirable female students including a former Miss Texas.

After college, he joined the Cheerleading Supply Co., which was founded by the legendary figure Lawrence Herkimer, known affectionately in the US as 'Herkie', the father of modern cheerleading. He patented the pompom and invented the Herkie Jump, as well as ensuring cheerleading was an aspirational pursuit for millions of young people in America. It was also big business.

Kenny had charm and charisma, working his way up the company's executive ladder. He was sent to Los Angeles in the late 1980s and everything changed for him there: 'I was a Texas boy who went to LA and just went "Wow".' He became a rich man in his own right as the West Coast sales director. Unsurprisingly, he didn't tell his parents that he'd realised he was gay in his twenties. He joked, 'It was the big pink elephant in the room.'

Even George wasn't completely sure that Kenny was gay when they met. He asked him out for dinner. Kenny observed, 'I think he thought, "Maybe I'm picking up this straight guy", which he wasn't.'

George still wasn't sure Kenny was gay on the first dinner date: 'The second night, I became *very* sure he was gay.' This was no example of 'Fastlove'. By the end of their first week together, George was so sure this was something special that he decided to call his mum. On the phone, he told her all about Kenny and how he was head over heels in love. She was so pleased for him. They had been able to share so much more since he'd told her he was gay and revealed his torment over Anselmo's death.

She told him lightly of a medical scare concerning a small lump they had found on her shoulder. His father Jack recalled that it was just a little dark spot: 'You don't look at these things.' Kenny later remembered that she downplayed it, but it preyed on George's mind.

He flew back to London to prepare for his first proper live concert for three years. The first thing he did was take delivery of his new car, a superfast Jaguar XK8 with blacked-out windows and a state-of-the-art stereo. Considering how rich he was, George didn't splash out every day. Cars, however, were his weakness, although he spent most time behind the wheel of a less flashy Range Rover. Hippy would jump in the back and George would drive to Hampstead Heath for the Labrador's daily walks.

The *Unplugged* concert in October 1996 at the Three Mills Studios next to the River Lea in East London took place in front of an audience of just 300 fans. George hadn't performed a proper solo gig for five years, so rehearsed meticulously for a week at a secret location in Bermondsey; he hadn't lost his desire for perfectionism.

He was on top form for his mum, who was in the audience. On reflection, George considered it one of his finest performances, made more special by how pleased he was that his mother was there. Between songs, he caught sight of her. His face lit up into the brightest of smiles and he said simply, 'Hello Mum', and raised his hand in a brief acknowledgement. If you blinked you missed it, but for a few seconds he was her Yogi and he could not conceal his happiness at seeing her. She had sat proudly through so many of his concerts but this was the only time he said anything directly to her. It was the last time she would see him perform.

For a change he opened with 'Freedom! '90' and went on to sing many familiar favourites, including 'Fastlove', 'Father Figure' and 'Praying for Time'. Two beautiful ballads were possibly the highlights: 'You Have Been Loved' and a new number, the wistful 'I Can't Make You Love Me'. Originally it had been a hit in 1991 for the blues singer Bonnie Raitt, but became one of George's most popular songs after it was the B-side of the single release of 'Older'.

George was as sparing as ever with his interviews although he decided to speak at length to *The Big Issue*, a magazine he admired. It came about by accident. The founder and editor, John Bird, had been having a coffee in a café in Crouch End, North London, six months earlier when a young woman sat at his table and started praising his publication, saying how much she and her brother were great followers of it.

As she was leaving, she dropped the bombshell that her brother was George Michael. It was Melanie. He pleaded with her to ask George if he would grant a cover interview. She observed that the press was puerile and only interested in his private life. George hadn't given a proper interview in six years, she told him, because he wanted to keep his life private.

To John's surprise, he heard back from George Michael's office and the interview finally took place that autumn. George invited the writer Adrian Deevoy for several mugs of tea at his home in Hampstead and a chat during which no question appeared to be off-limits.

Adrian asked him about Anselmo and about his current sex life, which apparently was 'fantastic'. His new relationship with Kenny wasn't yet common knowledge. Inevitably, he was asked about his sexuality. George answered, 'I don't believe in people making public statements about their sexuality.'

Incredibly, he wasn't considered to be officially 'out' by the media even though in the same interview he referred to Anselmo as 'someone I truly loved' and spoke of his grief that was always there. It was absolutely transparent that George Michael was a gay man, but he steadfastly refused to make a big announcement. The world, it seemed, wanted him to admit his sexuality by making a heartfelt confession and saying six Hail Marys. 'My sexuality is no one's fucking business,' he declared. Ironically, George was far happier talking about smoking dope: 'I can't see myself giving grass up as a writer.' His drug-taking was never a secret.

The interview appeared as a cover story and greatly increased sales, which was a satisfactory outcome for everyone. A few weeks later, John saw George sitting with friends in Café Rouge in Highgate. He introduced himself and George promptly sat down at his table and talked earnestly about the problems facing his vendors. 'I was amazed at his passion,' recalled John.

The plight of the homeless, as emphasised by *The Big Issue*, prompted George to start volunteering at a shelter where he served soup and sandwiches to the men and women living on the streets. He loaded up the back of his Range Rover and used it as a temporary food stall for them. He wanted to do more than just write a cheque for money he would never miss and would spend several hours in the middle of the night chatting to young runaways and those facing a bitterly cold night outside.

His presence, dressed in jeans and a baseball cap, was so unexpected that nobody recognised him. Occasionally, he would be told he looked like George Michael but he would shrug 'I wish' and laugh. Eventually, word got out and he had to call a halt when photographers started hanging around hoping to catch a picture of the superstar.

His mum's condition was still giving cause for concern before Christmas. Lesley was admitted to King's Oak Hospital in Enfield for some exploratory surgery but was allowed home to spend what would turn out to be a last Christmas at home in Radlett. She appeared to be in remission, although her family believed she knew how serious it really was.

After the New Year, she was readmitted, this time to Charing Cross Hospital in the Fulham Palace Road, where it was confirmed that her condition was terminal. George stayed at her bedside, inconsolable, during the last days of her life as her family gathered to say goodbye.

He stayed away from the BRIT Awards, where he won Best British Male Solo Artist. Elton John presented the award and knew his friend wasn't going to be there to accept it because he had a scribbled note in his pocket. George had sent his apologies and thanked everyone including his family and friends who had helped to make music his life for the past fifteen years. He didn't explain his absence but Elton sweetly added how proud he was of him: 'George is a dear friend,' he said.

The following day, 26 February 1997, Lesley Panayiotou died with Jack, Yioda, Melanie and Georgios beside her. She was fifty-nine. She was one of those rare people about whom the old cliché of never having a bad word to say was actually true. Those who met her through George, from childhood onwards, thought she was a lovely person. She cared about the right things and he inherited his empathy from her. Tony Parsons said simply, 'Lesley was a warm, kind-hearted woman whose life was built on the foundations of family.'

For the most part, George kept his grief hidden from the world, just as he had done four years earlier when Anselmo died. In reality, he descended into what he called a 'black hole'. He retreated behind the gates of his home, turned to Prozac and resumed smoking too many spliffs to help him through the day. The funeral was a simple, understated occasion and Lesley Angold Panayiotou was buried in a family plot at Highgate Cemetery, well away from the prying eyes of tourists. The Panayiotous were so intent on a private occasion that they organised a decoy event to ensure the press did not ruin the genuine service.

George admitted 'being on some other planet for weeks', but after a month he faced the world at a Help a London Child charity lunch. He had already been working on a song that would form a perfect tribute to his mother. Called 'Waltz Away Dreaming', it was a duet with a young Irish singer called Toby Bourke, who was the first artist to be signed to Aegean Records, a new label set up by George and his cousin Andros.

By coincidence, Toby's former father-in-law was receiving cancer treatment at Charing Cross Hospital at the same time as Lesley. He and George would work on the song in the morning and then go to the hospital in the afternoon. Toby explained, 'I think he saw the phrase "waltz away dreaming" as being a fitting epithet for what had happened with his mum and her slow and sleep-filled death.'

Tellingly, the demo of the song was already in his CD player when George drove away from the hospital after she died; it started playing when he turned on the car engine. He added some words to the existing track and went back to the studio a few days later to record them. One verse speaks directly to his father who, he says, will see his wife again in her children's eyes. He sings, 'Every grown man cries with his mother's eyes.' Andros observed, 'It's the most moving track I've ever heard.'

Capital Radio would play the song on Easter Sunday afternoon. Listeners would be invited to pledge money to hear it and he would match every pound raised for Help a London Child. He told the guests that he hoped his father would find some comfort in the song and the children it would subsequently help: 'My mother was a woman of great compassion. Thousands of children still experience few acts of compassion except through this charity.'

'Waltz Away Dreaming' reached number ten in the charts but, more importantly, the bidding raised £35,000, which he promptly doubled with a £70,000 donation. He then decided to give another £96,000 so that the amount would eventually exceed £200,000.

George rather lost interest in Aegean Records after that. 'He was in the midst of deep grief,' said Toby. George admitted that he felt 'cursed' by the deaths of Anselmo and his mother: 'I've lost two people in the last five years I have loved very much and one of the great lessons is how incredibly short life is.'

He later admitted that this was the closest he had come to saying, 'I don't want to live', but he would never do that to his family. He continued to struggle with a huge depression, referring to it as 'such a dark period of my life'. He said he was on some other planet for weeks. His best friend, David Austin, was so worried about George's state of mind that he didn't know what to say to him. The simple truth, as George himself observed, was that he was just not prepared for his mother's death.

One of the people George did not reach out to was Princess Diana. They hadn't spoken for a year. He had rung her the previous summer to wish her a happy birthday. They had chatted merrily away about Elton and she complained about the royals not being a very loving compassionate family. He called her 'darling', which he tended to do when he felt comfortable with people. He also confided that he was in love.

Sadly, they didn't arrange to meet up because Diana was too involved with the legal matters surrounding her divorce. He wished he'd made a better effort at keeping in touch: 'I was always reluctant to call her up. It was almost like a mate of mine who doesn't want to call me up too much in case it looks strange – because he thinks that everybody is calling me up. I would presume it was an intrusion to call, when actually they're lonely and would love to hear a friendly voice.'

When Diana died in a Paris car crash on the last day of August 1997, George was in Los Angeles with Kenny and had just bought a new house in Beverly Hills. He was very upset and made a public statement praising the Princess as 'the greatest ambassador for compassion and humanity in modern times'. If he'd been at his home in St Tropez, he would have seen her just before she died because he had an invitation to go on her boyfriend Dodi Fayed's yacht while they were holidaying on the Riviera.

George came back to London almost immediately so that he could attend the funeral at Westminster Abbey. He arrived with Elton John and his partner, David Furnish, and they sat together during the service. While Elton kept his emotions in check, George was sobbing, especially when his friend got up to perform 'Candle in the Wind 1997': 'I had forgotten my hanky and I was really streaming. I was one of the few people in that part of Westminster Abbey that was really blubbering and I remember thinking, "God, this is going to be so embarrassing".' Fortunately, images of distress among the congregation were not broadcast.

The special tribute version of Elton's classic song sold 33 million copies worldwide, but behind it at number two in the charts was 'You Have Been Loved', the final single release from *Older*. Many assumed that it too honoured Diana, not realising it had been available on the album for more than a year. While it was obviously written about Anselmo, it conveyed universal feelings that captured the sadness of her death – and that of his mum, Lesley. George subsequently donated it to a charity album in aid of the trust set up in Diana's memory.

While these major events were going on in George's life, he kept his blossoming relationship with Kenny hidden. He decided to return to Los Angeles and they began living together in the new house on Calle Vista Drive, an exclusive street in Beverly Hills. The property had all the features George liked – high ceilings, swimming pool in the sun, private gardens and the man he had fallen for to share them.

George spent his days ostensibly working on new songs, but, in reality, he hadn't written a line worth saving since his mum died. He was about to receive a wake-up call. On one sunny day in April 1998, he and Kenny had been for a relaxed lunch in Beverly Hills. They had enjoyed a glass of wine or two, probably a bottle and a half, but not enough to need to go home for an afternoon nap.

Kenny remembered that they went off to do their own thing in the afternoon. Later, he got a message from George saying, 'Darling, please call this number.' Kenny rang straight away and the person who picked up stated clearly, 'Beverly Hills Police.'

18

CRUISE CONTROL

Kenny had to do a rapid trawl around the local cashpoints to withdraw enough cash to pay the $2,000 bail. George couldn't tell him on the phone the trouble he was in, so he assumed it to be a DUI (Drunk Under the Influence) after their nice lunch.

George was going 'stir crazy' at the police station in Rexford Drive. In the end, Kenny only needed to pay over $500, but he dutifully sorted out the paperwork before George, with all eyes on him, walked down the corridor from the cells to the exit. He still wouldn't tell Kenny what had happened and waited until they were safely at home behind closed doors.

Kenny was sympathetic when he heard the details of his arrest for 'lewd behaviour', observing, 'Oh darling, I don't think it is going to be that big of a deal. I think you will get away with it.' George, however, was adamant: 'I am not going to get away with this, Kenny.' He would be right.

The drama had unfolded in the Will Rogers Memorial Park, a well-kept public space with palm tree-lined walkways, fountains and manicured lawns. Will Rogers had been one of the most famous silent movie stars in Hollywood and the first honorary mayor of Beverly Hills in 1926. The park was less than a mile away from the house on Calle Vista Drive and George would often pop there to walk the dogs. Sometimes, Kenny would go with him and there were as yet unpublished pictures of the two of them sunbathing with their shirts off.

Tucked away in the trees near the main entrance opposite the Beverly Hills Hotel were the public toilets. They were at the time a popular spot for cruising, a fact that George well knew when he ambled into the park just before 5pm and made his way over to the men's restroom. The police had received complaints about what was going on and had strengthened their patrols. George, dressed in jeans, a denim shirt and a DreamWorks baseball cap, looked like an ordinary member of the public out for a stroll.

Outside the toilet he made eye contact with a good-looking, well-built young man who it later transpired was a plain–clothes police officer called Marcelo Rodriguez. Apparently, George beckoned the officer inside and was subsequently observed while he exposed himself and engaged in some solo sexual activity.

Officer Rodriguez then left the toilet and a uniformed colleague went inside to arrest George for performing a lewd act in a public place. He was the second man to be arrested there that day. George had gone into the toilet as a private individual, Georgios Panayiotou. He came out as George Michael, superstar. He could not keep his two worlds separate this time.

He was unable to provide proper ID for the officers and was subsequently handcuffed and taken to the station, where he was fingerprinted and, as they do in the US, photographed holding his crime number: BH9802756. That's when he was allowed to call Kenny.

As always seems to happen in Hollywood, it took less than a minute for the story to go around the world. While helicopters whirled over his house the next morning, the media dusted off their favourite hand-wringing descriptions of his 'gay sex shame' or sniggered at him being caught with his pants down. *The Sun* famously carried the front-page headline, 'Zip Me Up Before You Go Go'. Some reports suggested that George had broken down in tears when arrested, but there was no evidence of that and he subsequently strongly denied that had been the case. He maintained that his principal emotion was anger.

Not everyone was hysterical in their reaction. Former *EastEnders* actor Michael Cashman, a founder of Stonewall, the leading charity promoting LBGT rights, gave a more reasoned response. He explained that 'cottaging' happened all over the world and 'the whole reason for going to such places is that no one recognises you or remembers you; that is part of the deal.' He had met George at a small gathering at Elton John's house and was struck not just by his shyness, but also by how supportive he was of gay rights and the work that he was doing.

Michael readily understood the pain George would feel for his family and those closest to him: 'What happened to George Michael in Los Angeles was sad. He should have been allowed to seek sexual satisfaction in a more dignified way. Whether he knows it or not, he has advanced the rights of lesbians and gay men. In time, people across the world will be saying, "Who cares?"'

He thought the most important thing for George going forward with his life was that he 'can now be himself, he can celebrate his sexuality, who he is and who he loves.'

Michael also wondered if George was in any way entrapped. Lt Edward Kreins of the Beverly Hills Police Department was quick to head off any suggestion of that in the media: 'There have been several complaints about the park but it was sheer coincidence that the officer went in when George Michael was there.' He confirmed that the officer did not recognise that he was a pop star and that George had been co-operative throughout.

George found support from an unexpected source when his father phoned him. Far from being outraged, Jack told him, 'Tell them to fuck off. You are what you are.' George was both grateful and impressed by his dad's reaction. His sisters and his close friends were also supportive, and so was Kenny: 'I wasn't angry. I didn't say, "What were you doing?" or "Who the fuck does something like that?" or "I'm leaving you". We moved on.' His love at this time was hugely important to George, whose biggest fear in the aftermath of what had happened was that Kenny would not forgive him.

His lawyer Tony Russell and manager Andy Stephens, a former CBS executive who had taken over from Rob Kahane, were on a plane from London straight away to help him get through it. George needed their advice on what to do next. He decided, as his father had suggested in a manner of speaking, to go on the offensive, considering the loss of his mother and Anselmo to be far more significant in his life than this incident. He spent a couple of days lying low at David Geffen's mansion before deciding that was quite enough time hiding and went out for dinner.

George did not go to a discrete bistro but to Spago, which on any night is going to have a smattering of celebrity diners. The fashionable restaurant was just half a mile from the police station. The Hollywood star Tony Curtis was one of the first to greet George and ask how he was coping: 'He replied, "I'm feeling great. I'm doing fine. I could not be better." I told him to keep smiling and he said, "I will." I wish him all the best. He is a very nice guy.'

George happily signed autographs for well-wishers but politely told journalists to leave him alone. He left at 11.30pm with Andy and Tony and went home to Kenny. He first appeared on television the next day when he gave a lengthy and disarmingly frank interview to CNN. He wasn't about to apologise in some grovelling manner just to please the media. The first point he made was to add perspective to what had happened, pointing out that many people knew he had endured a tough time in the past few years: 'This is not going to finish me off, this is really nothing compared to the bereave-ments I've had to deal with or some of the other stuff, even the legal stuff, I've had to deal with.'

He made it clear that he was not ashamed as the newspapers had wrongly assumed: 'I feel stupid and I feel reckless and weak for having allowed my sexuality to be exposed in this way but I don't feel any shame. I don't think I should.' He even acknowledged that this was something he had done before by refusing to say if this was the first time it had ever happened.

He also revealed that he was in a relationship with a man at the moment. One of the less reported remarks he made concerned the truthfulness of his songwriting. That was very important to him. He wanted his fans to know that his early songs like 'Careless Whisper' were about women: 'The songs I have written since have fairly obviously been about men. So I think in terms of my work I have never been reticent about defining my sexuality.'

It was a defiant performance. Obviously it didn't draw a line under anything and George would have to talk about being 'outed' in every interview for the foreseeable future. By this time the world also knew the identity of the man in his life. Kenny observed: 'It outed him and it outed me. He hadn't told the public. What a way to do so, but it turned into a positive thing though.'

They managed to retain a sense of humour despite the storm around them. In private, while the media wanted them to be trembling, they were laughing with each other as they had always done. Kenny loved George's self-deprecating take on what was happening: 'He said, "The most horrific thing that happened was that I was photographed with my shirt off and I was fat. Can you imagine two worse things than being fat and gay?"'

The day after his CNN interview, George's sister Melanie spoke on air to Capital Radio DJ, Neil Fox, in London to tell him that George was concerned about missing the annual charity appeal. She told listeners her brother had called her from Los Angeles and said, 'Do me a favour, sis, please phone Foxy and give him £50,000 for Help a London Child. He wanted you to know that just because he was away it doesn't mean he's not thinking of you.' It was the fifth year in a row that he had donated at least that amount.

Neil suggested, 'It must have been a stressful week for you and your family.' She answered, 'Less stressful than you'd imagine, actually.' George's family and closest friends already knew all about his sexuality, so there was nothing for them to feel shocked about. Neil invited her to request a record on behalf of her brother and thought 'Careless Whisper', voted yet again the nation's favourite, might be a good choice. Melanie, however, decided that 'Move On', one of the lesser-known, jazzier tracks on *Older*, would be more appropriate.

Fortunately, George didn't attend the Los Angeles Municipal Court when his case was heard in May 1998. He had flown to Europe to start work on putting together his greatest hits album. His lawyer had already entered a no-contest plea to engaging in a lewd act, so his presence was not required.

In his absence, the judge fined him $810 and ordered him to perform eighty hours of community service. He was also told to undergo counselling and was banned from entering the Will Rogers Memorial Park. Ironically, the park had become a great deal more popular since his arrest, with tourists posing for pictures while clowning around in front of the men's toilet.

Now that the legal proceedings were concluded, George was able to talk more freely about his feelings. He quite obviously felt he had been entrapped and would say so in many a subsequent interview. He also offered an entirely different view about being 'out' during an online interview: 'There is a world of difference between being "out" – which in normal terms means telling all of those in your circle of friends, and your family, that you are bisexual or gay – and being "out" as a celebrity, which apparently means making sure the entire world, including people who don't give a toss, know who and what you are doing with your genitals.'

After all that happened, George might have wanted to celebrate his thirty-fifth birthday quietly at home with Kenny. Instead, he decided to organise another of his spectacular parties in order to tell the world that George Michael was alive and well and getting on with his life. It was a public relations exercise. He made sure the invitation raised a smile by including the warning: 'Please go before you come as all conveniences will be locked to protect the host'.

The fancy dress theme was 'Cowboys and Angels', a reference to one of the most popular ballads on *Listen Without Prejudice Vol. 1* and a personal favourite that he would include in subsequent tours. There were plenty of picture opportunities as celebrities arrived. Most of them were familiar faces in George Michael's world, including Martin Kemp and his wife Shirlie, who came dressed ready for a John Wayne movie.

The Kemps had endured a traumatic couple of years, with Shirlie helping to nurse Martin back to good health after he suffered two brain tumours that required operations. She was also declared bankrupt when she gave up work to look after her family. George remained a close friend throughout their ordeal.

Pepsi was one of the three hundred or so guests, but Andrew Ridgeley didn't make it, although his partner Keren Woodward attended with her old bandmate Sara Dallin from Bananarama. Another guest, dressed as an angel, was a much newer member of his inner circle – the mercurial Geri Halliwell, who had left the Spice Girls earlier in the year.

As a young teenager, Geri had idolised Wham! She went to school just a couple of miles from Andrew's home in Bushey and most of her friends would gather outside the Ridgeley house after lessons in case he was there. Geri always liked George best, however, and would give a poster of him on her bedroom wall a goodnight kiss before getting into bed.

She went to see the group on the *Big Tour* at the NEC, Birmingham, in December 1984, when she was twelve. They were performing 'Freedom' and when he got to the last line, George pointed at Geri and sang 'Girl, all I want right now is you.' She was absolutely in love and decided on the spot that they were going to get married. She was a Spice Girl when she eventually met him in person at the Capital Radio Music Awards in early 1997, soon after his mother had died.

Geri was deeply impressed that he could speak of his mother so openly. 'I was floored by that,' she recalled. She waited for her moment to grab his attention and try a bit of flirting because she still fancied him, but didn't get anywhere despite exchanging phone numbers. Eventually he called her: 'He dropped in the phrase "my boyfriend" and my jaw just dropped, I was so shocked.'

She barely saw George again until she left the superstar girl band at the end of May 1999 and he invited her to relax for a couple of days at Chez Nobby in the South of France when he and Kenny were staying there. She recalled fondly how sweet he was to her: 'I was supposed to go for a weekend and stayed three months. He was so kind and made me laugh.'

George became very fond of Geri as well as expressing his admiration for her, believing her contribution to the Spice

Girls had been undervalued. He observed, 'Geri is one of the most remarkable people I have ever met. I really think she was the Spice Girls. No disrespect to the others. I met them and they are all great girls, but, let's be honest, who were you looking at when you watched a Spice Girls performance?'

Geri was very down when she left the group but George and Kenny helped to rebuild her confidence. The three of them would go out for meals and laze about in the sun all day. George understood better than most her poor body image because he too had struggled with that. She would later disclose that she had been a victim of bulimia for many years and was surviving on SlimFast drinks. He always made sure she had a proper dinner when she was staying with him and Kenny. George, she said, was a 'mentor, father figure and friend' all rolled into one; he saved the day when she needed a kind word to help her prepare for her solo career.

While he had much to deal with himself, George was often there for Geri. He went with her to Battersea Dogs Home to help her choose the right pet and then comforted her when she burst into tears at the number of old, abandoned dogs that were living there. Eventually she chose a loveable Shih Tzu, who took a shine to George and wouldn't stop licking his face. Geri thought it was a shiatsu until he pointed out that was a massage and not a breed of dog. Harry, as she named the puppy, would be her constant canine companion for the next sixteen years.

George also gave Geri moral support before her first solo singing performance. He went with Kenny to her dressing room to wish her good luck before she went on stage at the Royal Albert Hall to sing 'Happy Birthday' to Prince Charles at his fiftieth birthday concert. 'You'll be wonderful,' said George.

George, too, had to gear himself up for some important times ahead. He was promoting his first single since his now notorious arrest and it remained to be seen how his sales and standing with the general public would be affected. Once again, he tackled the subject head-on by releasing 'Outside', a satirical look at what happened. *Rolling Stone* called it a 'lush disco track about the illicit thrills of fucking in the great outdoors'.

The track was accompanied by one of his most memorable videos. Vaughan Arnell, who had directed the 'Fastlove' video, as well as 'Angels', which transformed the career of Robbie Williams, filmed a series of gay and straight couples kissing and having sex outdoors. They couldn't film in the Will Rogers Memorial Park because of George's ban, so the set moved fifteen miles away to Marina Del Rey, where Vaughan transformed a women's toilet into a disco and used it as the main location.

George dressed up as a police officer, showing some fine disco moves clutching a nightstick. The real policeman involved in his arrest, Marcelo Rodriguez, filed a $10 million claim for damages against him. He alleged that George profited by mocking his arrest in the video and by suggesting in interviews that the officer had set him up by pretending to be a gay man wanting sex. Eventually this was thrown out when a court ruled that, as a public official, he could not recover damages for emotional distress.

The moral majority were outraged at the video, upset that George could show such little regret at what had happened to him and was in effect sticking two fingers up at the Los Angeles Police Department. Even Mary Whitehouse, the veteran campaigner, said, 'I hope nobody will buy this video or broadcast it. That is the best way of showing Mr Michael we do not think his behaviour is funny.' Her intervention was always just the sort of publicity a project needed and 'Outside' went to number two in the UK charts when it was released in October 1998, kept off the top by Cher's massive seller, 'Believe'.

George did his bit for publicity by undertaking a new series of interviews and again adopting his natural, self-deprecating humour as the best way of deflecting any criticism. He expressed surprise that the general public had not realised he was gay, given he wore a moustache 'that makes you look like you've failed a Village People audition'.

He went on Michael Parkinson's chat show and began by telling the host what an honour it was to be there: 'When I was eight or nine years old, my mum would allow me to stay up beyond a certain time in the evening only to watch the *Parkinson* show. I am very privileged to be here. She probably wouldn't be quite as thrilled to learn I had to take my willy out to get on here.'

Parky didn't usually socialise with his guests before the show started but he made an exception in George's case and took him out to dinner. He had realised how nervous the singer was about his appearance and wanted to make sure he was all right: 'I asked him what he was prepared to talk about and he just said, "Everything".'

George gave one of his more thoughtful interviews to an American LBGT newspaper, *The Advocate*, in which he declared that he wasn't sorry it happened and wondered if subconsciously he allowed it to happen. Kenny agreed that might have been the case: 'I think he wanted to get caught. I don't know if he liked the danger but it's a hell of a dangerous thing to be doing.'

His greatest hits album, *Ladies & Gentlemen: The Best of George Michael*, was finally released as part of his prior agreement with Sony. Nobody quite knew if the title was tongue-in-cheek – 'Ladies' and 'Gentlemen' were the signs on the doors of thousands of British public toilets. There were twenty-eight songs arranged over two CDs. The first one contained the ballads and was called 'For the Heart'. Disc two opened with 'Outside' and was 'For the Feet'.

The AllMusic review online called the collection 'a monster', revealing the 'true depth of his talent'. He might not have been so pleased that *The Advocate* called him a 'veteran singer' at the age of thirty-four. As well as 'Outside', there were two previously unreleased tracks: 'A Moment with You' and 'As', the smooth Stevie Wonder hit that George sang with Mary J. Blige. Disappointingly, their version wasn't included on the American release – apparently her record company was not keen – but it reached number four in the UK.

The album scraped a million sales in the US but was further evidence that he was no longer as popular there as he once was. George acknowledged, 'I don't think I will ever be a big star in America again.' In the UK it sold more than twice that and was number one for Christmas 1998. He was the best-selling male artist in the world outside of the States.

Pleased with that success, George opted for a quiet Christmas, joining David Austin at his parents' house in the beautiful seaside town of Kinsale in southern Ireland. Kenny had travelled home to Dallas, so George tucked into a traditional turkey dinner and enjoyed a post-lunch stroll around the marina with old and trusted friends. It was the first time he had been over to see Michael and Maureen Mortimer since they had left London to run a pub.

George politely signed the odd autograph when asked but liked the fact that, for the most part, people left him alone even if they recognised him. It was a time for reflection after a helter-skelter year. He needed to make some changes in his life. Enjoying the country air in Ireland made him realise he might enjoy the same back home. He found a house he thought would be perfect in the lovely English village of Goring-on-Thames in Oxfordshire.

19

SHOOT THE DOG

George was fed up writing about his pain. He wanted to be more upbeat. He wanted his next album to be about something joyful. He had experienced lower points in his life than he ever thought were possible but he had come through them. 'I have to write a "fuck-off" hit record,' he declared.

Unfortunately, the best art is often written, composed or painted at a time of personal struggle and internal suffering. George was no different than the majority of creative people who found inspiration in pain, loneliness and uncertainty. He was not finding it pottering happily about in the garden at Goring.

The village is about eight miles north of Reading and an hour and a half on a bad traffic day from his other main home in North London. They were worlds apart. Goring is well kept and traditional – the sort of place you never wanted to leave.

The sixteenth-century house, which was next to the village church, was very private so he could just open the French windows, let the dogs out and inspect the flowers while still in the grey Gap flannel loungers that he would wear most of the day. If it was sunny, he would make a mug of PG Tips, grab a bowl of his favourite Coco Pops and just sit quietly on the patio.

Kenny moved over from Los Angeles and for a while they were like an old married couple. He recalled, 'We were happiest at the country house.' George loved it, content to stay in bed and watch television all day, eating tubs of his favourite Ben & Jerry's Chunky Monkey ice cream. The two of them could scarcely boil an egg between them so the pristine Aga in the kitchen remained untouched. George would frequently have the munchies thanks to his continued spliff smoking. Kenny laughed, 'He was a pothead. I'd get McDonald's all the time. He liked anything as fattening as possible because he was stoned all the time.'

George still loved *Coronation Street* most of all and was a devoted fan, although he also kept up to date with *EastEnders*. He liked *This Morning with Richard and Judy*, *Loose Women* and anything with Caroline Aherne in it. He thought she was hilarious as the spoof chat show host Mrs Merton, as well as later in *The Royle Family*, and even arranged to meet her in Manchester one day.

Sometimes they would venture out to walk the Labradors – Hippy and their newest arrival, Mo. Nobody bothered them if they decided to hold hands or put their arms around one another. That was one of the nicest outcomes of the world knowing they were a couple. George was happy to chat to neighbours when he popped into the local newsagent's for cigarettes and magazines. He was down to earth and friendly and, in return, the locals didn't gossip about him to the press.

George commissioned an architect to make some changes to the property, including designing an outdoor swimming pool, bar area and pool house, which was completely hidden from prying eyes and telephoto lenses by newly planted trees.

While it had five bedrooms and was very spacious by British standards, the rooms were smaller and the ceilings much lower than those in his other homes, particularly the ones in the US. He'd lived most of his life in airy villa-style houses and this was cosy by comparison. He installed a library, although the antique books were more for show than reading: 'They're kind of furniture rather than cultural input.'

Kenny was always amazed at how George learned the songs he sang. He never heard him practise at home, but he recalled going to watch him perform at the *Concert for Linda* in April 1999, a charity tribute honouring Linda McCartney. She had died a year earlier, aged fifty-six, after a long battle with cancer. George sang two Beatles songs that Kenny wasn't aware he even knew, let alone get up on stage and sing note perfectly.

George received a standing ovation when introduced by comedian Eddie Izzard and gave him a peck on the cheek. He told the audience how much he admired Linda and also that the night had a special meaning for him: 'My mother lost the same fight that Linda lost.' After 'Eleanor Rigby' and an exquisitely poignant interpretation of Paul McCartney's classic 'The Long and Winding Road', he dusted off 'Faith' and the crowd loved him.

Afterwards, he was quite happy to go home with Kenny and put the telly on. One of his habits that would prove to be beneficial to many people was pledging money if something took his fancy. One morning he was watching Richard and

Judy when they announced the *This Morning* Christmas Appeal in aid of needy children. George picked up the phone, still in his pyjamas, and gave £50,000 on the strict understanding that the donation was not publicised. He had transferred the money before the programme came off air.

Richard Madeley rang George that evening to thank him and when he discovered that George also had a home in North London, invited him over for Sunday lunch. Judy Finnigan thought she was going to faint when she heard her husband so casually invite one of the most famous people in the world round for a roast. When Richard put the phone down, he turned around to see Judy 'standing with her hands on her head, her mouth opening and closing like a goldfish.' They were obviously used to celebrities but George Michael was a class apart.

They need not have worried. Sunday lunch proved to be the start of a long friendship. George was on a diet – one of many he would try from time to time – and cornered Judy in the kitchen to insist on 'no carbs'. Dutifully, she took the roast potatoes off his plate only to find he would pinch all the ones from hers during lunch.

Richard thought George was a perfect guest: 'He was fiercely intelligent, witty and self-deprecating and genuinely thankful for what he referred to as "my gift", his voice.' George liked them, especially as they didn't talk about him in public. During the last edition of *This Morning* he phoned in to wish them well on air: 'Thank you for easing me into the day. You will be sorely missed.'

Both Richard and Judy realised early on that the most important thing in earning George's friendship was gaining his trust; he was disarmingly honest with those that had it. But sometimes even his closest friends would fall out of favour completely if he felt they had in some way betrayed him. Loyalty, more specifically his perception of loyalty, was of crucial importance to George. Most notably, he never spoke to Andros Georgiou again after they fell out in 1998. George never revealed the reason, although his cousin had given an interview and some private photographs to *Hello!* magazine that may or may not have been the trigger. Andros, however, claimed they had a silly argument over lunch about Geri Halliwell, who he didn't like, that ended in a mutual 'fuck off'.

Andros would continue to speak to the press about George in the coming years, which was hardly likely to bring him back into favour. He published an autobiography in 2012 that was primarily about his famous cousin and the times they had spent together. Unfortunately, their falling-out meant that George did not see his godchildren. He was godfather to Andros and Jackie's first two sons but did not meet their third.

Andros had been an important friend to George. Their quarrel was a significant moment, but in practical terms, Andros now lived in Los Angeles and George was shying away from the world of Beverly Hills. Over the years, Andros had never been particularly close to Andrew Ridgeley or David Austin. One member of the inner circle observed, 'They never had any time for him.'

Another friend George cast asside was Tony Parsons. They had fallen out over a series of articles that Tony wrote about him for the *Daily Mirror*. Tony had offered some of the best insights into George's character over the years and obviously liked him very much: 'George is unlike every other celebrity in one crucial respect – he doesn't think he's the centre of the universe. When you are with him, it's very easy to forget that he is one of the biggest stars in the world because he is such a nice, unpretentious, down-to-earth bloke.' Like Andros, he was to have no contact with George for nearly twenty years.

George had a potent dislike of tabloid newspapers, so that can't have helped where Tony was concerned. He won a legal battle with *The Sun* banning them from printing his address. The problem with any star gaining a victory against a newspaper is that they run the risk of more negative publicity; George would learn that lesson in the future. 'I would have to advise a young version of me that these days celebrity and secrets don't go together. The bastards will get you in the end.'

He wasn't much bothered by ridiculous stories that he was involved in some *ménage à trois* with Geri and Kenny. He was genuinely fond of Geri, though. For her twenty-seventh birthday he presented her with a 1960s blue Mercedes, similar to one he kept at Chez Nobby for driving along the beautiful coastal roads near St Tropez. Three hundred guests arrived at St Paul's House, the converted monastery in the Buckinghamshire village of Wexham, which she had bought at the height of her Spice Girls fame. George just pitched up, parked the convertible on the lawn and said, 'Happy birthday.' You knew you were in with George if he bought you a car.

A week later Geri was staying at his villa in France when news came through that her second solo single, 'Mi Chico Latino', had reached number one. George wouldn't have minded some of that success for his first recording venture after his greatest hits, a project he put together simply for his own enjoyment. He recorded an album of covers of his favourite songs called, amusingly, *Songs from the Last Century*, even though it was released in time for Christmas 1999. He had secretly flown to New York to work with Phil Ramone, one of the great producers of modern times.

The first of fourteen Grammies Phil had won was in 1965 for engineering one of George's favourite albums *Getz / Gilberto*, which had stimulated his love of the Brazilian bossa nova music of Antônio Carlos Jobim. George had harboured ambitions to work with Phil ever since he first heard it.

He simply phoned up the producer and asked if he would be interested in the project. Phil was flattered, knowing that George normally took sole responsibility for his albums. He admired George's passion for songs that ranged from old standards including 'Brother, Can You Spare a Dime' to modern classics such as 'Roxanne', one of the early hits for The Police. For many, the stand-out track was a version of 'The First Time Ever I Saw Your Face', which had been a US number one for Roberta Flack in 1972.

After the fanfare and fuss of *Outside* and the *Ladies & Gentlemen* greatest hits, the album almost slipped under the radar, although it did reach number two in the UK charts, the only George Michael collection not to reach the top. Considering it was an album of covers, worldwide sales of 3.5 million were very decent. The most disappointing performance was in the US, where George's belief that he would never again be a big star seemed correct when it peaked at number 182.

George did little to publicise the album and critics were lukewarm. The BBC review online thought his singing was technically excellent but had reservations: 'Maybe it's just that his voice lacks the lived-in, world-weary quality needed to do some of these songs justice.' Perhaps because so many of the songs are classics, the album has aged well and could have been recorded at any time during George's career.

The BBC made the interesting point that his fans would have preferred some original material, which showed no sign of happening soon. He wanted to reconnect with the pop side of his character and be more upbeat. When he was at home in Goring or at the house in Hampstead, he would work while soaking in the bath.

He had a studio at Goring but seldom used it. Instead he would spend hours in the bath, concentrating, as he always did, on one particular song until he felt he could take it to the studio, where he would work on putting it painstakingly together. When George was locked away in the recording studio, Kenny would spend his time absorbed in London's galleries and museums, unlocking a passion for art that would be important to them both in the future. If he became bored traipsing around looking at pictures, then there was always shopping with Geri.

Progress in the studio continued to be slow, so there was much time for those stress-free days in London. Eventually, in early 2002, George emerged with a new single called 'Freeek!' George was aiming to tap into the fashionable electronic world of Daft Punk and met with the groundbreaking French duo in Paris. They worked on some things together, although not specifically this track. This was dance-floor music at its then most modern.

While one critic thought the record 'a triumph', another

made Mary Whitehouse appear liberal by describing it as the stuff of which few parents would or should encourage their children to listen to: 'Perhaps "Freeek" should convince his few remaining die-hard fans that it is now time to turn our backs on the singer and call a halt to his musical parade of sexual perversion.' Even Elton John, usually one of George's biggest admirers, didn't think the song was one of his best, although he did try and make up for it by adding, 'We've all made those kinds of records.'

George had to fly to Los Angeles to shoot a video for the song, which was rumoured to have cost £1 million and was futuristic in the manner of *Blade Runner*. Beautifully shot by the innovative director Joseph Kahn, it featured more of George on film than we'd seen for years. He appeared as himself, a gay man, wearing a red rubber suit while presiding over a trance-like sci-fi orgy and mild bondage scenes. George, as ever, was trying to be part of something groundbreaking and innovative but 'Freeek!' failed to generate the same sensational headlines as 'I Want Your Sex' had in the 1980s.

The most distinctive quality of 'Freeek!' was that it didn't sound like any other George Michael song. The change was probably too much for a British audience that had loved *Older* and the song only made the lower reaches of the top ten. There was no US release but the European feel found favour in Spain, Portugal, Italy and Denmark, where it was his first number one since 'Careless Whisper'.

The song probably would have performed better had it been banned, but sex no longer seemed to generate enough controversy. Only seventy viewers complained when it was shown on *Top of the Pops*. Ironically, the B-side was his peerless version of 'The Long and Winding Road', which almost certainly would have been a much bigger hit. The number one single at the time was the old chestnut 'Unchained Melody' by the toothsome Gareth Gates.

If 'Freeek!' failed to attract enough publicity, then the next single, 'Shoot the Dog', was, for a while, the most talked-about song in the world. George was putting the finishing touches to the track at Air Studios in Hampstead when everyone stopped to watch the TV screen. It was 11 September 2001 and a plane crashed into the Twin Towers in New York. Then the second plane hit and they all realised it was a deliberate act. As he watched, transfixed by the horror, tears streamed down George's face.

George told Piers Morgan, then editor of the *Daily Mirror*, how he felt: 'I cried simply because it was such a shocking, sickening attack on humanity beyond any callous acts that you could ever remember. It was just the worse thing to even conceive of doing something as evil as that.'

At this stage 'Shoot the Dog' was a record reflecting his concerns over the relationship between Tony Blair and George W. Bush. He immediately realised he would have to reconsider the song in the aftermath of the tragic events, particularly as he didn't wish to be seen as opportunistic.

He wasn't ready to unveil the song with some new lyrics for several months, but by the summer of 2002, he had formed strong opinions about the Middle East and the prospect of Britain being dragged by America into an Iraq War: 'Our Government needs to reassure the Islamic population that we are not going into the Middle East with a gung-ho attitude.

There must be a lot of Islamic people feeling very uncomfortable in Britain right now.'

George was thinking ahead of his time when he added, 'If we just storm in there now, there'll be a disaster that will destroy any chance of stability in that region for a very, very long time.'

George believed he should be allowed to voice his opinion: 'This is the first time I've really had the guts to go for something knowing I might get critically savaged for it. There's always been this nagging worry of people saying, "Look, mate, you're a rich, pampered pop star – what the fuck do you know about it?" But now I feel confident enough to just go for it. And I should have the right to say these things without being ripped to pieces.'

In the main he was ripped to pieces, at least in the US. The video increased the general mood of anger; it was a cartoon that poked fun at the relationship between President Bush and Prime Minister Blair. America, it seemed, did not appreciate the satirical intention. He was jeered by the audience when he appeared on live television. The *New York Post* called him a 'washed-up pervert'. George tried to maintain his dignity: 'I don't think there's any connection between what I'm saying and the fact that I'm a gay man.'

He continued to speak out about the Middle East and the prospect of the Iraq War even after 'Shoot the Dog' sold so disappointingly. In February 2003, he warned, 'We are about to light the touch paper of all those pockets of Islamic fundamentalism by doing something which is totally illegal. The West and the fundamentalist world are going to be at loggerheads for many, many years if we don't talk now.' The invasion of Iraq began one month later.

The disappointing performance of both 'Freeek!' and 'Shoot the Dog' led to the postponement of the next album and a complete rethink. An album consisting of ten similar dance tracks might be a disaster for his career, and his professional pride would not allow that to happen.

George put his house in Los Angeles on the market and went home to Goring to soak in the bath. Perhaps he needed some more personal, introspective songs after all.

20

ANGELS AND DEMONS

George wrote two songs for Kenny on the new album. One was called 'American Angel' and the other 'Amazing'. They were a thank you to the man who had saved his life emotionally by wiping away the tears. When *Patience* was eventually released in 2004 there was a photograph of a handsome, smiling Kenny holding a remote control. The picture was rather ironic because custody of the remote was one of the few things they had big arguments about.

The couple had an open relationship. George, perhaps in defiant mode, had revealed that they were not monogamous when he spoke to Piers Morgan: 'This is not an uncommon state of affairs in long-term gay relationships. It's not open at all in any emotional sense, just purely physical.' Ironically, this was now the lifestyle choice of a man who had written 'monogamy' on Kathy Jeung's naked back in the video for 'I Want Your Sex'.

George said they had a 'great relationship and loved each other very dearly.' Kenny, who clearly adored him, admitted it was open on both sides, although he did once confide, 'I don't think I was as open as George.'

In George's case, the openness would involve slipping a condom into his pocket and casually telling his partner he was popping out to Hampstead Heath when they were staying in London. His notorious arrest in the park had not, it seemed, curbed his desire for the passing thrill of cruising. He freely admitted that he was 'over-sexed' but also subsequently said he envied gay men who managed monogamy for ever.

Quietly, Kenny was facing his own demons while the world focused on George Michael and his new album. His mother died of cancer in 2000 and his father of a stroke three years later in late 2003. His dad had apparently failed in a suicide attempt a few days earlier when, according to the local police department in Texas, he had shot himself in his own front yard.

Kenny, who is refreshingly honest about things, admitted to the *Dallas Morning News* that he had a huge amount of guilt due in no small measure to having 'no relationship of any kind with this man who tried to kill himself'. He acknowledged a growing reliance on prescribed sleeping medication. He was already seeing a therapist three times a week at George's suggestion but, despairingly, checked himself into a rehab centre in Arizona to try and cure his addiction. He spent five weeks at The Meadows in Wickenburg, a small town sixty miles north of Phoenix. He said his stay there helped him to realise how he had come to find himself in that position. George had to stay away, fearing that a media circus might ruin his partner's treatment.

George was by now fully immersed in the launch of his new album – finally. *Patience* was in the shops eight years after his last album of original material. Somewhat unbelievably, after all that had gone before, he had returned to Sony after a two-single deal he had signed with Polydor resulted in neither side taking up the option of the next release.

This time around he agreed to do his fair share of publicity and invited a few trusted journalists around to the house in Hampstead for his usual candid interview. He was waiting to move his London base into a new house he had bought, not far away in equally fashionable Highgate. The six-bedroom Grade II-listed mansion was in a millionaire's row where Sting, Kate Moss and Jude Law were among his celebrity neighbours. You could look out over Hampstead Heath from the top floor. He didn't need to dip into his savings too much because he sold the house in Beverly Hills for $2.75 million to Ken Warwick, the executive producer of *American Idol*.

His old home had lost some of its lustre when he was burgled and had his £100,000 Aston Martin DB7 stolen from outside the house. The car was later found abandoned. To make matters worse, a fan actually lived under the house for four days. At the back were stilts, propping up the house against the hillside, and she had hidden there. He only discovered her when she called out his name as he was chatting to a friend in the garden.

The appeal of new George Michael material combined with a higher profile took *Patience* straight to number one, selling 275,000 copies in the first week. One of the songs about Kenny, 'Amazing', was released as the first single. 'Freeek!' and 'Shoot the Dog' were conveniently forgotten for promotional purposes but were included on the album. The critics loved it. The *Mail on Sunday* thought the track 'soulful, hummable and sung with his trademark ease'. The *Daily Mirror* described it as 'a swish multi-layered piece of deluxe, designer soul with George the maestro asserting his authority over pop minnows'.

'Amazing', was co-written with Jon Douglas, who he had worked with on the *Older* album. It didn't provoke the strong reaction that his two previous singles had done. It was undemanding, polished and very catchy – the sort of song that you would sing in the car. Released in the US, it reached number one in the *Billboard* Dance Club Chart, which was a decent achievement after the performance of his last few records.

Once again though, the more intense ballads on the album were the most memorable compositions. Alexis Petridis, in *The Guardian*, thought 'My Mother Had a Brother' a 'remarkable piece of writing', telling the story of Uncle Colin who had killed himself and, George had later learned, struggled with being a gay man in the early 1960s: 'The effect is heart-rending in the extreme,' said Alexis. 'Round Here' was a delicately nostalgic piece about his early life and one the critic found 'sublime'.

The overriding impression was that here was an intelligent man producing a thoughtful record. The American critics were not as enthusiastic as their British counterparts, though. *The Philadelphia Inquirer* said it was a 'maudlin, naval-gazing affair'. *The Washington Post* described it as 'unremittingly mid-tempo and irrelevant'.

In addition to the two songs for Kenny, there was a tribute to his lost love called 'Please Send Me Someone (Anselmo's Song)'. As seemed to be the case with every album, there was one poignant track co-written with David Austin. This time it was the wistful 'John and Elvis are Dead' about a coma victim who wakes after thirty years to discover his heroes have died and asks how it could have happened if there was a God.

David talked very little about George over the many years of their friendship, testament to the strong bond they had. They fiercely protected each other's privacy. He did explain, though, that he understood what inspired George musically: 'The right chord change can be a platform for him to take off. You can't manufacture that sort of relationship.'

'John and Elvis are Dead' and the even more melancholic 'Through', which closed the album and seemed to suggest he was done with being George Michael, were the two tracks that George would feature most strongly in his future repertoire. Who could have known that a song called 'Through' would be the final track on the last album of original material from George Michael? He had made just four new albums in the eighteen years since Wham!'s *Final* concert, but would not make another.

While George was enjoying the success of *Patience*, he crashed a new BMW convertible on the A40 in Acton. Apparently, he careered into some railings and was lucky to escape unhurt although badly shaken. Nobody thought much of it at the time – just an accident involving a famous celebrity – but it was the start of a notorious succession of incidents involving driving and cars.

The episode was an early indication that some cracks were appearing in George's life. Rumours had surfaced that all was not well between him and Kenny after they had been seen having a heated row on their way home from the tenth-anniversary party for the gay magazine, *Attitude*. The tabloid newspapers suggested that George had been seen in the company of a gay porn star.

And then he fell out with Elton. He had been a good friend and mentor for many years so it seemed a huge shame for the two to start a feud. It began when Elton was quoted in *Heat* magazine giving his opinion on the younger man's life. He said George was in a 'strange place … smoked too much grass' and that there was a 'deep-rooted unhappiness in his life'. For good measure he added that *Patience* was disappointing.

George was outraged and dashed off a letter to the same magazine: 'Elton John knows very little about George Michael and that's a fact. Most of what Elton knows about my life is limited to the gossip he hears on the gay grapevine, which is, as you can imagine, lovely stuff. Sadly, I was always aware that Elton's circle of friends was the busiest rumour mill in town and that respect for my private life was not exactly guaranteed.

'Other than that, he knows I don't like to tour, I smoke too much pot and my albums still have a habit of going to number one.' He also had a dig at the older star's music, claiming he relied on his old hits to make millions, adding that his own 'passion and drive is still about the future'.

Elton tried to patch things up but George refused to take his call on five occasions. He revealed, 'Poor George, I tried to call him up at Christmas to sort things out but he wouldn't come to the phone. I spoke to his partner Kenny but he couldn't persuade George to talk to me.'

Elton, who had fought his own battle with drug addiction, maintained that he was only saying what needed to be said: 'I've been in the place George is in at the moment and I know you need someone to tell you the truth. It's a shame. I obviously struck a nerve and he took it all the wrong way.'

One of the saddest aspects of this quarrel was that it was conducted in public. It received much more publicity than George quietly donating all American royalties from the album to the Elton John AIDS Foundation. According to DJ Paul Gambaccini, Elton was 'very upset'.

There was no duet when they both appeared at the Live 8 concert in Hyde Park in July 2005. Instead, Elton sang the old T. Rex hit 'Children of the Revolution' with Pete Doherty as well as performing his perennial hit 'Saturday Night's Alright for Fighting', which seemed an odd choice for a charity concert highlighting the problem of world poverty.

George did not perform a solo spot because of a bad throat, but near the end he bounced on stage to sing 'Drive My Car' with Paul McCartney, who was headlining the event. Wearing designer sunglasses and stubble, he looked much better than had been suggested in the press when he was spotted shuffling around Hampstead, buying tubs of ice cream.

George was buoyed up by getting back on stage and receiving such an enthusiastic reception. He hadn't appeared at a big charity event for five years. He thought seriously for the first time about undertaking another tour – his first since 1991. He recognised that the musical landscape was changing with the biggest acts like Paul McCartney, Elton and U2 – all of whom were at Live 8 – no longer simply promoting a record. They were receiving applause for their musical history – their complete catalogue. He too had a legacy that deserved to be heard.

He also understood early on that the digital age would change the way we listen to music and that downloads would be the future. He released 'John and Elvis are Dead' as a download-only single. The video was a collage of famous faces we have lost; Elvis Presley, John Lennon and Marvin Gaye feature in the song. The approach was quite retro in that unusually it simply featured George singing to the camera, harking back to the old days of 'A Different Corner'.

George flew to Dallas the same month as Live 8 for the opening of the Goss Gallery. While George was in the UK, Kenny had been spending more time back in Dallas, where they'd bought a beautiful $2 million condominium in the upmarket Turtle Creek area. When he came out of rehab, they talked about their future together and decided that Kenny needed more point to his life than just being the partner of George Michael. He found it in a love of art that had been inspired by those many afternoons wandering around the galleries of London.

They had very different tastes. While George these days liked an antique feel to his home surroundings, Kenny much preferred a more modern approach with a touch of Asian influence: 'He's much more conservative than I am. He prefers old masters and comfy, cosy things with big cushions.'

George, however, was determined to give Kenny his total support in realising his ambition of establishing a gallery in his home town. One of the most important aspects of the whole venture was that Kenny used his own money to get his dream up and running. That was important for his self-esteem.

George was able, however, to introduce Kenny to some of the friends he mixed with in London, including the celebrated artist Tracey Emin, who shared a Cypriot heritage on her father's side and who hilariously lost his phone number after he'd written it on a scrap of paper for her one drunken lunch-time in The Ivy.

Together they also began collecting works by the leading British modern artists of the age who included not just Tracey but also Bridget Riley, Damien Hirst, Sarah Lucas, Marc Quinn and Michael Craig-Martin. Many of the works were edgy, including a Hirst – 'Saint Sebastian, Exquisite Pain' – that depicted a calf in formaldehyde being slaughtered by arrows, and several of the Lucas' signature penis sculptures.

Kenny's first exhibition was a display of the work of the acclaimed portrait photographer David LaChapelle. He had been responsible for 'Kissing Sailors', the iconic poster used in a 1995 Diesel campaign that had been one of the first advertisements to show a gay couple kissing. He also directed several of Elton John's best videos.

The Goss Gallery was going to specialise in promoting and selling the leading British artists Kenny had discovered in London. He loved the childlike paintings of Stella Vine and introduced her work to George, who promptly bought one of her most controversial pieces for £25,000. The piece entitled 'Murdered? Pregnant? Embalmed?' depicted Princess Diana in a blue evening gown with those words on the wall behind her.

Stella said he had seen it on her website: 'I was inspired to paint it after reading Diana's body was embalmed, destroying any possible evidence she may have been pregnant.' While George was appreciative of the painting's directness, he really bought it as a gift for Kenny, who hung it in the dining room in Dallas.

At the gallery opening, Kenny said simply, 'I hope George is proud of me.' He clearly was because, contrary to the negative reports back home, they talked for the first time of a civil partnership. They had already exchanged gold rings, which were photographed for the *Patience* booklet opposite the lyrics to 'Amazing'.

George was delighted that civil partnerships would become legal in Britain in December 2005, declaring it to be 'long overdue'. He had argued that gay couples should have the same legal rights as heterosexual relationships: 'The idea that if anything happened to myself or Kenny that our families would have all the rights and that we would have none is just ridiculous.' In the end they never got round to it, which is surprising considering how strongly George had spoken out in favour of equal rights for the gay community.

He was busy preparing another greatest hits package as well as his first tour in fifteen years while Kenny was occupied with the gallery. Once again, however, the private man spilled out into the public arena when in February 2006 a passer-by noticed George asleep and slumped behind the wheel of his Mercedes while parked near the Hyde Park Corner roundabout.

The member of the public was worried he was ill and called an ambulance, which wasn't needed, and the police, who promptly arrested George on suspicion of being unfit to drive. They also found some class C drugs – believed to be cannabis and liquid ecstasy (GHB) – when he was searched, and these were sent for analysis.

After examination by a duty doctor, he was found to be fit to drive and was de-arrested for that offence but was still bailed to face possible drug charges. George, knowing that the press would enjoy his predicament, released a statement: 'It's my own stupid fault as usual. I was in possession of class C drugs, which is an offence, and I have no complaints about the police, who were professional throughout.

'The only thing I care about is that people know that I was properly tested by the police doctor on Saturday night, who stated to the officers present that I was not impaired in any way and should be allowed to drive home.'

At least he didn't need Kenny to bail him out and the duty solicitor kindly gave him a lift home. George added a PS to his statement: 'I promise I won't make a record out of this one – even though it is tempting.' He made no mention of the various sex toys and bondage gear the tabloids gleefully alleged were also found in the car – although one can only speculate on how they came upon that information. He subsequently denied there was anything of that nature in the car.

He did, however, have the idea of a new song the following day. Called 'An Easier Affair', it was one of his relaxed mid-tempo numbers and contained a personal message that he was not going to give in to the haters and the name callers but intended to live his life as he wanted, as a gay man. He sang that he had nothing to hide from anyone.

A month later, George slipped quietly into Belgravia Police Station at 7am to receive an official caution after admitting possession of cannabis. That should have been an end to his driving adventures for the foreseeable future except that the following month he was seen pranging three parked cars near his home one Sunday morning. He later called police to admit he was driving the Range Rover Vogue involved.

Making the most of his discomfort, the *Daily Mirror* tracked down singer Toby Bourke to Ireland, where he talked about recording 'Waltz Away Dreaming' with George back in 1997: 'He was stoned all the time. It was pretty much a haze of dope the whole way through the recording sessions.' Apparently, George was getting through at least twenty potent skunk joints a day, all prepared for him by a 'lackey' and kept in a Marlboro box.

While the interview was treated in a sensational way, Toby

did share a genuine concern among people outside looking in that George needed proper help. He observed sadly, 'Drugs have turned him into a stoned waster and made him depressed.'

Andros Georgiou also gave an interview in which he revealed that he rolled the spliffs for George in the studio and that they had been 'smokers of spliffs for twenty years'. He also claimed that the reason his cousin was by himself during those driving incidents and not chauffeur-driven was that he was cruising: 'That's what he does. That is a big part of his life.'

George was back on form, joking and on the offensive when he went on *Parkinson* the following week to announce his world tour. He made the audience laugh as he explained that both driving incidents had been blown out of all proportion. In the first, he had simply fallen asleep at traffic lights. In the second, it was a parking accident as he tried to manoeuvre his car out of a space on a steep hill.

The incidents certainly guaranteed that the tour would be newsworthy. It would celebrate his silver jubilee as a pop star and would coincide with the release of an album called *Twenty Five*. Initially there would be about fifty dates in Europe and he felt that, despite what he'd said in the past, he would enjoy it this time. His fans cared nothing about any adverse publicity and the British dates for the *25 Live* tour sold out in two hours.

You could be forgiven for thinking that George's life was dominated by drugs, cruising and inappropriate driving, but, for the most part, he and Kenny continued as normal. They held a baby shower for Geri, who was expecting her first baby with Sacha Gervasi. Kenny was godfather when her daughter Bluebell was born and they invited the new mum to stay with them for as long as she liked.

George watched comedian David Walliams swim the Channel in aid of Sport Relief and the next day donated £50,000. The problem was that while his acts of kindness went unreported – often because of his insistence on anonymity – he kept on giving the media an open goal.

The paparazzi would not leave him alone. While it wasn't on the scale of the hounding of Princess Diana, he was followed onto Hampstead Heath by photographers who snapped him coming out of the bushes at a well-known cruising spot. George told them to fuck off and shouted angrily, 'I'm not doing illegal. I'm a free man. I can do whatever I want. I'm not harming anyone.'

The *News of the World* tracked down a fifty-eight-year-old unemployed man and alleged he had an assignation with George. Kenny, who was in London at the time, had to face up to reporters banging on the front door of their Highgate home. He told them George would not be making any statement: 'This is behind us. That is everything we are going to say on the subject. We are getting on with the rest of our lives.'

George did have more to say when he rang Richard and Judy on their new Channel 4 talk show. He said, again, that he was not ashamed of cruising and had no issues with it. He was upset at untrue reports that Kenny had called off the wedding. He told the hosts that they had just celebrated their tenth anniversary together: 'Kenny is fine. We're fantastic.'

The media it seemed were seriously out of step with the general public, who loved George and turned his tour into the most successful in the world during 2006/7. He ended up playing 106 shows in 41 countries and grossing $200 million.

The opening show in Barcelona met with universal approval and set the tone pretty much for the entire tour. *The Independent* pointed out that even 'Shoot the Dog' worked a treat live. For someone so reluctant to tour, George devised a two-hour show that featured him in the spotlight for two hours with none of the pyrotechnics that were so fashionable. 'I'm going to be less of a showman and more of a singer,' he declared.

When the show came to Manchester, Alexis Petridis thought it would remind audiences about his 'music rather than his drugs and cottaging, and what you might charitably call his unique interpretation of the Highway Code'. George received an almighty scream from the crowd when he said the album *Twenty Five* was expected to be number one. 'Yeah,' he shouted back. 'Fuck 'em.'

Twenty Five did indeed go to number one. On its release in November 2006, George announced that he would play a free concert for NHS nurses at The Roundhouse in Camden Town. He had made a promise to his family that if he ever toured again he would perform for nurses as a thank you for the wonderful care they had given his mother.

Applicants for tickets had to give their NHS registration number and were then entered into a draw. The lucky 2,000 were treated to a concert at a venue much smaller than the stadiums and arenas the singer had been playing. He did fifteen songs, including 'Last Christmas', especially for them and said between songs, 'This room is full of heroes. Thank you to every single one of you. I salute you.'

Afterwards, a ward sister from Cheshire said happily, 'He's made me feel so special and valued tonight.'

21

CONVICTION

He should have been celebrating the triumph of his home-coming shows, but instead George Michael was sat in Colindale police station, North London, listening to the arresting office charge him. He had again been discovered slumped and asleep at the wheel of his Mercedes. This time he was blocking traffic at lights on Cricklewood Lane, ten minutes from home. It was 3.20am.

He received a caution for possessing cannabis and bailed on suspicion of being unfit to drive. Kenny was at home and told reporters he was fine before they left the next morning to take a private plane to his concert in Lyon.

George followed his well-tried policy of being interviewed about his latest scrape with the law. He told Melvin Bragg, the genial host of *The South Bank Show*, that he was enjoying his life, and smoked a joint in front of the cameras. He declared, 'This stuff keeps me sane and happy', although he did concede that it was not very healthy, especially if you have anything to do.

The problem was that he was giving the media a stick with which to beat or poke fun at him. If he had been struggling with a heroin addiction, he would have received more sympathy and understanding. Instead, a review of his new single 'This Is Not Real Love', an enchanting duet with Mutya Buena, the former Sugababes singer, described him as a 'weedhead'.

At least the concert reviewers remained impressed. Tim de Lisle in *The Mail on Sunday* thought his performance at Earls Court in December 2006 was 'top class' but made a thoughtful point: 'George Michael has turned into two people: the cannabis smoker who insists on taking his car into the West End late at night, and the confident live performer who has returned from a fifteen-year exile with all his powers intact.'

In Dublin, Kenny and his family were joined by Tracey Emin when he appeared at The Point. She could not believe how joyful the whole experience was, especially when George pointed over to them and shouted, 'This song's for Kenny, Kenny the love of my life.' He then sang 'Amazing'.

George's driving charge eventually came to court. Blood tests had revealed a cocktail of liquid ecstasy, cannabis, sleeping tablets and antidepressants. His solicitor told the court that his condition on the night was due to prescribed drugs and tiredness as opposed to illegal drugs. In a typically honest interview with Michael Parkinson, George admitted, 'I know I have a very self-destructive tendency.' He acknowledged his dependency on prescribed drugs for his 'constant insomnia' and admitted once more that marijuana was his drug of choice.

The day before he was due to play the first-ever gig at the new Wembley Stadium, George appeared at Brent Magistrates Court for sentencing. He was given one hundred hours of community service and banned from driving for two years. Afterwards, he called the media coverage 'farcical' and said, 'I have been sentenced today on the basis of unfit driving through tiredness and prescription medicines, which I fully accept responsibility for. I am glad to put this behind me and now I'm off to do the biggest show of my life.'

The concert was a landmark event for George. He was chosen above all artists to launch a new era at the iconic venue. *The Guardian* approved: 'When the history of the new Wembley is written, this will be remembered as a worthy opener by someone fast approaching national treasure status.'

George appeared for the first time on the long-running radio show, *Desert Island Discs*, in 2007 and reinforced his position that he had been done for sleeping pills and not other drugs. Amusingly, for his luxury object he chose his Aston Martin DB9 because there would be nobody on the island to know he didn't have a licence. 'I'm obsessed with cars,' he told presenter Kirsty Young, 'and for the next two years I am not going to get to drive one.'

For his book, he asked for a collection of short stories by the revered novelist Doris Lessing, who the same year had won the Nobel Prize for Literature. 'I am not going to take a jolly book,' explained George. His castaway's favourite record was the melancholic 'Love Is a Losing Game' by Amy Winehouse, whom he praised, saying, 'This is the best female vocalist I have heard in my entire life.' He thought the troubled singer needed support because she was a fantastic talent. 'Please understand how brilliant you are,' he said. Amy was twenty-seven when she died from alcohol poisoning in 2011. 'Love Is a Losing Game' was her last single release.

George's use of prescription drugs mirrored the problems that had plagued his partner Kenny. The factor in this drama that George kept hidden from the public was that he and Kenny were no longer helping each other. Amy's mournful record could have been their song; they were in a dysfunctional relationship. His partner continued to battle a dependence on alcohol. They were literally as bad as each other, except with different addictions. Their friends were worried for them. One recalls, 'They got to a stage where it was combustive. It really was. I think there was probably denial on both sides. You know the sort of thing – "You're alleging I'm this." "No, I'm not." "Yes, you are." They were both as bad as each other in terms of their intake.'

Kenny did his best to help, flushing down the toilet any drugs he found around the house, hoping that George wouldn't notice because his prolonged use of marijuana had made him rather absent-minded. That did not mean, however, that they sat around every day drunk and stoned. Kenny took his work very seriously. The Goss Gallery had become the Goss-Michael Foundation, helping young artists flourish, as well as raising money for causes close to their hearts. They supported programmes combating hunger and starvation in the Third World, as well as HIV prevention.

They raised millions for the MTV Staying Alive programme, which aimed to empower and educate young people about the dangers of HIV. George shared its vision of a world where no young person contracts HIV or dies of AIDS. Kenny explained the simple philosophy: 'We give money back and we help people. That was George's deal.' From being a commercial enterprise, the Foundation became a non-profit organisation and a significant player on the international art scene. Over the years, their formidable collection of works by YBA (Young British Artists) would grow to more than 500, worth many millions.

For his part, George was fully occupied with the tour and completing his community service, which was not a chore in any way. He worked at a centre in Camden for the homeless – something he would have found worthwhile whatever the circumstances. He cleaned rooms and cooked for the first time in his life. He made chicken fajitas, which were a great success. These days he had two housekeepers on his payroll and he had obviously been paying attention when they were in the kitchen. Most of all, he enjoyed talking to people about their problems, especially those addressing mental health issues. He dressed simply as he always did – in jeans, trainers and a baseball cap. One resident remarked, 'He was down to earth, a good man.'

The success of the tour gave George the confidence to be in the public eye a little more. He didn't mind sending himself up either. He appeared in the hilarious Christmas special of the Ricky Gervais comedy, *Extras*, in a sketch set on a 'queer bench' on Hampstead Heath. George, as himself, rolls up, smoking a joint and eating a kebab, and asks Andy Millman (Ricky) and camp friend Bunny, 'Any action?' George only has twenty minutes, as he is on a lunch break from community service, picking up litter. He tells Andy to keep a lookout for paparazzi as he disappears into the shrubbery.

He again played himself in American TV comedy-drama *Eli Stone*, starring a youthful Jonny Lee Miller, who plays the title character, an attorney whose life is thrown into disarray when he begins to suffer hallucinations. He keeps seeing and hearing George Michael, who appeared in several episodes as himself. He acted a little and sang 'Faith', 'Older' and 'Feeling Good'. The series was short-lived but it did reveal a friendlier, more natural side to George ahead of his first North American tour since 1991.

George genuinely didn't know what to expect, but his reception there was wildly enthusiastic and affectionate. The audience at the Los Angeles Forum sang 'Happy Birthday' to him. In Vancouver, Charlie Smith reviewed his performance for *The Georgia Straight* newspaper: 'George Michael is remarkably honest, sincere, lacking in pretentiousness and ego – a true gentleman, which runs contrary to the tabloid rubbish that so many of us consume like imbeciles.' Charlie had gone to the concert expecting it to be some sort of festival for his city's gay community. Instead, he observed, 'The women at this show *love* him. It's a love that appears to run deeper than I've seen at other shows.'

George came back to London for two nights at Earls Court that were billed as *The Final Two* concerts. He told the audience he would be releasing a Christmas song for charity. He ended his 'goodbye' show with a wave, said, 'See you next time', and was gone. The *Daily Mirror* said he radiated 'sheer joy'.

The following month he was arrested yet again at a toilet on Hampstead Heath when he was found to be in possession of a class A and a class C drug – crack cocaine and cannabis. This time he received a caution and the police said they would take no further action. He issued an apology for 'screwing up again' and promised to 'sort myself out'. It was clearly becoming a recurrent theme.

George was rumoured to be the front runner for the Lifetime Achievement Award at the BRITs of 2009 but that unconfirmed idea was quietly dropped. In the end, the award was given to the Pet Shop Boys. George never received it.

He released 'December Song' in time for Christmas that year, putting into practice an idea he had wanted to try for a long time: you could download the song for free and were invited to make a charitable donation. He had originally written it with David Austin for the Spice Girls as part of their reunion tour the previous year. Kenny played it to Geri Halliwell and their manager, Simon Fuller. They were keen but George didn't finish it in time.

He decided to record it himself. In his hands, the song was sweet and soft but not sentimental as he wished for all your New Year dreams to come true. While it would never become a classic in the manner of 'Last Christmas', the song was infinitely more interesting lyrically.

George had been able to take it easy since the tour finished. Most mornings he would get up late and start the day with a coffee from Starbucks fetched by one of his staff. He kept an office at the house in Highgate, where he would check emails and do some work if he felt like it. More often than not he would just bounce around on a gym ball, spliff in hand, talking to whoever was around about random events. Then he might retire to catch some daytime TV.

On one memorable occasion he was watching *Deal or No Deal* when one of the contestants, a young woman from Lancashire, told how she had been struggling to conceive using expensive IVF treatment. She and her partner needed

£9,000 to continue. The next day, George rang the programme and gave her the money anonymously.

While he could change other people's lives for the better, his own was not going so well. George and Kenny were on the verge of splitting up. They went to counselling to try and resolve their problems and the psychiatrist encouraged them to stay together, but in the end they just drifted away from one another. Kenny was already spending six months of the year in Dallas and no one else was involved. It was the end of what Kenny would call a 'really good, sweet relationship'.

For many years, Kenny had been a reassuring presence in his life but now they just seemed to be dragging each other down even further. Unlike Elton and David Furnish, they never did enter into a civil partnership or subsequent marriage. George had never wanted children. He once said he thought he would be a good dad but would be too neurotic – he would be worrying about them all the time. They didn't have those traditional bonds that sometimes keep couples together.

All George's friends loved Kenny, and would continue to do so. Perhaps they were too similar – gentle, shy men who had faced many years coming to terms with their sexuality and who needed help to beat their addictions. Kenny went back to the US to live. At home there, he would still listen to his favourite George song, 'A Different Corner', and think fondly of the man he called the love of his life.

Kenny managed to complete a successful recovery programme for his alcohol dependence while George battled on alone, despite many friends urging him to seek professional help. David Furnish appeared on the Victoria Derbyshire radio programme and said that George's friends often phoned up, saying, 'You have to do something. George is in a bad way, he's in a bad state.'

David observed, 'George has to want to help himself. If he wants help, we are here for him. If he doesn't want help that's fine, that's his choice, too.' But George was none too impressed with the prospect of help from Elton, who was now *Sir* Elton John: 'He will not be happy until I bang on his door in the middle of the night saying, "Please, please help me, Elton. Take me to rehab." It's not going to happen.'

On a day-to-day basis he seemed content jogging along with life. Without Kenny around, he didn't eat out so much, although his sister Melanie lived across the road and ran her own bijou gift shop on Highgate West Hill. Kenny would come and visit from time to time, which gave people the wrong impression that they were still together, especially when they were seen in restaurants. They managed to keep their separation secret for more than two years, which at least spared George the agony of being asked about it incessantly.

Kenny was not with him when he crashed his Range Rover into the front of Snappy Snaps in Rosslyn Hill, Hampstead, in 2010. There was nothing he could say afterwards to justify or mitigate what had happened. Apparently, he had spent the day at the Gay Pride celebrations in Central London and was driving between his Highgate and Hampstead homes. It was 3.35am. Once more, he was found by police slumped across the steering wheel.

When it came to court, George admitted driving under the influence of cannabis. He said he had smoked a small quantity of the drug and taken a sleeping pill. The judge immediately banned him from driving and told him, 'I make it clear all options remain open including powers to imprison. It is a serious matter. Your driving was extremely poor and there was an accident.'

In the three weeks between the proceedings and sentencing, George at last entered a detox programme. In an open letter to his fans he wrote: 'Personal problems which I had tried to deal with myself had clearly got the better of me, and I am sorry that my pride has prevented me from seeking help before now.'

Kenny flew over to support him at Highbury Magistrates Court. His defence barrister, Mukul Chawla, QC, said, 'It is no exaggeration to describe him as a very kind, considerate and loyal man, constantly concerned for the plight of others. The prospect he could have put anyone else in danger is an appalling prospect for him.'

District Judge John Perkins issued him with a five-year driving ban, a fine of £1,250 and an eight-week prison sentence. The judge told George, who was wearing a smart grey pin-stripe suit: 'On this occasion you drove your vehicle about a mile while suffering from a dangerous and unpredictable mix of drugs. Your record is of concern. Despite the resources at your command, it does not appear that you took proper steps to deal with what is clearly an addiction to cannabis. That's a mistake which puts you and, on this occasion, the public at risk.'

George was led away to spend his first night behind bars at Pentonville Prison in North London – ironically a jail much in the news concerning prisoners' drug use. On the second day, Kenny went to see him for a couple of hours and told reporters afterwards, hesitantly, that he seemed to be doing OK.

George abandoned any thoughts of appeal and after three days was transferred to Highpoint Prison in Suffolk. Martin Kemp, who made a point of not talking about George as much as possible, told breakfast television, 'He is one of my best friends and he is the most wonderful man I know, absolutely without a word of a lie, he is fantastic. If you're watching today, George, I hope you're well.' While inside, George was delighted to receive 'lovely' letters from Elton John, Paul McCartney and even Boy George, who had been in Pentonville the previous year after being convicted of imprisoning a male escort.

Most days, George spent by himself, reading the literally thousands of letters of support he received from fans all over the world. Sometimes he would take a break to watch *The Jeremy Kyle Show* or play a game of pool. He made a short statement through his lawyer: 'I have been treated with kindness by fellow inmates and prison officers and, as far as I can tell, have received no special treatment whatsoever – unless some of the guys here are letting me win at the pool table.' He made sure that every member of staff had his autograph before he left.

Kenny – and a chauffeur – collected him from jail and drove him home to Highgate at the end of his sentence. He served twenty-seven days. He came out to speak to the news crews waiting outside. 'It's a beautiful day,' he said. Reflecting on what had happened, George was able to rationalise the experience by saying that he deserved it: 'It's so much easier to take any form of punishment if you believe you actually deserve it.' Unsurprisingly, he did not want to go back to prison.

The ordeal did not lead to a great creative rush, however. He released a version of the New Order song 'True Faith' for Comic Relief in 2011, but it sold poorly, peaking at number twenty-seven on the UK chart. Much more successful was his appearance in a sketch with comedian James Corden, which became the prototype for the hugely successful 'Carpool Karaoke'.

He once more displayed his ability for self-deprecating humour. James, in character as Smithy from the sitcom *Gavin & Stacey*, has to go to the Comic Relief offices to try and save Red Nose Day. George wants to go too but James says he can't possibly walk in with him: 'Comic Relief is about help-ing people like you.' George sulks until they turn on the radio and it's 'I'm Your Man', and they both sing along exuberantly in the car – something he actually used to do in the old days. Then, for good measure, they sing 'Freedom'. George was being a good sport.

When James began his second career in the US as host of *The Late Late Show*, he tried to persuade stars to take part in the Carpool Karaoke segment but received a lukewarm response until he sent Mariah Carey the tape of himself and George. She agreed immediately and told him, 'If it's good enough for George then it's good enough for me.'

He was evidently getting some of his sparkle back, as demonstrated after Jeremy Clarkson had a dig at his sexual promiscuity. George tweeted that he was a 'pig ugly homo-phobic twat!!!'

While he was not ready to release a whole album of new material, he was energised enough to announce another tour

– something he hadn't planned at all after the demanding *25 Live*. This was a grand project, featuring George, his band and singers, and the Symphonica Orchestra, which in effect was the Czech National Symphony Orchestra.

During the first concert at the State Opera House in Prague in August 2011, he introduced emotionally a new song called 'Where I Hope You Are', disclosing for the first time that he and Kenny had split. He had never sung it in public before and wanted the world to know the background of a song that was clearly autobiographical, as were so many of his. He acknowledged that Kenny had fought his own terrible battles with alcohol that were 'the scariest thing I have ever seen.'

He continued, 'I am so sorry for any pain I have caused him although he is cool about that. I am so sorry things have worked out the way they have. But in truth Kenny and I have not been together for about two and a half years and all I can say is that I love him very much, but sometimes people should know when their demons are more interested in each other than they are.'

He wanted to be honest about what had happened: 'My love life has been a lot more turbulent than I have let on.' The song was almost too personal, an apology to a man he loved very much, that he shared haltingly with the audience. The concert itself wasn't relentlessly sad, but another highlight was a version of 'Love Is a Losing Game', which he sang as a tribute to Amy Winehouse who had died the previous month. *The Mail on Sunday* said the show was 'distinctly melancholic, and all the better for it. His finest songs are marked by a profound and almost tangible sadness, without which his oeuvre wouldn't be half what it is.'

His much-publicised spat with Elton John was completely forgotten when George played a one-off concert at the Royal Albert Hall that raised nearly £1 million for Elton's AIDS Foundation. As Elton himself watched approvingly from the audience, his faultless vocal performance that night would form the basis of George's only live album.

The tour could not have been going any better when, after forty-five dates, George fell ill in Vienna in late November 2011. He was struggling to breathe after he checked into the Hotel Imperial. At first it seemed like a bad chest infection and he went for a lie-down, but it was much worse than that.

George was rushed by ambulance to hospital with a virulent strain of pneumonia – streptococcus pneumoniae bacterium. He was in a coma and needed an emergency tracheotomy to help him breathe. For a couple of weeks, it was, he later said, 'touch and go'.

22

INTO THE WHITE LIGHT

Georgios Panayiotou left the safety of his Highgate home, dressed in a long dark overcoat and grey woolly scarf, to face the world as George Michael and tell the reporters and the TV crews waiting outside how he had nearly died. He stood in front of a large Christmas tree in the little green across from the house, by himself, with no assistants or bodyguards to shield him. He was a vulnerable man, grateful to be alive.

George had been lucky to be in Vienna when he fell ill because the city's AKH hospital was one of the best in the world for treating his illness. He was clearly still very weak and struggling for breath as he tried to keep his emotions in check and thank those that had saved his life.

He admitted that he had just endured 'by far the worst month of my life' but now felt 'amazing'. He said, 'I am incredibly fortunate to be here.' Thoughts of his family and all the people he still wanted to play for had kept him going in the darkest hours. 'I have plenty to live for. If I wasn't spiritual enough before the last four or five weeks then I certainly am now.'

He was tearful but managed to prevent himself from breaking down when he concluded, 'I have spent the last ten days thanking people for saving my life. I have never had to do it before and never want to have to do it again.'

He hoped everyone had enjoyed the mince pies he had brought out and wished the crowd a very merry Christmas before retreating back to the safety of his home. It was a brave performance, one that made you want to put your arm around him and sit him down in a comfy chair by the fire with a blanket and a cup of hot chocolate.

The splendid Christmas tree he stood in front of was one he paid for every year as part of the anonymous donations he made towards making the festive celebration special for the local community. He was the biggest private sponsor of the annual 'Fair in the Square', the highlight of holiday time in Highgate Village.

He was just pleased to be home for Christmas. This year he could share it with the new man in his life, a very handsome, strapping Australian called Fadi Fawaz, who'd been a constant presence at the hospital while George was battling his illness. He even issued bulletins to reporters about the patient's progress. They were quick to call him George's boyfriend.

Fadi liked to tweet what was going on and happily wrote that George would be home in time for Christmas: 'I cannot stop smiling today, the best day ever. He is getting better and better. Nothing to worry about, happy days.'

George had been unable to publicly acknowledge Fadi while the world still thought he was with Kenny. Now that he had revealed the painful truth about their break-up, he could at least be seen with someone else without snide headlines implying there was something untoward going on.

George had met Fadi, who was ten years younger than him and originally from the Lebanon, when he stayed in Sydney during his short *Live in Australia* tour in early 2010. He played three concerts in Perth, Sydney and Melbourne that grossed $15 million. Those lucky enough to see one of these thought he had never been more brilliant.

During his short time there, George had loved Australia. He had been there a few times before, during the mad Wham! days, and the *Faith World Tour* that he'd found so stressful. After finishing his concert commitments, he stayed on in Sydney, enjoying the sun and the lively nightlife without his every move appearing in the papers. He bought a beachfront mansion in Palm Beach, one of the exclusive areas to the north of the city, for $5.8 million. As ever, it was a magnificent house and a shrewd investment.

Fadi was taller than George, with a ready smile and an affable personality. His family lived in Brisbane but he had travelled to Sydney as a young man to seek work. Newspapers would later suggest that he had made a porn film, but he denied this. He certainly worked as a hairdresser before becoming interested in interior design and fine art photography.

After a quiet Christmas getting his strength back, George was well enough to go on holiday to the Maldives and then on to the house in Sydney. He and Fadi looked like any other couple in the sun, holding hands as they walked along the waterfront and posing for photographs in front of the Opera House. George didn't hide away and they went out to eat at a number of popular restaurants and hired a boat to cruise around the harbour before docking for some serious sun bathing. George seemed very relaxed and happy, recovering much quicker than expected.

He showed everyone that he was in better shape when he made his first proper public appearance at the BRITs in February 2012 to present Adele with the premier award for MasterCard British Album of the Year. George rather stumbled through his introduction, but that was overshadowed by Adele being cut off in the middle of her thank you speech by host James Corden because they were running short of time. She flipped the finger to a table of executives as she left the stage.

The newspapers next day ignored George and concentrated on the controversy surrounding Adele. At least he had demonstrated that he was recovering well. Understandably, the rest of the *Symphonica* tour had been cancelled for the time being, but he was working again − his near-death experience had inspired him to write a new song called 'White Light'. He planned to perform it for the first time at the closing ceremony for the Olympics in London in August. The lyric was about a man at the crossroads of life and death, keeping breathing while a God decides if this is his day. In the end, he declares joyfully that he wants to live: 'I'm Alive.'

'White Light' was a hypnotic dance track and not, as fans might have expected, one of his more dramatic ballads. The video began dramatically with a ventilator and a man lying on a stretcher. George's lifetime fascination with models continued with many shots of his neighbour Kate Moss at her most stunning. For once, though, George held centre stage, a man singing from the heart.

At the Olympics, he probably would have pleased millions if he had performed 'Wake Me Up Before You Go-Go' followed by 'Careless Whisper'. Instead, he sang 'Freedom! '90' followed by 'White Light', which nobody really knew. These songs were more important to him emotionally. Afterwards, he held one of his fabulous parties in the garden of his home, playing host to many stars, including Liam Gallagher and all the Spice Girls except Posh. Geri had given him a puppy to celebrate his recovery.

He resumed the tour at the beginning of September back in Vienna, where he gave a thousand tickets to the staff at the AKH hospital. He was the same performer, except that his dark suit was now adorned with a very large crucifix. His voice, it seemed, had been unaffected by the trauma he'd faced. In Paris he gave an inspired performance at the Palais Garnier opera house, a venue steeped in a classical music tradition. George had first noticed the building many years before in his early twenties. He'd been spellbound by its glorious architecture, but never dreamed he might appear there one day.

His concert in the French capital was in support of the French AIDS charity, Sidaction. He was also guest of honour afterwards at a fundraising dinner. The evening was subsequently made into a documentary in which he paid tribute to Phil Ramone, who'd given George some of his happiest days in a recording studio. He called him a 'wonderful man' and the 'most accomplished producer of the twentieth century'.

George had resumed the tour in fine voice, which was a relief to his fans. The *Birmingham Mail* said after his show in that city, 'The hits oozed like warm honey. His pitch-perfect voice is, if anything, richer than it was in his heyday.'

The first indication that all was not well with George came in the autumn, when he cancelled the planned tour dates in Australia. The strain had taken its toll on him: 'I was wrong to think I could work my way through the major anxiety that has plagued me since I left Austria last December.' He decided that after the set of British concerts, he would receive the 'treatment which is so long overdue'. He performed live for the last time at London's Earls Court on 17 October 2012.

Georgios Panayiotou, it seemed, was not as tough as George Michael, and he never really recovered. He disappeared from view amid rumours that he was receiving treatment for his anxiety at a rehab centre. Dramatically, he reappeared, being airlifted to hospital after an incident on the M1 near St Albans. He never properly explained what happened when he fell out of the passenger seat of his silver Range Rover and ended up on the carriageway.

Drivers in the cars following managed to miss him. Somehow he escaped with a few cuts to his face and various bruises. Fadi said he was 'perfectly fine' but knew nothing about the accident. A motorist, who had slammed on her brakes and stopped, said one of the other passengers in the car had told her that George had been trying to shut his door, which was open, when he fell out.

George spoke to the police, who decided that after taking statements no further action would be taken. He then completely disappeared from view, keeping out of sight behind the doors of his Highgate home. Fadi was there and David Austin was at his side to help him through the days, but there were no interview or TV appearances. He announced his next album would be called *Symphonica* and that he had worked behind the scenes with Phil Ramone to perfect a live album that sounded like it was made in the studio.

Phil had sadly died in March 2013 and *Symphonica* was the last album he would ever work on. George was 'heartbroken' that he was not alive to see what they had accomplished together. The singer kept a very low profile when the album was finally released the following year. He hadn't been well enough to sign off on everything before then. He even missed the launch at the Hamiltons Gallery in Mayfair when the press were given a first listen and could also inspect the exclusive photographs taken by his friend, Caroline True. She had first met him on the set of the *Fastlove* video when she was working for the Virgin record company, and it was thanks to George that she changed careers from music to photography.

While the album was a curious mix of live and studio, the critics liked it. *The Guardian* said his voice still sounded 'incredible throughout', while pointing out that it had been a decade since *Patience*. Caroline Sullivan wrote, 'he can croon the stuffing out of the most well-worn covers.' The album reached number one in the UK, so more than served its purpose of reminding people that George was still a major artist.

The recordings were, in effect, more than two years old, and the reality of George's life was better illustrated when he was rushed to hospital again after falling ill at home in Highgate. His loyal spokeswoman, Connie Filippello, who had been with him practically all his professional life, said he was 'well and resting' after he was discharged, but declined to say what the matter was.

Privately, friends were concerned and David Austin came to stay in the house in Highgate to make sure he was all right.

While his neighbours thought George had turned into a recluse, he had in fact slipped quietly out of the country and flown to Switzerland. He was finally persuaded that it would be best if he spent some time at an exclusive addiction treatment centre, and Fadi Fawaz, who he referred to as his 'better half', dutifully flew out to be with him in Zurich. George spent the best part of a year at the treatment centre called the Kusnacht Practice, which apparently cost as much as £190,000 a month.

George had clearly put on weight when he was pictured out and about in the city, holding hands with Fadi. Eventually they moved into an apartment while George continued as an outpatient. The only public statement he made was via Twitter in response to a story in the newspapers in which Jackie Georgiou, his cousin's ex-wife, was quoted in *The Sun*: 'He was smoking crack. Before he went away he got to the point where he would be shaking, saying "I need it".' She added that 'it was pretty dark and getting darker'.

George responded, 'To my lovelies, do not believe this rubbish in the papers by someone I haven't see for nearly eighteen years. I am perfectly fine. Love, The Singing Greek.'

When he came back to England, he decided to move full-time into the house in Goring, which was quieter and freer from the temptations that plagued him in London. Villagers barely saw him. Occasionally, he would walk his dogs or have a meal out with David or Fadi, who stayed in London at a mews house George owned near Regent's Park.

Some days, George would travel to the house in Highgate to check all was well there and perhaps have a visit from his osteopath, who had been treating him for thirty years for the natural wear and tear that resulted from performing on stage. He had come through the worst of his addictions and was looking forward to working properly again. There was talk of a collaboration with the fashionable producer Naughty Boy and also of a new documentary about his life called *Freedom*.

He still loved seeing friends and had invited those closest to him, including Martin and Shirlie Kemp, to Goring to wish them a happy Christmas. George enjoyed the holiday time but it was still a sombre few days for him, remembering his mother Lesley, whose birthday fell on Christmas Eve.

The day after, on Christmas Day 2016, Michael Lippman, who had returned as George's manager, issued a statement on behalf of the family at 11pm: 'It is with great sadness that we can confirm our beloved son, brother and friend George passed away peacefully at home over the Christmas period. The family would ask that their privacy be respected at this difficult and emotional time. There will be no further comment at this stage.'

Somebody famous always seems to die on Christmas Day but George Michael was a complete shock. He was only fifty-three. He had been discovered dead in bed by Fadi Fawaz on Christmas morning.

Conspiracy theorists and the press wildly speculated that his death was drug-related or that he had committed suicide, but it would subsequently turn out that he died of natural causes. Michael Lippman said that there was no question of foul play and that he had died of heart failure. Fadi was overcome, tweeting: 'It's a Xmas I will never forget, finding your partner dead peacefully in bed first thing in the morning. I will never stop missing you.'

He had made the 999 call, telling the emergency services that he had found George and had tried to revive him but he was dead. The police confirmed that there would be a post-mortem because the death was unexplained – although there were no suspicious circumstances.

George's sister Melanie had called Kenny Goss at home in the US to break the news. He spoke eloquently: 'I'm heart-broken by news that my dear friend and long-time love George Michael has passed. He was a major part of my life and I loved him very, very much. He was an extremely kind and generous man. The beautiful memories and music he brought will always be an important part of my life and those who loved and admired him.'

Kathy Jeung, who has never spoken of her time with George, tweeted, 'I can barely encompass in words what George means to me. I treasured our special friendship – to just scratch the surface with no exaggeration, he was the most generous, hilarious, brilliant, talented true friend. For now I'll just say, I love you Yog.'

Andrew Ridgeley said he was 'heartbroken at the loss of my beloved friend Yog'. George's family took a day or two to compose themselves after the shock. Connie Filippello issued a statement for them: 'Contrary to some reports, there were no suspicious circumstances surrounding his death, and from the bottom of our hearts we thank those who, rightly, have chosen to celebrate his life and legacy at this difficult time.'

The family were horrified when a transcript of Fadi's 999 call was leaked to the press, a recording they called 'personal, painful and clearly confidential'. Much was made by the media of the fact that Fadi had apparently slept in his car outside the house and only discovered George when he went inside to wake him up. That was a red herring because George always preferred to sleep alone and would have been discovered dead by whoever went to wake him.

As well as the celebrity tributes and those from distraught fans, the true extent of George's generosity and philanthropy gradually became apparent. Kenny said that George had given away tens of millions of pounds, and that was only the donations he knew about. George supported well-known organisations but it was the smaller acts of kindness that touched a nerve with the public when they were discovered. He once overheard a student nurse in a bar worried sick about her debts. He calmly wrote out a cheque for £6,000 and left it for her.

The inquiries into his death dragged on, meanwhile, which was especially hard on those seeking closure. The first post-mortem apparently proved inconclusive. Every newspaper seemed to have a 'source' who could offer inside information on George's state of mind. Shirlie Kemp, who actually was a friend, said he had been 'laughing' and 'happy' the last time she'd seen him and that her family had been looking forward to seeing him over the holiday.

While the formal inquiries into his death continued, there was a chance for public tributes to be paid. At the Grammys, Adele, who the family had particularly asked for, sang a slow, bluesy version of 'Fastlove' in front of video clips of George projected onto a large screen. She fluffed the opening and stopped, saying, 'I can't mess this up for him.' Second time around she was perfect.

At the BRITs, Chris Martin performed 'A Different Corner' with an orchestra. He may not have had the clear angelic tones of George Michael, but he brought a powerful emotion to the song that won a standing ovation. Andrew, Shirlie and Pepsi paid tribute to a man they loved. They all spoke beautifully of their friend, but Andrew summed up his legacy: 'George has left for us in his songs, in the transcendental beauty of his voice and in the poetic expression of his soul, the very best of himself.'

And still there was no cause of death. Andrew said afterwards that everyone was in limbo, waiting to be able to move on and they had not had closure.

George's cousin Andros rather stirred things up by declaring in a national newspaper that Fadi Fawaz would not be invited to the funeral because the 'family hate him'. Fadi was unimpressed: 'That someone who is saying all this rubbish about the funeral has not been part of George's life for nineteen years. Can we cut the crap now for once and for all? Let's have some respect for George (the poor man). George's family are very loving, respectful and decent people, there is nothing more to say.'

Finally, on 7 March 2017, the coroner confirmed that George had died of natural causes. The official cause of death was given as dilated cardiomyopathy with myocarditis and a fatty liver. In other words, he died of heart disease. Alcohol or drug abuse over a period of time could be a factor in a fatty liver. The weakness caused by his pneumonia might also have played a part. In some ways George was unlucky: if he had collapsed outside a hospital then there was a possibility he might have been saved. But he was sleeping peacefully in his bed and so nobody knew.

Kenny Goss was of the opinion that George's body had just given up on him, which was probably about right. The coroner decided there was no need for an inquest. Fadi was relieved the findings were now public: 'I have managed for five years not to be famous. I would like to go back to that. Every day it has just been horrible.'

The funeral of Georgios Kyriacos Panayiotou took place at Highgate Cemetery at midday on 29 March 2017. The details were kept secret just as they had been for his mother, Lesley. It had been thirty-six days since the death of George Michael had shocked the world and now his family and friends had the chance to say goodbye to the man, not the legend. A place next to his mum had been prepared in a private part of the cemetery away from the public trails.

There was no solemn funeral procession and no more than fifty people walked quietly into the church to say goodbye to Yog, as many of them knew him. They were not famous people. Martin Kemp and his wife Shirlie were an exception, but the great majority were his family, close friends and the loyal staff who had been with him for many years.

Kenny Goss flew over from the US and Fadi Fawaz was the last to arrive. He was a little late, causing consternation among those already seated. Andrew Ridgeley was there but Geri Halliwell – now Geri Horner – and Kate Moss, who would have been celebrity distractions, politely stayed away. Ironically, George's cousin Andros was the one who was not invited and he did not attend. As one friend of George observes, 'That particular rift was never healed.'

Melanie had organised a simple, normal service to be followed by tea and sandwiches back at his house. His two sisters sat by their father in the front row, together with their thoughts and memories. Mel, as George called her, gave the principal address about a much-loved brother. One of the mourners saying goodbye remembers, 'The church was filled with many people who loved him dearly. There was a mixture of tears and smiles. It was absolutely beautiful.'

As they stood to leave and pay their respects to Georgios Panayiotou for the last time, instrumental music drifted around the church. It was a George Michael song, 'You Have Been Loved'.

ENCORE

Thursday, 7 September 2017

It's unmistakably George. 'Fantasy', the first posthumous George Michael recording, has arrived. Chris Evans had the exclusive, playing it on his Radio 2 breakfast show just after 8am. It's very catchy. Perhaps it's a disappointment if you were hoping for a soaring ballad that showed off one of the greatest voices of all time. Instead, it's a 'retro' disco-influenced track from the late 1980s that didn't make the final cut for *Listen Without Prejudice Vol. 1*.

That period was a particularly creative time in George's career and I can understand how this song never quite sat comfortably on an album that contained such sublime compositions as 'Praying for Time', 'Mother's Pride' and 'Freedom! '90'. It doesn't set the same lyrical challenge.

According to David Austin, who has taken over the role of manager of the singer's professional affairs since his death, George wanted to release 'Fantasy' as one of the lead singles for the album, but 'somehow the track got lost in the ether'.

The new version has been put together by Nile Rodgers, the legendary force behind Chic, the disco giants of the seventies. George had asked him in 2016 if he would like to collaborate on some new studio work because, as David Austin said, 'they spoke the same musical language'.

George was a great fan of Chic, dancing enthusiastically as a teenager to their classic hits 'Le Freak' and 'Good Times' when he was a club boy. He even included the latter track as the encore on Wham!'s first UK tour in 1983 when it was the perfect choice to send the fans home happy.

'Fantasy' harks back to carefree days when George would jump on the 142 bus for a night out in London with his girlfriends from school, or with David, Shirlie and Andrew. They were grand times and he liked nothing better than showing off his latest moves. It's easy to picture him hitting the dance floor if 'Fantasy' came on the turntable.

One of the best stories about George dancing away to his own music, as he always did, took place at a party one night around the pool at Chez Nobby in the South of France. George was joined by another famous pop star for some serious showing off to a succession of Wham! hits. It was Robbie Williams, who had just abruptly left Take That in the summer of 1995. Fortunately their joie de vivre was not spoilt by the click of the paparazzi cameras.

George performed 'Fantasy' on the *25 Live* tour and you can hear it on the *Live in London* DVD, recorded at his Earls Court concerts in 2008. His original version is also on the B–side of the US release of 'Freedom! '90' and the UK single 'Waiting for that Day', so it's been around the block. Live, it featured a boisterous brass section that had a much richer sound than the new release.

The purpose of bringing out the single now is to make everyone aware that a remastered *Listen Without Prejudice Vol. 1* and his *MTV Unplugged* performance from 1996 will be out soon, a project George was heavily involved in before he died. Confusingly, his earlier version of 'Fantasy' had already been included in the deluxe reissue of *Faith* in 2011.

Nile Rodgers found working on the new mix after George's death 'extremely emotional'. His trademark guitar sound certainly lends more funk to the original but the BBC Music reviewer thought the track 'felt more like an off-cut than an undiscovered gem'. He also drew attention to the use of speeded-up vocals, which came across as a 'rare mis-step for Rodgers'. *Rolling Stone* was more upbeat and thought it a 'quintessential disco groove' and praised George's 'vigorous vocals'. The *Guardian* said 'Fantasy' was 'a reminder that George Michael could invest a dancefloor with sex and wit like few other pop stars'.

Coincidentally, I did hear a proper undiscovered gem earlier in the summer when a friend played me the earliest recording of 'Rude Boy', made all those years ago by The Executive, George and Andrew's first group. I loved its youthful exuberance and could hear the song in my head being chanted by a terrace of football fans – definitely a big hit.

George's fans were very positive about 'Fantasy' when I checked Twitter, although their happiness at hearing something new was tinged with inevitable sadness. By coincidence, trending at the same time was a campaign launched by Stonewall, the LGBT rights charity much admired by him.

Their initiative entitled 'Come Out for LGBT' was enthusiastically embraced online, with many supporters showing pictures of themselves wearing a T-shirt bearing this slogan. The television host Clare Balding and her wife Alice Arnold held up a mug with those words emblazoned on it. She wrote: 'Love and happiness to anyone who chooses today to come out to parents, friends or colleagues at work.'

It was a decision that tormented George for years, although, as he himself said on many occasions, he was out to the people that mattered to him by the time of the notorious incident in Will Rogers Memorial Park when he was thirty-five. He became a vocal supporter and active ambassador for LBGT rights for the rest of his life.

The following year, in 1999, George performed at a concert celebrating Stonewall's tenth anniversary at the Royal Albert Hall in London. When it was over, the audience were given a promotional record entitled *An Early Xmas Present from George Michael*. It consisted of three superb tracks he had worked on with Phil Ramone for the *Songs from the Last Century* album: 'Secret Love', 'My Baby Just Cares for Me' and 'I Remember You'.

After George's death, Stonewall said, 'George Michael is a musical icon whose visibility and artistry had such a positive influence on the LGBT community.' He would undoubtedly have enthusiastically backed their new campaign, understanding that there was still much to be achieved.

The civilised world is a very different place for the LGBT community today than it was in the 1980s when George was a teenager struggling with his sexuality and the arrival of AIDS cast a long shadow. One of the things I noticed about the newspaper coverage of George after his public outing was the number of times he was referred to as a 'gay' pop star, as if that was a stigma or some sort of handicap. George's definitive word on the subject was unequivocal: 'I never had a moral problem with being gay.'

In another coincidence, 'Fantasy' was released on the same day as the new single by another supreme vocalist, Sam Smith, who brings emotion to a song in a manner that George was always able to do. Sam came out in May 2014, the same month as his debut album, *In the Lonely Hour*, was released. His sexuality didn't matter one bit and has in no way affected his popularity.

Sam has never faced the negativity that George had to put up with and which led him to declare, 'I think the media is a real demon.' Strangely, though, George invariably gave interviewers a great deal of time, taking them seriously and answering questions thoughtfully. It was as if he treated the conversations as a session on the analyst's couch and he was talking through his problems.

Many of his private thoughts, of course, he kept to himself. It seemed as if, in a way, he was trying to protect Georgios by not giving away too much. Sometimes he couldn't help it. He was passionate, kind and a generous spirit. He once admitted that he didn't have the armour for the game he was in. The image of George Michael that he created could protect Georgios – or Yog – only up to a point.

As I write this it's nearly six months since the funeral in late March. Highgate Cemetery is a tranquil and peaceful oasis, the quiet broken only by birds calling and the whirr of lawnmowers keeping the grass looking neat and tidy. It's a popular destination for tourists, but not overrun. There are many trails and paths to wander and perhaps stumble across a gem, such as the grave of novelist George Eliot, comedian Max Wall or the impresario Malcolm McLaren, and the famous tomb of Karl Marx, of course.

They are all on the east side and George is buried on the west, and isn't included in any specially arranged walks. He has his privacy in death. At the top of the hill leading into Highgate Village is the little green, which has become a shrine to George Michael for fans, his 'lovelies' as he called them, visiting from all over the world. It is immaculate. So many of the messages pinned to a favourite picture of George are clearly heartfelt. One said simply, 'Thank you for making my life happier with your music', while another carried the words, 'You brushed my eyes with angels' wings.'

George had his share of sex and drugs but no rock and roll. He was a creator of pure, unadulterated pop and he took it very seriously. So what's his legacy? It's two-fold, I think. Musically, as George Michael, he created a wonderful catalogue. But he was not very prolific – life always seemed to get in the way. In the end, we have just two original Wham! albums and four solo offerings. He released two greatest hits collections, a set of cover versions and a live album.

But almost every George Michel track is memorable. In my opinion, he was the very best British singer of a ballad, a beautiful voice allowing him to convey the melancholy or heartache that so many of his songs demanded. It's not surprising that there are so few covers of his songs because it's hard for any artist to match the original. George liked Mariah Carey's version of 'One More Try' in 2014 and she said she was honoured by his endorsement. But even Mariah, for all her brilliance, cannot convey his vocal anguish.

For me, George is also the very best interpreter of other people's songs. Mainly, he bettered the original; sometimes he merely matched a great vocal, as with the timeless Freddie Mercury classics, Roberta Flack's 'The First Time Ever I Saw Your Face' or 'As' by Stevie Wonder. After Live Aid, when George sang 'Don't Let the Sun Go Down on Me', Elton John observed backstage, 'He's a superb talent and also a great voice – sheesh!' Elton's songs really seemed to suit George and his treatment of the little-known 'Tonight' is among his very finest work.

An onstage collaboration with another great artist is something he never avoided. As well as his acclaimed duet with Elton, George sang with Paul McCartney, Aretha Franklin, Beyoncé and even Pavarotti. One of his finest hours was again performing 'Don't Let the Sun Go Down on Me', this time with the master tenor at one of the Pavarotti & Friends concerts at the Parco Novi Sad in Modena, Italy.

These humanitarian events were for worthwhile causes around the world and in 2000, when George appeared, the beneficiaries were children's charities in Cambodia and Tibet. Pavarotti sings his part in Italian and Elton's timeless classic has never sounded so majestic – truly a hidden gem.

We all have our favourite George Michael songs. For many they represent different stops along life's journey. The one I played after hearing of his death was another he didn't write, the achingly beautiful 'I Can't Make You Love Me'. The lines are almost too sad: 'Here in the dark, in these final hours, I will lay down my heart ...'

The second part of George's legacy is the private world of Georgios Panayiotou, a man who did not want recognition for the thousands he helped through his generosity and patronage. This was the real man of whom George Michael, the superstar, was only a part. His former partner, Kenny Goss, remarked, 'The man on the stage being George Michael was a stranger to me and he didn't like that person. He liked being at home, behind closed doors.'

The defining event of Georgios' life was falling in love with Anselmo Feleppa at the age of twenty-seven and trying to cope with his tragic early death. Losing his beloved mother a few years later shaped his future life. It was something subtly acknowledged in a letter to loyal fans from his sisters Yioda and Melanie on the day 'Fantasy' was released. They sign it from 'Jack, Yioda, Melanie and David ... and Yog, Lesley and Anselmo ... smiling down and all together ...'

George wasn't perfect – thank goodness – but the private man, Georgios, adopted his mother's philosophy of living life, 'hopefully happy without harming anyone or anything'. He saw the world as she did and perhaps that should be our enduring memory of him: 'The worst thing you could do was to be thoughtless of other people.'

GEORGE'S STARS

This is someone whose great creative talent and strong courageous drive towards personal honesty provides a shining beacon to all who would be true to themselves.

Jupiter, planet of wisdom, grace and fortune, is beautifully positioned at the top of the chart and in the crusading sign of Aries. This suggests both professional success and also a desire to engage in matters of fundamental importance to humanity – protecting others, leading them to gain knowledge. Above all, Jupiter here provides a pioneering spirit in terms of the recognition and acceptance of people as individuals.

For many, the journey towards living confidently, baring aspects of themselves that an intolerant society might condemn, is a hard one, and this would have been true for George. Several important planets occupy a chart area associated with a need for seclusion. There is an image of sacrifice with these planetary placements – a sense that in giving oneself to the collective, one forfeits a personal life. Additionally, the shy, sensitive and imaginative sign of Cancer rules both his Sun and Ascendant, indicators that the first instinct would be

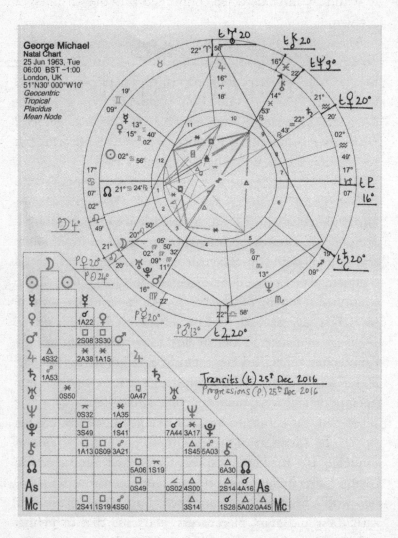

to withdraw and hide when confronted with the harshness of the world.

As a counterbalance, the Sun's ruler, the Moon, is found in noble, sunny, charismatic Leo, suggestive of warmth, generosity and an integral need for appreciation and recognition. This strong need to be seen, valued and take centre stage is complicated by a negative link to critical Saturn. The message here? Fearlessness comes slowly to those made to feel unworthy, but recognition is vital and to be won at all costs.

Two other chart features are interesting in their pointing to a life struggle. First, the presence of the North Node in an area associated with personal identity. The Nodes are considered indicators of past and future, where one has come from, where one is going, for many astrologers referencing past life as well as the present time on Earth. For George, the need was to leave behind a tendency to merge with the group, and move towards standing proud as an individual.

Of greater importance is the dominant presence of Chiron, the planet named after the half-man, half-horse son of a god. The most central aspect of this centaur's story revolves around his inadvertent wounding, a terrible injury that would never mend and which, as an immortal, he could not escape through death. He was a creature who could heal others, but never himself – thus the planet's appellation as the wounded healer. Joined to the highest point in the chart, it is a clear indicator of someone who would bring wisdom to his profession, wisdom won through vulnerability and courage and the fight to be honoured for his true identity. This planet forms many positive, flowing links within the chart, not least to the inspirational and creative Neptune, and most clearly shows the route through which George would gift the world, receive personal validation, and attain long-lasting fame.

Uranus, planet of originality and truth, intense and regenerative Pluto, and courageous, assertive Mars, together make up a powerful cluster of planets in a sign, Virgo, and the chart area associated with communication. These form positive links to Neptune, which, empowered by position, creates a simply enormous wealth of artistic, imaginative, sensitive, intelligent musical talent. Not only can this man write songs of profound emotional truth and vocalise them with utter melodic beauty, but he will enable healing through his moving, imaginative singing, creating a bridge between the harsh realities of life and a vision of something so much better. His talent is transcendent, unique and extraordinary, and in an artistic league way beyond that of so many gifted performers.

George's home was one with a strong work ethic and parents for whom the dream of a solid, prosperous life would be turned into reality. Much forceful effort would have gone towards rising above the status of the previous generation. Usefulness would be considered a virtue, as would acceptance of social norms and orderliness. There would be openness to material advancement and improvement.

The position of Mercury, the planet associated with siblings, joined to harmony-loving Venus reveals a close interdependent bond with his sisters. In fact, there is a suggestion that in some circumstances a sibling may act in a parental role. Mercury is in Gemini, its sign of rulership, suggesting a family who loved relating through conversation and ideas. There would be a high value placed upon talking and sharing news, and a certain restlessness, a coming and going, and also some dissension within the home.

The position of Mars, however, suggests a difficulty in getting along with a parent. A desire to be more in charge of who he was, a need to be seen more clearly, heard more truly, may have conflicted with a yearning for approval and, as a result, certain feelings and emotions would have been repressed. Consequently, there may have been unexpected explosions and/or deep depression, probably shared with siblings. The strong links forceful Mars makes with Pluto, Uranus, Mercury and Venus can often come out as intense anger directed towards those who are most loved, a pattern that would have been prevalent early in the home and later in adult relationships.

This is, essentially, a sensitive, intelligent and enormously loving man, whose highly self-critical nature and some disapproval by others would have forced doubts on his own worth. He would have been driven throughout his life by an urge to improve and refine himself, to please and make proud those he loved, and these battles in the early years would be the training ground, teaching a hesitant star how to assert himself and ultimately fight for others too.

How did George experience his parents? The astrological picture is subtle and complex. Main significators are the luminaries, the Sun, for father, and the Moon, for mother, both planets in this chart linked by being in each other's sign – termed 'mutual reception'. Although he will have had individual relationships with each of them, and despite any differences between them, they are nonetheless represented in the chart as a unity, a pair, whose approval he needed and whose dreams he may have been keen to protect, probably to his own disadvantage. That aside, together with the planet's signs considered, it would seem George's mother's need for security and position were met by his father, whose goals for a family life were fulfilled by her – a conventional arrangement which works well enough for many. His mother would have loved being generous and glamorous, and 'loyalty' could have been her second name. Tolerant, warm-hearted, there may have been times when she was too proud to ask for help. There would have been a restless streak that could, in early years, have resulted in George experiencing some sense of emotional distance from her – it may simply be that she herself lacked ease with emotions, or was sometimes prone to fearfulness. The Moon linked to Jupiter reveals her as an adventurous, inspiring force, validating his charisma and entertaining potential and supporting his ambitions.

His father, with the Sun linked to Uranus and Saturn in aloof Aquarius, would have a strong if distant presence and be something of an outsider. He would be proud of his traditional values and close to his wider family. He could have smothered George with love and yet not managed to see his individuality or encourage him to recognise what made him unique. The child would be seen as an extension of him, not regarded in his own right. Mars and Pluto, positioned at the bottom of George's chart, the area representing roots and life foundations, are suggestive of buried anger, with one parent fuelling accomplishment.

The issue of being not seen and validated would have followed George into the classroom. While the group planets, Uranus, Pluto and Mars, link positively to Neptune in facilitating his creativity, a harsher aspect to Chiron hints at a subconscious fear of being weak and damaged, with little trust in his ability to assert his thoughts and views. It is possible that in order to compensate, George may on occasions have acted in a passive-aggressive way, getting into rucks with others and authority figures. It's equally likely that he would be the target of bullying. Either way, school would have meant power struggles and unfavourable circumstances compounding a lack of confidence. Attempts to fit in would be counterproductive – only when he could follow an alternative route would doors open and recognition follow.

A preponderance of water planets and the Moon in fiery Leo hints at a lifetime of emotional drama for George, fuelling the creative process. As should be clear, this would have started from the moment he drew breath, but subsequent relationships would also be the arena for passionate encounters that engendered growth and, most vitally, helped develop the sense of self. The positive link between feeling Moon and uplifting Jupiter results overall in great optimistic buoyancy, although sometimes the demands of the heart might seem insatiable. As Jupiter expands all it touches, massive despair can be as predictable and all-engulfing as great joy can be life-enhancing. Moreover, this is a risk-taking combination; it is adventurous, suggesting George will gain the security he needs only through courageous commitments and actions which expose him and seem perilous. This would not be easy, as a complex link to the Moon from fearful, cautious Saturn would urge restraint. Jupiter represents faith and belief, and in order for George to function emotionally, he would need to hold on to a sense that humanity is good and that he could work to bolster fairness. Consequently, George would need a partner with a similar life path, whose humanitarian outlook and energy would be devoted to the justice of a particular calling.

The planets Mars and Venus are also linked to romance and play a part in the narrative here. Mars joined to Pluto, Lord of the Underworld and all that is taboo suggests burial of the sexual instinct, a rejection of masculine energy – not something that it's healthy to endure long-term. Fortunately, the desire for truthfulness, shown by a link between Uranus and the Sun, would prevail. The Moon–Jupiter link also reveals this great respect for honour and honesty. Equally revelatory is the position of Venus, hinting at the urge to transcend separateness and merge with something far greater than the self – a love is desired that knows no boundaries. This is an idealistic Venus, one that will make sacrifices for the one it loves but that ultimately needs seclusion, peace and escape from reality.

Looking at the chart area associated with marriage reveals the influence of restrictive Saturn, suggesting delays. For George, early criticism would have resulted in feelings of being unlovable – he would hesitate in exposing his heart. Further, a strong sense of vulnerability in terms of social acceptability may have stalled involvement. While Saturn slows down, it does not always deny. It would, though, bring a certain seriousness to partnerships and often indicates that one or other of a couple will act protectively as a father figure.

George Michael's Sun was positioned in an area of the chart called the Twelfth House, often associated with fame but also indicative of compromised vitality. This is because it is linked with the planet Neptune, associated with spiritual realisation, the collective unconsciousness of all humanity and other-worldliness. This Sun placement is often read as a reluctant soul – someone who incarnates, but hesitantly, not keen to face the battles of life – fairly ready to slip away again. People with a dominance of Neptune in the chart, as George has, struggle to live with the harshness of reality and frequently seek seclusion and other means of escape. Commonly, this can be through music, love, beauty, drink or drugs. There are implications of sacrifice; the artist can lift the hopes and dreams of others through the pain of artistic creation, allowing a sense of merging with something greater than themselves, alleviating the crippling sense of alienation and separateness that can destroy happiness. But they may pay the price – the sensitivity needed for their gift can destroy them.

The planet ruling George's Sun, giver of vitality and life, is the Moon, placed in Leo, which is associated with the heart. It sits between 20 and 21 degrees of Leo. Opposite, forming a stressful link, is restrictive Saturn. Placed in the sign of Aquarius, Saturn occupies a position often associated with problems of the circulatory system, the nervous system and the heart. On the day of George's death, there were many transiting planets forming exact links, at 20–21 degrees of various signs, to the Moon. This is very clear to see on the chart illustration. These links are suggestive of a life that has reached a turning point, someone with a readiness for change, a soul seeking a passage home.

About a fortnight earlier, a stressful link between Pluto, Lord of Darkness, and George's Jupiter suggests some inner spiritual struggle, but in the following weeks, Jupiter and the mighty outer planets, Uranus and Saturn, were moving steadily to positions of ease. They would form a rare kite pattern suggestive of inner balance and harmonious equilibrium. George had reached a state of grace and now had only to wait for the call of loved ones. This was delivered by fast-moving Venus, planet of love, moving speedily through the Eighth House of Death and Rebirth and forming an exact link for one day, on 25 December. George was ready, job done, for this song, this welcome from those he cherished and who had already passed – a joyous welcome home.

Astrology can be used in a pragmatic way – if you have hit a difficult patch, it can tell you when this will recede and more; it can provide the insight for you to better navigate the period that follows by adjusting the way you approach your life. But many astrologers see it as a confirmation of something greater – a confirmation of the spirit and how we keep returning in order to give and grow. Certain souls seem to exist especially for the collective good – providing the wisdom and joy so many need in order to themselves live a better existence, providing an example of courage. George Michael can be seen as a channel – someone who channelled that joy and honesty to the collective – an outer-planet person whose significance moved beyond the personal out towards the group. Such souls leave their gifts to us and their chart lives on – when significant transits occur, we are reminded of their contribution from the great beyond, and their goodness helps us yet again.

Madeleine Moore
September 2017

LIFE AND TIMES

25 June 1963: Georgios Kyriacos Panayiotou is born in East Finchley, London. He has two elder sisters – Panayiota, known as 'Yioda', who is four, and Melanie, aged two. His father Jack is an assistant manager in a restaurant.

Jan 1964: George's uncle – his mother's brother – Colin Harrison, dies from an overdose of barbiturates at the house in Lulot Street, Archway, where his mum grew up.

Sept 1968: George starts school at Roe Green Infants in Burnt Oak. The family is living above a nearby launderette but soon moves a short distance into the first home of their own, a semi-detached house costing £4,000 in Redhill Drive. Jack becomes a partner in an Edgware restaurant.

Sept 1974: George starts senior school at Kingsbury High but only stays a year because his father plans to move the family to leafy Hertfordshire.

Jan 1975: George's father buys a house in Oakridge Avenue, Radlett, but the family stay in a flat above his restaurant for six months until building work is completed.

Sept 1975: Begins life at Bushey Meads School, having turned down the chance to go to a private school. On his first day, Andrew Ridgeley volunteers to look after the new boy.

May 1976: George attends his first concert to see Elton John at Earls Court. Elton sings 'Don't Let the Sun Go Down on Me.'

July 1978: Listed as Georgios Panayiotou, he performs his own composition, a drum solo, at a Bushey Meads school concert. Proudly signs his then girlfriend Lesley Bywaters' programme.

Nov 1979: The Executive, the band George has formed with Andrew Ridgeley, play their first gig on Bonfire Night at the church hall known locally as the Scout Hut in Bushey Heath.

Jan 1980: The Executive record two songs: Beethoven's 'Für Elise' and 'Rude Boy', written by George and Andrew, at the Profile Recording Studios in Wheathampstead.

Feb 1980: Meets future girlfriend Helen Tye on a school trip to Stratford-upon-Avon to see *Othello*, starring Donald Sinden.

Sept 1980: Breaks up with Helen at a pub in Bushey just before she goes off to university. They agree they might want to date new people.

Feb 1981: Appears on television for the first time in a documentary about Spandau Ballet. George is shown with other clubbers dancing at the popular Le Beat Route in Wardour Street.

June 1981: Before leaving Bushey Meads passes two A–levels in Art and English. He had already given up music theory after his first year in the sixth form.

March 1982: George and Andrew sign a contract with Mark Dean from Bushey, who is a rising star in the music business and has started his own label, Innervision.

June 1982: The newly named Wham! release their first single 'Wham Rap! (Enjoy What You Do)', which peaks at a lowly number 105 in the UK chart.

Oct 1982: Wham! get their first big break when an act drops out of *Top of the Pops* and they stand in. George performs a *tour de force* singing their second single 'Young Guns (Go for It)'. He is now definitely the leader, while backing singers Pepsi and Shirlie help to give the band a sexy look. The song rises to number two in the UK charts.

Dec 1982: Andrew and George return to Bushey Meads to play a special concert just for pupils.

May 1983: George hates their new record, 'Bad Boys', even though he wrote it, declaring it to be an 'albatross around his neck'. The fans disagree and it, too, reaches number two in the UK.

June 1983: While filming the 'Club Tropicana' video on Ibiza, George tells Andrew and Shirlie he is gay. They advise him not to tell his parents and his sexuality remains hidden to all but his closest friends.

October 1983: Wham!'s *Club Fantastic* tour opens in Aberdeen. The band begin legal action against Innervision to release them from their contract. George appears with Andrew live on *The Tube* surrounded by a host of teenage girls. Tells interviewer, 'We don't feel terribly safe.'

March 1984: The High Court finds in their favour and Wham! finally leave Innervision and sign to Epic Records.

June 1984: 'Wake Me Up Before You Go-Go' is Wham's first UK and US number one. George goes to Miami to shoot the video for 'Careless Whisper'. Filming costs an extra $60,000 after it is stopped and restarted so that George can have his hair restyled by sister Melanie. His parents give him a ring for his twenty-first birthday, bearing his nickname Yog, which becomes one of his most treasured possessions.

August 1984: 'Careless Whisper' is George's first solo number one. It would top polls of the nation's favourite song for many years.

Sept 1984: Wham! are widely criticised in the media for using backing tapes at the miners' benefit concert at the Royal Festival Hall in London.

Oct 1984: Wham!'s second album, *Make It Big*, is released and tops both the US and UK charts.

Nov 1984: George sings the third segment of the Band Aid charity record 'Do They Know It's Christmas?' during an all-star recording at the Sarm West Studios in London.

Dec 1984: The *Big Tour* 1984 begins at the Whitley Bay Ice Rink. All tickets cost £6.50. 'Last Christmas' is kept off the UK number one spot by Band Aid but becomes the biggest-selling single not to top the charts. To date, sales top two million.

March 1985: Elton John calls George the 'greatest songwriter of his generation' when he presents him with the Ivor Novello Award for Songwriter of the Year, the youngest person ever to receive the accolade. 'Careless Whisper' is named most-performed work.

April 1985: Wham! become the first Western pop group to play in China. They perform concerts in Beijing and Guangzhou.

July 1985: Sings 'Don't Let the Sun Go Down on Me' during Elton John's Live Aid set at Wembley Stadium in front of an estimated global audience of 1.9 billion people. Is introduced backstage to Princess Diana.

Oct 1985: Contributes backing vocals to Elton John's melodic ballad 'Nikita'. Also features on another hit, 'Wrap Her Up', from Elton's album *Ice on Fire*.

Feb 1986: Norman Tebbit presents Wham! with an Outstanding Achievement Award at the BRITs. George parts company with managers Jazz Summers and Simon Napier-Bell after learning of their plans to sell their company.

April 1986: 'A Different Corner' becomes his second solo UK number one, revealing George to be a master of the emotional song.

June 1986: Wham! The Final takes place at Wembley Stadium in front of 72,000 fans and less than four years since George and Andrew first appeared on *Top of the Pops*.

Feb 1987: His first post-Wham! release, 'I Knew You Were Waiting (For Me)', a duet with Aretha Franklin, reaches number one in both the US and the UK.

June 1987: Premiers controversial video to 'I Want Your Sex' in which he writes the words 'Explore' and 'Monogamy' on Kathy Jeung's thigh and back. The song is banned on UK radio but achieves a commercial boost when it features on the soundtrack of *Beverly Hills Cop II*.

Oct 1987: First solo album *Faith* is released and is a worldwide smash, eventually selling more than 25 million copies. Four singles from the album would top the *Billboard* chart in the US.

Feb 1988: Begins the exhausting *Faith World Tour* at the Nippon Budokan in Tokyo. He will play 137 shows in eighteen months.

March 1988: Wins first Grammy for Best R&B performance by a duo or group with Aretha Franklin for 'I Knew You Were Waiting (For Me)'.

June 1988: Sings three covers at the seventieth-birthday tribute to Nelson Mandela at Wembley Stadium. Performs 'Village Ghetto Land', 'If You Were My Woman' and Marvin Gaye's 'Sexual Healing'. Undergoes throat surgery to remove a cyst.

Dec 1988: Ends the year as the biggest-selling artist in the US and tops the *Billboard* Year-End chart of both album and singles with *Faith*, only the second artist to achieve this double.

Sept 1990: His autobiography *Bare*, co-written with Tony Parsons, is published when George is twenty-seven and before he has fallen in love for the first time. *Listen Without Prejudice Vol. 1* becomes his second solo number one album, selling more than *Faith* in the UK but performing disappointingly in the US.

Oct 1990: George doesn't appear in the £300,000 video for new single 'Freedom '90'. Instead, five of the world's top supermodels lip-sync the lyrics.

Jan 1991: Andrew Ridgeley appears on stage with George for the last time when he headlines two shows at the Rock in Rio II festival. Meets and falls in love with Brazilian fashion designer Anselmo Feleppa. Founds his own label, Aegean Records, with his cousin Andros Georgiou.

March 1991: Elton John is a surprise guest at the last Wembley Arena concert of the *Cover to Cover* tour. Their live version of 'Don't Let the Sun Go Down on Me' becomes a number one record on both sides of the Atlantic, benefiting children's, AIDS and education charities.

Dec 1991: Spends Christmas with his parents in Radlett worrying about Anselmo, who had told him he was HIV positive. His own AIDS test would be negative.

April 1992: Appears at the Freddie Mercury Tribute Concert for AIDS Awareness at Wembley Stadium. Sings '39', 'These Are the Days of Our Lives' with Lisa Stansfield and 'Somebody to Love'.

July 1992: Contributes three tracks, including 'Too Funky', to the *Red, Hot & Dance* album, a charity project to help raise awareness of HIV.

March 1993: Anselmo Feleppa dies of a brain haemorrhage in Rio de Janeiro aged thirty-six.

Oct 1993: Begins High Court action against Sony, claiming his contract is an unreasonable restraint of trade.

Dec 1993: Tops the bill at the Concert of Hope, a fundraiser for his friend Princess Diana's National AIDS Trust, at Wembley Arena on World AIDS Day.

June 1994: Loses case against Sony with total court costs to date of £6 million.

Nov 1994: Premiers 'Jesus to a Child', a tribute to Anselmo Feleppa, at the inaugural MTV European Awards (the EMAs) in Berlin.

July 1995: Finally settles dispute with Sony. He will record for DreamWorks in the US and Virgin for the rest of the world.

May 1996: Releases his first album for six years. Called *Older*, it is dedicated to Anselmo Feleppa and to the great Brazilian composer Antônio Carlos Jobim. Both the album and the single 'Fastlove' go to number one.

June 1996: Meets handsome Texan Kenny Goss in an upmarket spa in Los Angeles. Rings his mum to tell her and she confides that she has had a cancer scare.

Oct 1996: Performs an *MTV Unplugged* concert and says hello to his mother who is in the audience.

Nov 1996: Gives his first proper UK interview in nearly six years to *The Big Issue*. Admits he needed bereavement counselling after Anselmo's death. Begins volunteering at a homeless shelter in Central London.

Feb 1997: Cannot attend the BRITs owing to his mother's battle with cancer. Lesley Panayiotou dies in Charing Cross Hospital with husband Jack and her children by her bedside.

May 1997: Before iTunes and Spotify, George's company Aegean. net, the internet arm of Aegean Records, begins selling music for download. Releases 'Waltz Away Dreaming', a duet with Toby Bourke, featuring words inspired by the loss of his mother.

Sept 1997: Cries at the funeral of Princess Diana, which he attends with Elton John and David Furnish. Many radio stations play his new single 'You Have Been Loved' as a tribute to her, although it was actually written in memory of Anselmo Feleppa.

Nov 1997: Reveals that he was smoking twenty-five joints a day while grieving for Anselmo.

April 1998: Is arrested in the Will Rogers Memorial Park, Beverly Hills, for alleged lewd conduct in a public toilet. The following month he enters a guilty plea and is fined, receives community service and therapy orders, and banned from the park. Officially reveals his sexuality during a CNN interview.

June 1998: Throws a 'Cowboys and Angels' themed party in London to celebrate his thirty-fifth birthday. He is a cowboy and new friend Geri Halliwell goes as an angel.

Oct 1998: Uses his arrest as the inspiration for new single 'Outside'. Campaigner Mary Whitehouse calls for a ban on the video, which pokes fun at the incident; it is set mainly in a Californian toilet and George dresses up as a police officer.

Dec 1998: George's greatest hits album, *Ladies & Gentlemen*, spends the first of 200 weeks in the UK charts, becoming his biggest-selling album in Britain with sales of 2.8 million.

Feb 1999: Buys a five-bedroom country house for a reported £1.6 million in the picturesque village of Goring-on-Thames, Oxfordshire.

March 1999: Performs a moving rendition of 'The Long and Winding Road' at a memorial concert in honour of Linda McCartney, which will benefit cancer charities.

Oct 1999: Takes part in Net Aid at Wembley Stadium in aid of Kosovan and Sudanese refugees but is disappointed with sound problems.

Dec 1999: Jumps the gun by releasing an album of mainly jazz standards co-produced by Phil Ramone called *Songs from the Last Century* – the month before the Millennium.

April 2000: Takes part in the Equality Rocks concert in Washington's RFK Stadium and sings a duet of 'Freedom! '90' with country music star Garth Brooks.

Oct 2000: Buys John Lennon's piano at auction for £1.45 million. The former Beatle had composed 'Imagine' on the upright Steinway.

July 2001: Rings Richard and Judy on air during the final edition of their *This Morning* show to thank them for 'easing him into the day for the past decade'.

Feb 2002: George's house in Hampstead is burgled and thieves drive off in his Aston Martin DB7, which is later found abandoned. Stars in an advertisement called Fur and Against, part of a campaign strongly opposing the wearing of fur.

July 2002: Releases controversial single 'Shoot the Dog'. Tells Piers Morgan his biggest concern is that America will drag Britain into a war with Iraq. Is jeered by an American TV audience.

Jan 2003: Buys new home in Highgate for a reported £10 million. The six-bedroom Grade II-listed mansion has stunning views of Hampstead Heath.

June 2003: George meets the cast of *EastEnders*, one of his favourite programmes, when he makes a surprise visit to Albert Square as part of his fortieth-birthday celebrations.

Dec 2003: Gives his royalties from actor Shane Richie's version of 'I'm Your Man' to BBC Children in Need. Wins £32,000 with Ronan Keating on a celebrity special of *Who Wants to Be a Millionaire?* and donates his share to Macmillan Cancer Support, which provided the nurse who cared for his dying mother. Sells his Beverly Hills mansion for $2.85 million.

March 2004: His last studio album *Patience* sells 275,000 copies in its first week and goes to number one in the UK.

April 2004: Is named by the Radio Academy as the most played artist on British radio of the last twenty years.

July 2005: Sings the old Beatles' favourite 'Drive My Car' with Paul McCartney at the Live 8 concert in Hyde Park.

Dec 2005: *A Different Story*, a candid and entertaining documentary about George's life, is given a cinema release.

Feb 2006: Police arrest him after he is discovered slumped at the wheel of his car at Hyde Park Corner. He later receives a police caution for possession of class C drugs.

Sept 2006: Opens *25 Live* world tour at the Palau Sant Jordi in Barcelona. One hundred and six dates will gross more than $200 million.

Oct 2006: Openly smokes a joint during an interview for *The South Bank Show*.

Nov 2006: Returns to Sony for a new greatest hits collection, *Twenty Five*. Plays a free concert at the Roundhouse, London, for NHS nurses as a thank you for caring for his mum.

Jan 2007: Earns £1.78 million for singing at a Russian billionaire's New Year's Day party in Moscow. At nearly £24,000 a minute, it's said to be the largest fee ever paid to a recording artist.

May 2007: Pleads guilty due to tiredness and prescribed drugs to a charge of driving under the influence of drugs. George had been found asleep at the wheel at a junction in North London. Spends an estimated £20 million on works by the artist Damien Hirst.

June 2007: Sentenced at Brent Magistrates Court to 100 hours of community service and banned from driving for two years. The following day, plays the first ever concert at the new Wembley Stadium in front of 90,000 fans.

Sept 2007: Sends himself up in an episode of *Extras* in which he is cruising on Hampstead Heath. Chooses an Aston Martin as his luxury item on *Desert Island Discs* because nobody there would know he didn't have a licence.

Jan 2008: Makes a number of guest appearances as himself in the US comedy drama *Eli Stone*, starring Jonny Lee Miller – all the episodes of the first series are named after George Michael songs.

Sept 2008: Receives police caution for possession of class A and class C drugs after being arrested on Hampstead Heath. Goes on African safari with Kenny Goss.

June 2009: Joins Beyoncé on stage to sing 'If I Were a Boy' at her London O2 concert.

Dec 2009: Makes a guest appearance on the *X Factor* final singing a duet of 'Don't Let the Sun Go Down on Me' with eventual winner Joe McElderry.

July 2010: Crashes his Range Rover into the shop front of Snappy Snaps in Hampstead.

Sept 2010: Sentenced to eight weeks in jail after pleading guilty to possession of cannabis and driving under the influence of drugs. Begins sentence at Pentonville Prison in London before being moved to Highpoint in Suffolk.

Aug 2011: Introduces new song 'Where I Hope You Are' at the Prague State Opera House by revealing that he and Kenny Goss have not been together for two and a half years. Sings an emotional version of Amy Winehouse's 'Love Is a Losing Game'.

Nov 2011: Postpones concert in Vienna because of pneumonia. Taken by ambulance to the AKH hospital, where he undergoes a tracheotomy to help him breathe. New boyfriend Fadi Fawaz goes to see him every day. Eventually postpones all remaining gigs of *Symphonica* tour.

Dec 2011: George tells reporters outside his house in Highgate that it was 'touch and go for a while' and that he has endured the worst month of his life.

Aug 2012: Sings 'Freedom! '90' and new song 'White Light' based on his near-death experience at the closing ceremony of the London Olympics. 'White Light' enters the charts at number fifteen, his last UK top-twenty hit.

Sept 2012: Becomes the first international pop star to perform at the Palais Garnier opera house as part of the resumed *Symphonica* tour.

Oct 2012: George cancels his Australian tour dates, saying he is suffering major anxiety as a result of his serious illness. His concert at Earls Court on 17 October would be his very last live show.

May 2013: Is airlifted to hospital after he falls out of his chauffeur-driven Range Rover onto the carriageway of the M1 motorway near St Albans.

Feb 2014: Releases his last single, 'Let Her Down Easy', a cover of a Terence Trent D'Arby song.

March 2014: *Symphonica* tops the charts, becoming his seventh solo album to reach number one. He also had two with Wham!

June 2015: George is pictured out and about in Zurich with Fadi Fawaz. Spends most of the year in Switzerland receiving treatment for drug addiction at the Kusnacht Practice, which reportedly costs £190,000 a month.

Dec 2016: Dies peacefully from heart failure at his home in Goring on Christmas Day. Police say there are no suspicious circumstances.

March 2017: The coroner confirms that George died of natural causes. The private funeral takes place at Highgate Cemetery and George is buried in a family plot next to his mother Lesley.

Sept 2017: First posthumous single, 'Fantasy', is premiered on the radio. In a personal message to George's fans, his sisters Melanie and Yioda say their aim is 'to share and enjoy his precious legacy and to continue to bring you joy – through his extraordinarily beautiful music'.

Oct 2017: *Listen Without Prejudice Vol 1* is re-released and reaches number one – twenty-seven years after first topping the album charts.

Dec 2017: *Last Christmas*, the biggest selling single not to top the charts, re-enters the top forty and, yet again, peaks at number two. His family wished everyone a good Christmas: 'And as our darling Yog would say … take care.'

ACKNOWLEDGEMENTS

It's great for me when the people I speak to are filled with enthusiasm and affection for the subject of a book. That's certainly been the case with George Michael, whether it's childhood friends, those from the Wham! days or, latterly, when he faced the love and loss that shaped his life. My thanks to those who shared their memories, including Michael Burdett, Lesley Bywaters, Tony Bywaters, Ruth Coles, George Georgiades, Jamie Gould, Lucia Guanabara, Joy Mendelsohn, Michael Salousti and Helen Tye. I am grateful to Simon Napier-Bell, who kindly allowed me to use his excellent observations on his famous former client. Thanks also to those who did not want to be named – your insights were invaluable.

One of the things I most enjoy about writing my books is parking the car and just chatting to people in the old neighbourhoods where, in this case, George Michael was brought up and lived. That could be a shop owner on the Edgware Road, a school teacher in Bushey, a dog walker in Radlett or a church warden in Highgate. They all helped me to build a picture.

ACKNOWLEDGEMENTS

I am very fortunate to have such talented people backing me up. I couldn't have written this book without their help and expertise. First, my long-standing agent Gordon Wise continues to guide my career and give me the best advice. Thanks also to Niall Harman, his assistant at Curtis Brown, for his patience and efficiency.

My research team has been terrific as always. Thanks to Emily-Jane Swanson, who again did most of her work beside a pool in Ibiza, and to Alison Sims and Jo Westaway. The more they found out about George, the more they liked and admired him, and that was true for me too. In California, my good friends Richard Mineards and Cliff Renfrew were helpful as ever, while I am grateful to Beatriz Bilichuc for handling things so well for me in Brazil.

Astrologer Madeleine Moore has again excelled with a fascinating birth chart. She tells me that George's has been the most enjoyable chart she has done so far. She doesn't see anything I write in advance, so I love it when her findings mirror my own thoughts. She describes George as a beacon of hope and understanding, which is a sentiment I endorse.

Some old friends kindly gave me their time to talk about George. It was lovely to catch up with Spencer Bright, Patrick Humphries, Chrissy Iley and Rick Sky, who was part of the Wham! adventure to China.

Thank you to Jen Westaway for transcribing my interviews so expertly. This time she had to cope with me chatting to a friend of George's outside on a sunny day in Chelsea. I hadn't realised how noisy the King's Road can be! I am also grateful to Nicky Gyopari for her sterling work as copy-editor.

At HarperCollins, many thanks to Oliver Malcolm and my editor, Zoë Berville, for commissioning the book and guiding me so thoughtfully through the manuscript; Isabel Hayman-Brown for project editing; Claire Ward for her impressive cover design; Dean Russell in production; Laura Lees and Jasmine Gordon for looking after publicity and marketing.

You can read more about my books at seansmithceleb.com or follow me on Twitter and Facebook @seansmithceleb.

SELECT BIBLIOGRAPHY

Boy George with Spencer Bright, *Take It Like a Man: The Autobiography of Boy George*, Sidgwick & Jackson, 1995

Dessau, Bruce, *George Michael: The Making of a Superstar*, Sidgwick & Jackson, 1989

Halliwell, Geri, *Just for the Record*, Ebury Press, 2003

Michael, George and Tony Parsons, *Bare*, Michael Joseph, 1990

Napier–Bell, Simon, *I'm Coming to Take You to Lunch*, Ebury Press, 2006

Rogan, Johnny, *Wham! Confidential*, Omnibus Press, 1987

Steele, Robert, *Careless Whispers: The Life & Career of George Michael*, Omnibus Press, 2017

Summers, Jazz, *Big Life*, Quartet Books, 2013

PICTURE CREDITS

INDEX